A CRIME AGAINST HUMANITY

DEDICATION

To the mothers of South Africa, who bore the brunt of the crushing burden of apartheid repression.

We wish especially to remember Sophie Masite, ex-detainee, senior advice office worker and member of the Detainees' Parents Support Committee, first black woman mayor in South Africa, mayor of the Southern Metropolitan Substructure (incorporating Soweto) of Greater Johannesburg.

Sophie died on 26 April 1997, a few days after giving birth to twins.

To the memory of all those who died in the struggle for freedom and democracy in our beloved South Africa.

We remember especially our colleagues and co-workers Sicelo Dhlomo and David Webster, who both fell to the cruel hand of apartheid's assassins.

A CRIME AGAINST HUMANITY
ANALYSING THE REPRESSION OF THE APARTHEID STATE

Edited by Max Coleman

Human Rights Committee, Johannesburg

Mayibuye Books, University of the Western Cape, Bellville

David Philip Publishers, Cape Town

Mayibuye History and Literature Series, No. 91.

First published 1998 in southern Africa by David Philip Publishers (Pty) Ltd,
208 Werdmuller Centre, Claremont, 7700, South Africa; Mayibuye Books, University of
the Western Cape, Bellville; and the Human Rights Committee, Johannesburg

ISBN 0-86486-416-7

A CIP catalogue record of this book is available from the British Library

Typeset by User Friendly

Printed in South Africa by Creda Press, Eliot Avenue, Epping, Western Cape

Contents

List of figures

List of tables

List of abbreviations

ANC – African National Congress
AWB – Afrikaner Weerstandsbeweging
AZAPO – Azanian People's Organisation
CAWU – Construction and Allied Workers' Union
CCB – Civil Co-operation Bureau
CCAWUSA – Commercial, Catering and Allied Workers' Union
CODESA – Conference for a Democratic South Africa
COSAS – Congress of South African Students
COSATU – Congress of South African Trade Unions
COD – Congress of Democrats
CONTRALESA – Congress of Traditional Leaders of South Africa
CP – Conservative Party
CT – Cape Town
CWIU – Chemical Workers' Industrial Union
Dbn – Durban
DP – Democratic Party
DPSC – Detainees' Parents Support Committee
FF – Freedom Front
HRC – Human Rights Committee
IDASA – Institute for a Democratic South Africa
IFP – Inkatha Freedom Party
ISA – Internal Security Act
ISU – Internal Stability Units
Jhb – Johannesburg
JMC – Joint Management Centre
KZN – KwaZulu/Natal
KZP – KwaZulu Police
MDM – Mass Democratic Movement
MI – Military Intelligence
MK – Umkhonto weSizwe
NEHAWU – National Education, Health and Allied Workers' Union
NIS – National Intelligence Service
NP – National Party
NSMS – National Security Management System
NUMSA – National Union of Metalworkers of South Africa
NUSAS – National Union of South African Students
OAU – Organisation of African Unity
OFS – Orange Free State
PAC – Pan Africanist Congress
PE – Port Elizabeth
PSA – Public Safety Act
Pta – Pretoria

PWV – Pretoria/Witwatersrand/Vaal
RENAMO – Resistência Nacional Moçambicana (Mozambique National Resistance)
SA – South Africa
SAAF – South African Air Force
SACBC – Southern African Catholic Bishops' Conference
SACC – South African Council of Churches
SACP – South African Communist Party
SACTU – South African Congress of Trade Unions
SADF – South African Defence Force
SANSCO – South African National Students' Congress
SAP – South African Police
SASO – South African Students' Organisation
SOE – State of Emergency
SOSCO – Soweto Students' Congress
SSC – State Security Council
SWAPO – South West African People's Organisation
TBVC States – Transkei, Bophuthatswana, Venda, Ciskei
TEC – Transitional Executive Council
TRC – Truth and Reconciliation Commission
UDF – United Democratic Front
UNITA – União Nacional para a Independência Total de Angola (National Union for the
Total Independence of Angola)

Acknowledgements

Our thanks are due, first and foremost, to the teams of dedicated researchers who faced the daunting task of monitoring and recording our history in the making. At times it was a task that was overwhelming, depressing and stressful in the extreme. Every small victory along the way helped to rejuvenate their determination not to relax their efforts. The result of their tenacity is to be found in this book.

We owe a debt of gratitude to our many sources of information over the years, many of whom were rooted in oppressed communities throughout the country, often as victims of the myriad forms of repression described in this book. Another community which supported our monitoring activities and gave our work added meaning and relevance was the international community, including anti-apartheid movements throughout the world, foreign governments and their Pretoria-based diplomatic offices, United Nation agencies, and foreign donor agencies, all too numerous to mention individually.

Amongst other communities whose support and cooperation we enjoyed were the many human rights NGOs who unstintingly shared their information with us, human rights lawyers who unfailingly responded to our calls for help, and an important part of the media community, both 'mainstream' and 'alternative', who courageously printed or broadcast what we had to report even when they ran the risk of arousing the ire of the security police. All of these contributed to building up the record on which this book is based.

We have made use of two external publications which fit well into the structure of this book and we thank the authors for permission to do so. They are: *Manufacturing Violent Stability* by Nicholas Haysom; *Apartheid Terrorism* by the Commonwealth Secretariat.

A collection of cartoons relating to repression has been gathered over the years and some of these are used here to lighten up the rather austere subject matter. Artists and publishers are acknowledged in each case. Finally, we wish to record our thanks to the Truth and Reconciliation Commission for granting us a hearing at which this entire manuscript was submitted into their record on 27 May 1997.

Max Coleman, as editor of this publication, wishes to express his deep appreciation for the unflinching support and guidance given by HRC researcher Tim Marchant in the painstaking task of drawing together all the strands that make up this book.

Foreword by the Rev. Beyers Naudé

I feel greatly honoured to be requested to write this foreword to the publication of *A Crime against Humanity: Analysing the Repression of the Apartheid State*. Since 1981, over a period of 15 years, the organisation known first as the Detainees' Parents Support Committee then the Human Rights Commission and finally the Human Rights Committee compiled all available evidence on repressive methods and practices which were used by the apartheid state to sustain apartheid power. In this publication we find a distillation of the data and the information which was gathered during this period. It is divided into four sequential parts, the one part being as important and impressive as the other. Few have dared to challenge the correctness of the facts or the statistics published here.

In reading through this publication one is struck by the fact that the information is presented in a calm, clear, concise and objective manner with no intention to arouse feelings of anger or resentment. The fact that this compilation and presentation, almost clinically done, is presented in this way possibly has just the opposite effect; it evokes emotions of shock, disbelief and anger over the terrible injustice which apartheid inflicted on thousands and thousands of South Africans over many years: over 80 000 opponents of apartheid detained for up to 3 years without trial during the period 1960–1990, including about 10 000 women and at least 15 000 children under the age of 18. Another example: the whole system of banning or restriction which was implemented against approximately 3000 persons from 1950–1989. A third example: around 15 000 persons charged in the courts under security legislation since 1950, and probably ten times that number in

SAK, *Sowetan Sunday Mirror*, 1984

'unrest' trials. During these years I was one of the many persons who was actively involved in our resistance against the evil of apartheid and in seeking adequate measures to terminate this evil practice. Although many of these facts were known to me, in reading through this document and being reminded of so much which has happened, I constantly had to say to myself: 'Yes, this is what happened; yes, this is how it happened.' And yet, I find it incredible to believe that all this occurred during these years!

I wish to express my sincere gratitude to all those who were responsible for compiling this document and presenting this information. This is undoubtedly a very significant document, and the future will increasingly convince us of this fact. Apart from the tremendous value of all the facts and statistics which have been gathered in such meticulous and comprehensive manner, this document also reminds of us about the evil of apartheid and the injustice and the pain which it inflicted on millions of people who suffered and sacrificed themselves in order to ensure that this evil could be removed once and for all. It also challenges all South Africans, both now and in the future, to ensure that there will never be a repetition of what occurred during these years.

Allow me, on behalf not only of many South Africans but also millions of people around the world who assisted us during these years in our opposition against apartheid, to express our sincere gratitude to all those in the Detainees' Parents Support Committee and the Human Rights Committee who through all these 15 years have to a smaller or larger degree made their own contribution which led to the termination of apartheid and the establishment of a worthwhile non-racial democracy in South Africa.

INTRODUCTION

This is a book about repression. More specifically, it is a book about the repression of the apartheid state and particularly the repressive structures and methods which were devised and refined by the Nationalist government on its assumption of power in 1948 in order to safeguard and perpetuate that power in the face of a hostile and non-compliant majority. That is not to say that repression was not exercised in South Africa before 1948 or that apartheid did not exist before that date. On the contrary, the foundations for both were laid as early as the arrival of the Dutch colonists in 1652, and later in some earnest by the British colonists especially after the discovery of gold and diamonds. The divide-and-rule tactics of British colonialism so successfully practised elsewhere in the world were to set the pattern for the co-option of a privileged elite within the indigenous population of South Africa by according it limited power and providing the elite with the means to defend that power.

Notwithstanding the long history of colonial conquest and suppression, and of racial exploitation and discrimination, the year 1948 stands out as the time of a qualitative shift from the ad hoc art of control to the rigorous science of repression in South Africa. As such, it forms a natural starting point for this book on the repression of the apartheid state.

The need for this book

Need this book have been written? The HRC believes so for 2 compelling reasons. Firstly, there seems to be a great deal of ignorance, puzzlement and now – as a result of TRC hearings – curiosity within the South African public's mind about the gross violations of human rights that have been perpetrated in this country during the last 50 years, ostensibly in the name of an ideology of social engineering. Anything which can make a contribution to penetrating that ignorance and respond to the public's need for a clearer understanding of this terrible past, must have value. This book is an attempt to make just such a contribution; it is hoped at the same time to complement and reinforce the excellent work of the TRC by submitting this manuscript into its record.

Secondly, the very considerable accumulated data of 15 years of monitoring by the HRC and its predecessor, the Detainees' Parents Support Committee (DPSC), constitute a valuable historical resource which cannot be allowed to lie fallow. It was realised that this resource could and should be translated into a reference work, hopefully in an accessible form, for the benefit of the public at large, and for the interest of students, domestic and international, of recent South African history and with a particular interest in the subject of the repression wrought by apartheid.

The plan of this book

The design of the book divides the subject matter into four distinct periods from 1948 to the end of 1996. Part A covers the period of 1948 to 1989 during which 'total strategy' was conceived, born and matured as the classical form of apartheid repression. Part B is concerned with the incipient collapse of apartheid power that became evident from 1988 to 1990 and opened the way to a negotiated transfer of power. Part C then traces the 'destabilisation strategy' which emerged as the successor to total strategy and which accompanied negotiations during the period from 1990 to the first democratic elections in April 1994. Finally, Part D takes stock of the post-election period of May 1994 to December 1996 in an attempt to assess the completeness of the eradication of apartheid repression and destabilisation.

The style of this book

The book draws largely for its content from material published by the DPSC from its formation in 1981 to its banning in 1988 and by the HRC from its formation in 1988 to the present time. These publications have been incorporated in a sequence which fits naturally into the 4 parts outlined above, and have been joined together within this framework by appropriate narrative and commentary. No attempt has been made to modify the tense of original publications, but on the contrary every effort has been made to preserve the 'real-time' integrity of each document and to preserve the impression of a running commentary of the times and circumstances in which they were written. Readers are invited to immerse themselves mentally in the time of writing and to assist them in this the date of publication of the document is always prominently indicated. This immediacy of the material used is particularly strong in Parts C and D when the HRC was geared up for an intensive daily monitoring of events. However, Parts A and B, while often more backward looking, still rely heavily on publications which were written at critical times in our history and were reflective of their time of writing.

Another feature of this treatment of the material which has been incorporated into the book is the ease with which reference can be made by the interested student or researcher to a specific aspect of repression. For example, someone with a special concern about deaths in detention will be able to discover a complete publication on the subject in Part A, Chapter 3.

The title

The choice of title, *A Crime against Humanity*, was made for two reasons. Firstly, it is a matter of history that the United Nations General Assembly adopted a number of resolutions declaring the system of apartheid to be a crime against humanity and a negation of the UN Charter. These expressions of censure culminated in the adoption by the General Assembly (Resolution 3068) on 30 November 1973 of the International Convention on the Suppression and Punishment of the Crimes of Apartheid. The

Convention was entered into force on 18 July 1976. The following are extracts:

> Observing that the General Assembly of the United Nations has adopted a number of resolutions in which the policies and practices of apartheid are condemned as a crime against humanity,
>
> Observing that the Security Council has emphasized that apartheid and its continued intensification and expansion seriously disturb and threaten international peace and security
>
> Article I
> 1. The States Parties to the present Convention declare that apartheid is a crime against humanity and that inhuman acts resulting from the policies and practices of apartheid and similar policies and practices of race segregation and discrimination, as defined in Article II of the Convention, are crimes violating the principles of the Charter of the United Nations, and constituting a serious threat to international peace and security.
> 2. The States Parties to the present Convention declare criminal those organisations, institutions and individuals committing the crime of apartheid.

To emphasise international condemnation of apartheid and its practices as expressed within the world body, the General Assembly in 1974 refused to accept the credentials of the South African delegation, effectively resulting in the expulsion of apartheid South Africa from the UN and its agencies, and providing impetus to the growing isolation of South Africa from the outside world that would eventually bring apartheid to its knees.

A second reason for the choice of title is to be found in the content of this book itself. In it the reader will be exposed to the litany of brutalisation of an entire population which has left its impact on victims and perpetrators alike. Apartheid repression, as one of the most deliberate, systematic and ruthless expressions of the practices of apartheid, must surely qualify as a crime against humanity. The reader is left to judge the record.

The information bank

As already indicated, the basic sources of material for this book are the files and publications of the Detainees' Parents Support Committee and the Human Rights Committee (formerly known as the Human Rights Commission); there are two or three exceptions where documents have been externally sourced and these are acknowledged where they occur.

The DPSC was established in October 1981 to oppose and expose detention without trial in particular and repressive human rights violations in general. Its effectiveness received the acknowledgement of the apartheid government in the form of a restriction order in February 1988 banning it from any activity whatsoever. During its life the DPSC performed an intensive monitoring function, producing and disseminating over 50 detailed monthly reports in that time. The HRC was created to take up the cudgels and from 1988 to the present time has produced over 120 monthly reports in the course of monitoring over 20 000 incidents. This prodigious feat of sustained investigation and analysis must be ascribed to dedicated teams of researchers all determined to expose the inherently evil character of apartheid repression. Their work was the foundation for the numerous publications and documents which form the basis of this book.

Amongst the sources relied upon by the research teams for their information were thousands of victims, community organisations, the press, electronic media, political organisations, other monitoring groups, religious groups, trade unions, lawyers, and individual researchers as well as government sources and police unrest reports.

Zapiro, *Sowetan*, 2 April 1997

PART A
THE UNFOLDING OF
TOTAL STRATEGY
1948–1989

Introduction

'Total strategy' is a term with which most South Africans will be familiar. It came into common use during the era of P.W. Botha and was portrayed by its authors as the apartheid government's response to the perceived threat of the 'total onslaught'.

The total onslaught, the story went, was the threat posed to South Africa (and indeed to the Western world) by the Soviet Union's designs on the strategic value of South Africa as the industrial powerhouse of the African continent, the guardian of the sea lanes around the Cape of Good Hope, and in particular the possessor of enormous mineral wealth, which combined with the mineral wealth profile of the Soviet Union would enable that country to hold the world to ransom. Furthermore, there were revolutionary forces at work within South Africa which were intent upon supporting and fuelling this threat.

This ingenious invention was intended to serve many purposes:
* to win the support of Western governments;
* to justify draconian repression of the black population or that part of it displaying tendencies towards toppling white power;
* to brainwash the white population into closing ranks, particularly within the security forces (defence and police) and within the judiciary, even to the extent of mentally condoning torture and assassination of political activists;
* to justify destabilisation of South Africa's neighbours, through cross-border raids, through support for Renamo, Unita and other renegade forces and through military invasion of Angola.

The irony of the doctrine of total strategy was that it was designed to portray the apartheid government as the sole bastion of Western democracy on the continent of Africa, whereas the real purpose of total strategy was to maintain apartheid power in the most undemocratic manner imaginable, serving the interests of 13% of the population at the expense of 87% of the population.

Could there have been a total strategy without the spectre of a total onslaught? Certainly the justification to the international community and to the white population of South Africa would have been a lot more difficult. And perhaps the title would have been inappropriate. But undoubtedly the substance would have been the same for apartheid power had to be defended.

In Part A of this book, an attempt is made to reveal how multi-faceted and total the scope of total strategy really was. A hint of this totality was given by no less an authority than General J.V. van der Merwe, former Commissioner of the South African Police, in a submission to the Parliamentary Portfolio Committee on Justice during January 1995 on the desirability (or otherwise) of establishing a Truth Commission. We quote verbatim from a memorandum forming part of this submission:

> The National Party formulated a policy whereby a system was created to plan and execute counter-revolutionary measures to counter the threat posed by the actions of the liberation movements. The Nationalist government ordered the security forces to take abnormal action not covered by normal legislation. This created moral ground for justification for the contravention of existing laws.

As an example the so-called 'Simonstown Deliberations' of 1979 gave specific orders with regard to the gathering of information and cross border operations to the Security Forces. These orders gave rise to the creation and implementation of a national intelligence gathering capability directed at counter-revolutionary actions. This included the utilisation of the South African Police where the emphasis was placed on abnormal intelligence gathering methodology and not according to international norms and practices.

The 'Simonstown Deliberations' were followed over a number of years by decisions taken by the government of the day in conjunction with the heads of the Security Forces, the Department of National Intelligence and other security mechanisms in committees and structures like the State Security Council and the Co-ordinating Intelligence Committee. These structures gave orders concerning counter revolutionary actions on a continuous basis, whether by direct or implied authority. By mutual agreement it was decided that the SA Defence Force was to be responsible for the foreign dimension, the SAP for the internal dimension and the National Intelligence Service and the Department of Foreign Affairs would support both dimensions with intelligence back-up. Practical examples of this co-operation includes the 'Teenrewolusionêre Inligtingstaakspan' (Trewits), which was responsible for the identification of organisational structures and individuals involved in the armed struggle of the liberation movements. Another example was the Division for Strategic Communications, a sub-structure of the Secretariat of the State Security Council of which the SADF was the primary functionary and the NIS provided the administrative infrastructure. These structures were fully sanctioned by the Nationalist government and senior members of the cabinet were briefed on a continuous and structured basis.

The system used members of the public, academics, senior personnel in the public service, informers, agents and members of the security forces in a covert manner. Many of these people at present hold senior positions in society. Some current members of parliament and provincial legislatures, have unwittingly provided the system with strategic information. In view of the fact that terrorism is internationally accepted as a serious crime, the government had a close relationship with various foreign intelligence agencies to provide information.

The above extract provides an interesting insight into how widely the net was cast in marshalling various players in the total strategy and including not only the security forces, National Intelligence Service and Department of Foreign Affairs as well as specially created co-ordinating structures, but in addition members of the public in all spheres and even extending to foreign intelligence agencies. Much attention will be given to this network under 'Covert operations' (Chapter 6).

It must be pointed out that while total strategy has its origins in the cycles of repression and resistance dating back to 1948 (and earlier, many will argue), it was only subsequent to the Soweto Uprising of 1976 that the need for a total strategy was formally identified and the phrase came into common usage. In 1977, P.W. Botha as minister of defence at the time introduced a White Paper on Defence, in which the following occurs:

The process of ensuring and maintaining the sovereignty of a state's authority in a conflict situation has, through the evolution of warfare, shifted from the purely military to an integrated national action ... The resolution of conflict in the times in which we now live demands interdependent and coordinated action in all fields – military, psychological, economic, political, sociological, technological, diplomatic, ideological, cultural, etc. We are today involved in war whether we like it or not. It is therefore essential that a total strategy [be] formulated at the highest level.

And so was born total strategy and the National Security Management System as its vehicle of implementation and coordination. The Simonstown Deliberations of 1979 referred to by General van der Merwe above must have been one of the first gatherings of the designers of formal total strategy to take stock of the means available to them and determine how to put them to best use. In Part A, both the overt and covert components of this repressive armoury come under scrutiny.

Immediately following this introduction, the reader will find a chronology of major events which occurred during this period and also a statistical summary of the impact of repression in this time.

Calendar of major events during the unfolding of total strategy 1948–1989

Year	Internal events	External events
1948	National Party comes to power	
1950	Suppression of Communism Act	
1952	Defiance Campaign (over 8000 arrests)	
1953	Public Safety Act Bantu Authorities Act creates separate authorities for blacks	
1955	Congress of the People adopts Freedom Charter (26 June)	
1956	Arrest and trial of 156 Congress Alliance leaders (all acquitted March 1961) March of 20 000 women on Union Buildings (9 August)	
1958	Verwoerd becomes prime minister	
1960	Anti-Pass Law Campaign Sharpeville massacre (21 March) Banning of ANC and PAC (28 March) State of Emergency (30 March– 31 August)	
1961	ANC adoption of the armed struggle Republic declared	SA withdraws from Commonwealth
1962	Sabotage Act	
1963	Rivonia Trial 'Ninety-day Detention' Act	
1965		Rhodesia declares UDI
1966	Verwoerd assassinated (succeeded by B.J. Vorster)	
1967	Terrorism Act	
1970		SA expelled from Olympic movement
1973		UN adopts International Convention on Suppression and Punishment of the Crime of Apartheid
1974		SA barred from General Assembly
1975		Invasion of Angola by SA forces Independence of Mozambique proclaimed (25 June) People's Republic of Angola declared (11 November)
1976	Soweto Uprising (16 June)	

1977	Death of Steve Biko in detention Banning of 17 organisations and 2 newspapers	UN mandatory arms embargo

1978	P.W. Botha succeeds Vorster as prime
	  minister
		UN Resolution 435 providing for
		  Namibian elections

1979	National Security Management System
	  instituted
	Simonstown Deliberations on total
	  strategy	

1980		Rhodesia becomes Zimbabwe (18 April) SADC formed to counter SA influence
1982	Internal Security Act	
1983	United Democratic Front launched	
1984	Tricameral constitution adopted (3 September) Vaal uprising	Nkomati Accord with Mozambique

1985	Partial State of Emergency declared
	  (21 July)
	Over 32 000 SADF troops deployed in
	  96 townships	

1986	Partial State of Emergency withdrawn
	  (7 March)
	National State of Emergency declared
	  (12 June)
		USA adopts Comprehensive
		  Anti-Apartheid Act (CAAA)

1988	Banning of 17 anti-apartheid organisations	
1989	F.W. de Klerk succeeds P.W. Botha as state president	

Total strategy 1948–1989: A statistical summary

DETENTION WITHOUT TRIAL

No. of persons detained (from 1960–1990)	80 000
including children (under 18)	15 000
including women	10 000
Estimate of numbers tortured in detention	20 000
No. of deaths in security detention (1960–1990)	73
No. of political deaths in police custody (1984–1989)	37

BANNING OF PERSONS

Banning and restriction orders (1950–1989) – estimated	3000
Persons 'listed' (gagged) – estimated	600

POLITICAL TRIALS

'Security' trials persons charged – estimated	15 000
'Unrest' trials persons charged – estimated	150 000
Political executions (1963–1989)	49

ORGANISATIONS

Numbers banned and restricted (1950–1989)	100

GATHERINGS

Blanket ban on outdoor political gatherings (1976–1990)	
Bans on specific gatherings	many thousands

PUBLICATIONS

Newspapers closed down	8
Newspapers warned	8
Newspapers suspended	3
Publications banned for possession or distribution – estimated	10 000

DEATHS IN POLITICAL UNREST

Deaths from 1948–1983	1400
Deaths from 1984–1989	5600

MASSACRES

No. of major massacres (1948–1989)	46

COVERT OPERATIONS

No. of abductions recorded by HRC	30
No. of disappearances recorded by HRC	38
No. of assassinations recorded by HRC	150

CROSS-BORDER OPERATIONS

No. of major cross-border raids	12
No. of cross-border bombings	29
No. of cross-border abductions	20
No. of lives lost (excluding Angolan invasion)	147

1 THE MANY FACES OF APARTHEID REPRESSION

*Repressive regimes abound in the historical record but few can have raised repression to the level of an art form in the way that the apartheid regime managed to do. The breadth and intensity of its arsenal of weapons scaled new heights or, perhaps more correctly, plumbed new depths. In order to portray the sweep of apartheid repression, the HRC published a document entitled **Anatomy of Repression** in December 1989. This document summarises the many forms of repression evolved by apartheid forces and used by them from the time of the accession to power of the Nationalist government in 1948 right up to the dying days of the eighties, a period of 42 years. It is reproduced here to initiate the reader into the subject, and to provide a broad perspective on the evolution of apartheid repression as it appeared in December 1989.*

ANATOMY OF REPRESSION
HRC, December 1989

Repression is the response of the apartheid regime and its supporters to resistance against the policies of apartheid; resistance by the people of South Africa, resistance by South Africa's neighbours and resistance by the international community.

Repression takes many forms, from the blunt controls of legislation to the more subtle controls of what has come to be known as 'low intensity conflict'. The apartheid regime has become a pioneer in repression, not only adopting the techniques of other past and present-day repressive regimes, but refining them to a pitch of perfection and even evolving new techniques which have served as a model for others to follow.

This document sets out to list and categorise all these forms of repression and briefly to outline their history and current status (as at December 1989).

The following forms of repression are examined in turn:
1. Formal repression
2. Informal repression
3. Target repression
4. Financial repression
5. External repression

1. Formal repression

Formal repression includes those forms of repression with which the apartheid regime has empowered itself by means of legislation placed by it on the statute books of the South African parliament.

Repressive legislation

- The Internal Security Act, No. 74 of 1982 (ISA) is permanently in force (including and especially during periods when no State of Emergency has been declared) and confers wide powers of detention without trial, banning of persons, organisations, gatherings, publications, etc. It has been in force, in one form or another, since 1963, and is fully operational at the present time. All the so-called 'independent' homelands have their own versions of the ISA, which are virtually indistinguishable from the parent.
- The Public Safety Act, No. 3 of 1953 (PSA) enables declaration of a State of Emergency (SOE) granting even wider and more unbridled powers, capable of use on a mass scale. Partial SOEs have been declared in 1960 and 1985 and National SOEs declared in 1986,1987,1988 and 1989 extending uninterruptedly from 12 June 1986 up to and including the present time.
- The Public Safety Amendment Act, No. 67 of 1986 (PSAA) enables declaration of Unrest Areas, the idea being to have SOE-type powers within specified areas without actually declaring a SOE and suffering the international repercussions, both economic and political. Although it has been on the statute books since 26 June 1986, no opportunity has yet arisen to invoke this Act.

Formal repression of persons

Detention without trial

- Detention for interrogation or 'preventive' purposes, without access to the courts, lawyers, family or friends, has been widely practised by the apartheid regime ever since 1960. Such detention can be in solitary confinement and for virtually indefinite periods (many have experienced detention without trial for as long as 32 months).
- Conditions of isolation from the outside world are conducive to abuses, and there has been a continuous stream of allegations of torture and assault in detention over the years and up to the present time. Court records abound with such allegations and medical records attest to serious physical and psychological effects.
- A by-product of detention conditions has been an unending procession of deaths in detention, the first in 1963, the most recent in 1988, a total of 69 deaths in all. If one is to believe the inquest verdicts, nearly half of these were suicides. A small number of escapes from detention have been reported but some of these are of such a mysterious nature that they must more properly be regarded as disappearances from detention.
- Since 1960, over 75 000 persons have been detained without trial, about 52 000 of them (or 70% of the total) within the last 5 years.
- During this latter period children and young people have accounted for at least 25% of the total, and women have accounted for over 10%.

Dov Fedler, *The Star*, 7 February 1986

- In July-August of 1986, the detention cells were filled with nearly 9000 persons at one time.
- A determined and tenacious hunger strike which started in January 1989 resulted in the release of the nearly 1000 detainees being held at that time, most of them for considerable periods of up to 30 months or more.
- New detentions continue and over the last few months the daily detainee population has fluctuated between 100 and 600. This includes children under the age of 18 years, some as young as 14.
- Records kept over the last 8 years reveal that 75% to 80% of all detentions end in release without any charge in a court of law, and that finally only 2% to 4% of all detainees are convicted of any offence.

Banning and restriction of persons
Banning of persons under 'security' legislation has been in operation since 1950, whilst restriction of persons under emergency regulations was first introduced in 1985. In effect, they are identical.

The purpose is similar to that of 'preventive' detention (and in fact frequently follows it), namely, to neutralise political opponents and withdraw them from the political arena. It provides strict control over the movement, activities, public utterances and association of the person, while often interfering severely with his or her ability to earn a living, engage in study or pursue a normal social life. In its more extreme form, it amounts to house arrest, with time off to report twice daily to a police station. By comparison with straightforward detention without trial, the financial burden of support is shifted from the state to the victim.

Since 1950, the number of bannings and restriction orders served is conservatively estimated to be around 3000. The effective length of each order can vary from 1 to 5 years, but successively applied orders can extend the period well beyond this. The longest period on record so far is 26 years.

At the present time new restriction orders continue to be served, and between 500 and 700 persons are currently restricted, most of them having already suffered the vicissitudes of years in detention and weeks on hunger strike. There is great concern about their vulnerability to attack, because of the predictability of their movements in having to report to a police station. Already, 2 have been assassinated and several others attacked.

Political trials

Over the years increasingly heavy use has been made of the courts to criminalise political activity and to remove opponents from the political arena, either as awaiting-trial or on-trial prisoners (for as long as 3 years) or as convicted political prisoners.

Extensive legislation for this purpose includes the ISA (and its forerunners and homelands variants), the PSA and its Emergency regulations, the Defence Act, common law (treason, public violence, etc.), and countless others.

The accused might be engaged in totally peaceful opposition and yet face charges ranging from treason and subversion to possession of banned literature, attending an unlawful gathering or participating in a boycott. Alternatively, the accused may have been caught up in political unrest situations involving violence (often on the part of police or army) and face charges ranging from public violence and murder to incitement and intimidation.

It is impossible to estimate the numbers of trials, persons accused, and persons convicted over the years, due to the lack of adequate records. However, partial records maintained by monitoring groups since 1984 show the following for the 5-year-period up to and including 1988:
• treason trials: 17 trials, 82 accused, 35 convicted;
• ISA-type trials: 521 trials, 4548 accused, 973 convicted;
• 'unrest' trials: impossible to estimate with any accuracy, but a report that 25 000 persons were charged in 1985 alone suggests a total in excess of 50 000 were charged in the 5 year period.

In the first 8 months of the current calendar year of 1989, the following trials have been completed:
• treason trials: 3 trials, 16 accused, 9 convicted;
• ISA-type trials: 190 trials, 785 accused, 261 convicted.

Furthermore, as at 1 September 1989, records show 317 political trials still in progress, 3 of them for treason. In the first 2 months (August – September) of the defiance campaign over 2000 persons were charged for attending unlawful gatherings, etc.

Current population of political prisoners serving sentences for 'security offences' is

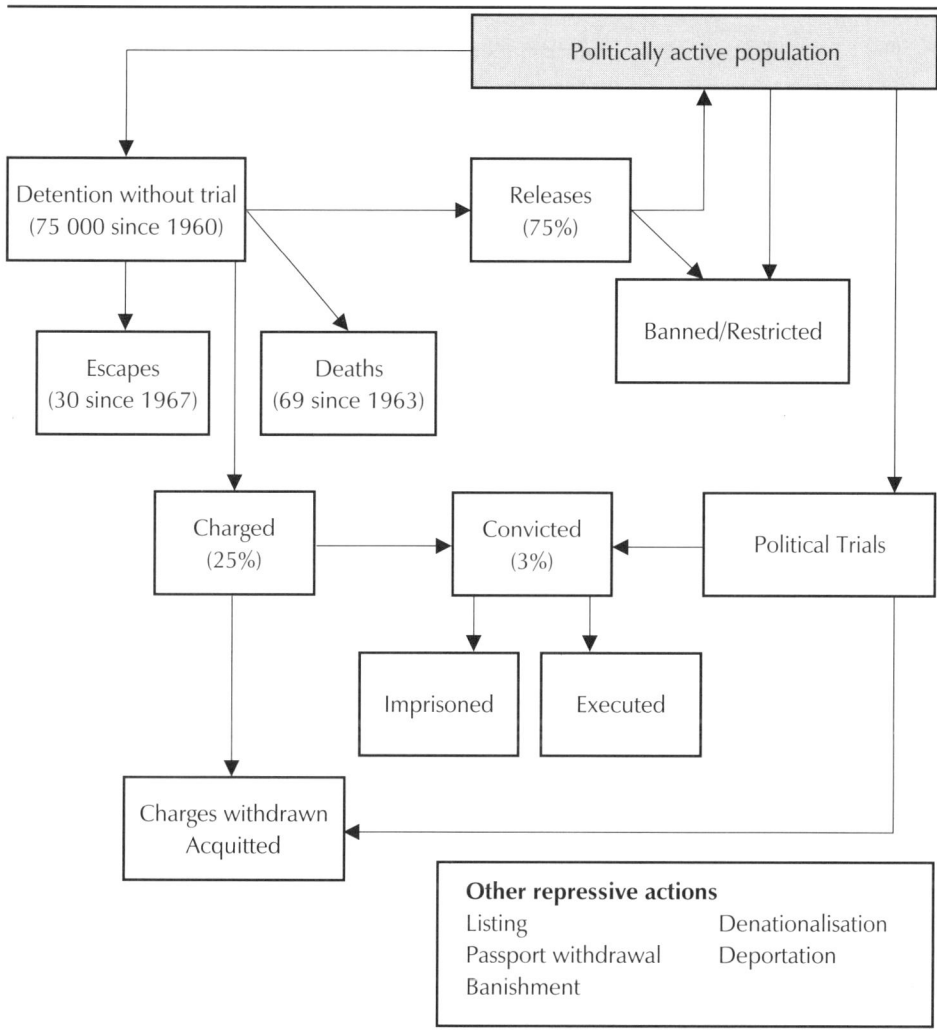

FIGURE 1
Formal repression of persons

about 350 and for 'unrest offences' is somewhere between 2000 and 3000. Included in the first group are over 20 women and also 14 serving life sentences, after taking into account those released in late October 1989.

Political executions
A special category of political prisoner is the condemned prisoner, convicted of murder under politically related circumstances, often through the legal principle of 'common purpose' as in the case of the Sharpeville Six.

During the last 2 years, 7 such prisoners have been executed by hanging and currently there are 84 on death row awaiting execution, including the Upington Fourteen. This latter number represents nearly one third of the total death-row population.

Other repressive actions against persons

- The Consolidated List, maintained under the ISA, is a list of persons who may not be quoted in any way (under pain of a prison sentence of up to three years). The list is reviewed annually, but can be amended at any time, to include names of those convicted of treason or security offences, and other categories. Newspaper editors must constantly maintain a thorough knowledge of this List, in order not to fall foul of the law, but several court actions against the media are currently in progress. The Consolidated List at present contains the names of over 500 persons, of whom 31 are deceased, 107 are living abroad and 350 are incarcerated in jails.

- Passports for South African citizens are a privilege, not a right, and may therefore be refused or withdrawn at any time, with no reasons given, and no possibility of a court challenge. Applications by many political opponents are constantly (and currently) being turned down. During 1988 there were 169 passport refusals.

- Banishment is a practice which was quite prevalent in the past and up to recent years (1987). It involves the removal of a person from a particular area for political reasons, and is most often combined with the subsequent confinement of that person to some remote area. Legislation used is the Riotous Assemblies Act, the ISA (forming part of a banning order) and homelands security legislation (especially in the Transkei).

- Denationalisation or the withdrawal of citizenship is a by-product of the creation of the 'independent' homelands. Besides the almost-endless repercussions on the daily lives of about 8 million people who have been deprived of their South African citizenship in this way, there are also political implications involving the refusal of admission into 'South Africa' of 'political undesirables', or their 'deportation' into their relevant ethnic homelands.

- Deportation or expulsion of South Africans has been practised for the last 10 years on the basis of their forfeited citizenship and by, in effect, declaring them undesirable aliens under the Admission of Persons to the Republic Regulations Act. During the last 2 years (1987–88) alone, 172 persons were deported in this way, 141 of them to Transkei, and the balance to Ciskei, Venda and Bophuthatswana.

Formal repression of organisations

Banning of organisations

Under the ISA (or its predecessors), once an organisation has been banned it becomes an unlawful organisation. Since 1950, 24 organisations have suffered this fate, with a further 42 under homelands security legislation.

Currently, anyone furthering the aims of 4 specified banned organisations may be charged with terrorism. These organisations are:
1. South African Communist Party (since 1950)
2. African National Congress (since 1960)
3. Pan Africanist Congress (since 1960)
4. Congress of South African Students (since 1985)

Restriction of organisations
Under emergency regulations there are currently 32 organisations which may not engage in 'any activities or acts whatsoever' other than purely administrative duties. In other words, they may continue to exist on paper, but may not function until the State of Emergency is lifted.

The Congress of South African Trade Unions (COSATU) is prohibited from engaging in a long list of political activities.

Funding restrictions
Restrictions on the receipt of foreign funding by organisations is dealt with elsewhere in this document.

Formal repression of gatherings

- Since 1976 there has been a blanket ban, renewed annually under the ISA, on all outdoor political meetings. During the last 4 years there has also been a blanket ban on all indoor meetings which advocate work stoppages, stayaways or educational boycotts.
- Since the 1950s, literally thousands of specific gatherings have been banned under security legislation and emergency regulations by ministerial, magisterial or police edict. Such gatherings have included public meetings, private meetings, protest demonstrations, rallies, commemorations, conferences, music festivals, concerts, carol services, detainee tea parties and fun runs.
- Funerals form a special category of gathering which has been severely restricted since 1985. Blanket restrictions are currently in force on all funerals in over 70 black townships, while specific restriction orders are constantly invoked on particular funerals in other areas (38 in 1988).
- Police are empowered to break up gatherings (whether banned in advance or not). For example, in August and September 1989 during the defiance campaign, over 50 marches and demonstrations were broken up, 28 with the application of force (including use of teargas, quirts, birdshot, rubber bullets, water cannon, batons, etc.).

While permission for some marches and other gatherings is currently being granted, others are being refused and the legislation empowering the banning and restriction of gatherings is firmly in place.

A recent innovation in interference with meetings takes the form of 'sitting-in' by the police. As many as 200 police occupy a block of seats in the hall and video-recordings of the proceedings are made in a prominent manner.

Formal repression of publications

- Individual publications (books, pamphlets, etc.) can be declared 'undesirable' and banned for possession or distribution under the Publications Act. Many thousands have been banned since 1963, about 500 per year being of a political nature. Nearly every Friday of the year a new list is gazetted.

- Newspapers can be closed down completely under the ISA. This has happened on 6 occasions. Newspapers can also be temporarily suspended under the SOE regulations after receiving warnings for repeatedly publishing 'subversive propaganda'. During 1988/9, warnings were issued to 8 newspapers and 3 of them were suspended for periods of up to 3 months. Currently, the *New Nation* is under warning of suspension
- Content of newspapers and other publications is severely restricted by an array of legislation. The ISA prohibits the quoting of a 'listed' person (see under Repression of Persons). The Police Act and the Prisons Act restrict reporting on the actions of the police and the conditions in prisons respectively. Other Acts serve to suppress 'sensitive' information on the production and procurement of armaments, petroleum products, nuclear products, etc.
- SOE regulations forbid the reporting of 'unrest', actions of the security forces, treatment of detainees, conditions of detention, etc. The regulations also prohibit the publishing or advertising of 'subversive statements', defined by a long list. During 1988 alone, 2240 reports of subversive statements were investigated. Blank spaces to indicate self-censorship are also forbidden. At present a number of prosecutions are in progress for alleged contraventions of the above Acts and regulations.

Formal repression of political actions

- A wide range of political actions is either banned directly under the ISA and under SOE regulations, or by implication under the definition of 'subversive statements' in the SOE Media Regulations and under the restrictions against political acts listed in the restriction order on COSATU.
- Boycott actions which are forbidden include educational, consumer, company, product, rent and election boycotts, as well as work stayaways and acts of civil disobedience.
- The creation and promotion of 'alternative structures' including people's courts, alternative education, alternative local government, and area, block and street committees are classified as subversive.
- Prohibited political campaigns include those calling for the release of detainees and political prisoners, the scrapping of detention without trial, the unbanning of banned organisations, the scrapping of local authorities and an end to compulsory military service. Other subversive acts include advocating disinvestment, economic and other sanctions, expressing solidarity with banned organisations, opposing new constitutional proposals and commemorating past political events.

2. Informal repression

Informal repression includes those forms of repression which lie outside the direct controls of formal security legislation and which are exercised by state structures at one end of the scale and by persons unknown at the other end of the scale. In order of descending overt links with the state, we have the National Management System (a parallel or shadow system of government); vigilante groups, whose state links are often but thinly disguised; and hit squads composed of unknown persons but whose political affiliation and intent are clear.

National Management System (NMS)

The NMS was until recently named the National Security Management System but the word 'security' has been dropped from the title, presumably to play down the real purpose of the system. The NMS, which has no constitutional status, was set up in 1986 by army generals and police chiefs and is designed to co-ordinate the counter-revolutionary warfare strategy of 'eliminating' or 'taking out' political activists while simultaneously 'winning hearts and minds' (WHAM) of the masses by token township upgrading.

At the top of the system is the State Security Council (SSC), which effectively is a secretive super-cabinet, whilst at regional, district and local level are the Joint Management Centres (JMCs), about 500 in number. The JMCs, with representation from the Security Police, Military Intelligence and National Intelligence Service (NIS), are responsible, inter alia, for gathering information in all localities about political activists and their organisations and identifying their places of abode and work, their movements and links. This and related information is fed upwards through various committees to the SSC. The SSC in turn digests this information from all areas and forms an overall security profile, on which it continually reviews security policy and sends down decisions and instructions to the JMCs.

The instruments for carrying out instructions on the 'security' side of the overall strategy at local level are the riot police, security police, army personnel, municipal police and *kitskonstabels* ('instant police'), all co-ordinated by the JMC for the area, and using powers of detention, banning, restricting, spying, monitoring and harassment. There are strong suspicions that such instructions also find their way to vigilantes and hit squads.

Vigilantes

Vigilante groups have their origins in the support systems which have grown up around the apartheid-created structures of homelands authorities and of black local authorities. As such they are squarely situated in the camp of apartheid supporters and collaborators. Like the NMS they began to emerge between 1985 and 1986, and, like the NMS, they form an important component of the strategy of counter-revolutionary warfare patterned on the models of Algeria, El Salvador, the Philippines and other countries, and involving the tactics of 'low-intensity conflict' (LIC). Low intensity refers to the level of profile rather than the degree of violence, and relates to the attempts to transfer the responsibility of violent action against anti-apartheid groupings away from the South African Police and army to elements ostensibly within the black community and thereby promote the idea of 'black-on-black violence'.

Easily demonstrable links exist between vigilante groups and homelands police, municipal police of black councils and *kitskonstabels*. Sometimes common facilities are used, and often the vigilantes serve as a recruiting source for these police structures, earning them the description of 'vigilantes in uniform'. Links with the South African Police are less obvious, but numerous claims have been made of free rein and even sponsorship being given to vigilantes by the SAP as a factor which has stimulated the growth of such groupings. Typical of these claims was the manner in which the vigilante group known as the *Witdoeke* accomplished in a few weeks what the state had failed to do in 10 years, namely the destruction of the Crossroads and KTC squatter camps housing 70 000 people.

Situations which invite vigilante intervention, always of extreme brutality, are, in the case of the homelands, resistance by communities to enforced incorporation or to the creation of new homelands; and in the case of urban communities, opposition to black municipal councils through promoting civic associations as alternative structures with popular support. Such vigilante intervention is lethal in intent and has as its express purpose the elimination of leadership and rank-and-file members of opposition organisations.

Internal refugees

The hunting down and rooting out of political activists by state security structures and by vigilantes in specific areas have created a phenomenon known as 'internal refugees'. These are people who have been identified and singled out for elimination in one way or another and no longer find it safe to live within their communities. They live a life on the run, away from their homes and in constant fear of discovery. Sometimes whole communities are uprooted in this way and forced into a twilight existence. The internal refugee population has at times numbered in the thousands.

Hit squads

Acts of violence by unknown persons against the opponents of apartheid are not new, but the sheer volume and sophistication of such acts during the last 5 years is a clear indication of the widespread existence and activity of well-organised units or hit squads. A high degree of expertise is evident, with skills in the use of explosives, weapons, incendiary materials, chemicals, lock-picking devices, etc. Abundant resources include equipment, materials and access to information not generally available to the public. Funding does not seem to be a problem. Speculation as to the base for such an operation inevitably leads to state security structures, particularly the security police which would also explain the virtually complete absence of success on the part of the police in solving these numerous mysteries. Apparent evidence of such security force involvement has been surfacing recently.

Hit squads seem to have as their purpose the elimination or intimidation of political activists, and/or the disruption or crippling of their organisations.

Actions against individuals range from straightforward assassination to harassment of all kinds including death threats, attacks on homes (bricks, shots, petrol bombs, teargas canisters, dead cats, etc.) and attacks on vehicles (petrol bombs, bricks, paint, tampering with tyres and brakes). Limited records kept over the last 5 years show at least 5 disappearances, 45 assassinations (11 during 1989), 160 attempted assassinations (28 in 1989) and 68 incidents of harassment (38 in 1989).

Actions against anti-apartheid organisations frequently involve the bombing or fire-bombing of offices or whole buildings in which they are housed. Another widely used technique for crippling organisations is to burgle their offices and remove records, computers, equipment, etc. Partial records show 79 attacks and 29 burglaries in the last 5 years (13 and 9 respectively during 1989). In addition, 9 places of worship have been attacked and 4 graves desecrated. Disinformation in the form of bogus newsletters, smear pamphlets and so on, often displays a high level of sophistication and inside knowledge, such as would be gained from the interrogation of detainees or through informers.

Since the section on hit squads was written, clear evidence has come to light of extensive police-based hit squad activity.

3. Target repression

A number of well-defined groupings of the population have become the targeted victims of apartheid repression. As will be seen from Table 1, these groups cover almost every aspect and sphere of our society, with some notable exceptions, such as the business community. The sheer comprehensiveness of this list seems to suggest a government which is at war with its people, and a population which questions the legitimacy and authority of its government. The impact of repression on some of the major targets is described below.

TABLE 1
Targets of repression

Community	Extra-parliamentary political bodies Civic and residents associations Rural bodies Women's organisations Youth organisations Children
Educational	Pupils, teachers, headmasters, inspectors University students, lecturers, professors Student bodies
Trade unions	Union leaders, organisers, shop stewards Union members, workers
Religious	Ministers Church officials, church workers Church bodies
Media	Journalists, photographers, editors Newspapers
Professionals	Lawyers Doctors, nurses, social workers
Cultural	Actors, writers, poets
Sporting	Sports administrators Sporting bodies

United Democratic Front and affiliates

The United Democratic Front (UDF), founded in August 1983 to oppose the introduction of a tricameral parliament and black municipal councils, has ever since become the prime target of state repression. Over 75% of all identifiable detainees during that time have been members of the UDF or its affiliates. In February 1988, the UDF was restricted from engaging in any activities whatsoever under the emergency regulations, which is its current status. It has also been declared an Affected Organisation, which prohibits it from receiving any foreign funds whatsoever. Virtually all of its leadership has been either imprisoned or restricted at one time or another, and many are still affected. A growing list of members have fallen victim to assassination and to killings by vigilantes.

Youth and students

These groups have been at the forefront of resistance to apartheid since 1976, and have as a result borne the brunt of repression, and continue to do so:
- Huge numbers have been detained (about 15 000 in the last 5 years).
- The major student organisation, COSAS, with over a million members has been banned out of existence.
- 12 youth and student organisations are restricted under SOE regulations from engaging in any activity whatsoever.
- Special SOE regulations are in force, which control the presence in or movement in and out of schools, and control what may be taught and what clothing may be worn.

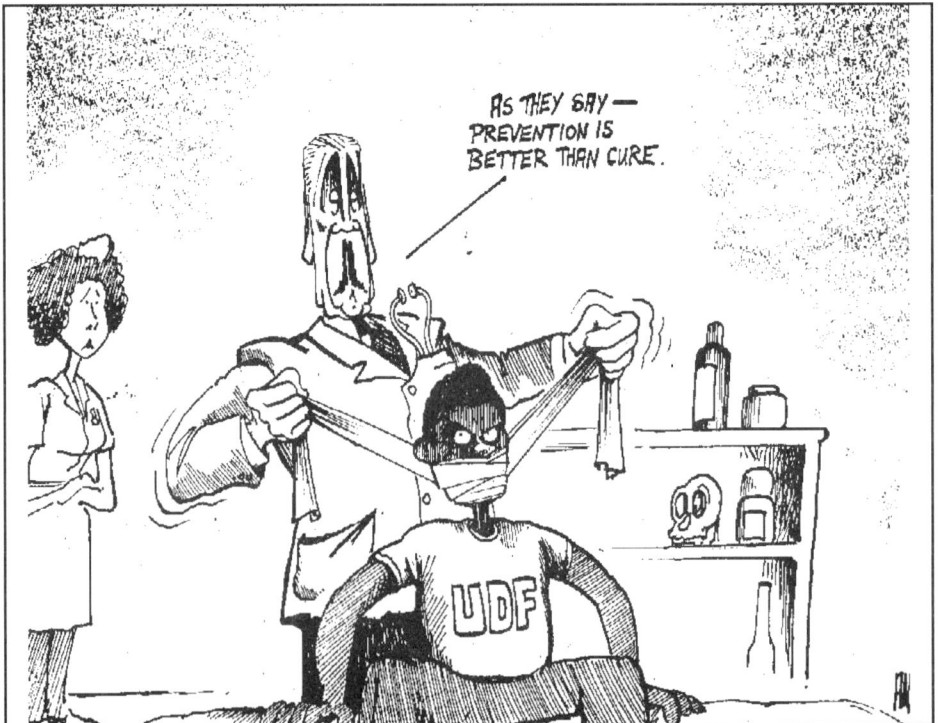

Andy, *Rand Daily Mail*, 25 April 1985

Educational boycotts are specifically forbidden.

- Leadership is heavily prone to detention, restriction, harassment and assassination.

Trade unions

The trade union movement is an extremely important factor in the struggle against the apartheid system. This has been recognised by the introduction of the Labour Relations Amendment Act designed to curb worker power.

Large numbers of trade unionists have fallen victim to detention without trial, and many have been restricted upon their release from detention while others have been tied up in lengthy political trials, and some are on death row. Many trade union members have been subject to arson attacks on their homes, and some disappearances and assassinations are on record. Vigilante action, especially in Natal, has been particularly prominent. The major federation, COSATU, has been singled out for restriction under the SOE regulations, prohibiting any activity construed as political. Its officials are refused passports, its members subjected to considerable police harassment and its offices constantly attacked and burgled.

Churches

The churches and church organisations are in a special position in the struggle against apartheid, having immunity not enjoyed by other opponents of apartheid. However, this 'immunity' does not protect its members or property from the following:

- hundreds of church workers have suffered detention without trial and have even reported being tortured;
- the churches and their leaders have been subjected to vitriolic propaganda attacks by the state-controlled TV and radio;
- hit squads have attacked numerous church buildings and have, for example, destroyed the headquarters of both the SACC and the SACBC;
- an attempt on the life of Revd Frank Chikane, secretary general of the SACC, was made recently through the use of a poison.

The media

Alarmed at the bad image being created in the outside world by security force action, the apartheid regime introduced special SOE Media Regulations on 11 December 1986, designed to impose a news black-out reminiscent of wartime. Such regulations have been reinforced and fine-tuned to a pitch of perfection.

The Media Regulations basically prohibit the reporting in any way of unrest incidents or actions of the security forces. Powers have also been introduced to warn and then suspend publications. During 1988, 6 publications received warnings and 3 newspapers were suspended for periods of up to 12 weeks. During 1989 a further 5 warnings were issued and another 2 newspapers suspended, with 1 currently under threat of suspension.

The latest form of harassment is a spate of charges against newspapers and journalists for contravening the ISA by quoting listed persons, or contravening SOE media regulations.

4. Financial repression

One of the expressions of the international community's rejection of apartheid policy is the providing of funds for the victims of apartheid. Not surprisingly the apartheid regime has responded with measures designed to repress foreign funding of this nature. Two pieces of legislation with this purpose in mind are currently in force:

Affected Organisations Act, No. 31 of 1974

This Act was introduced in 1974 and is still on the statute books. Its effect is to ban outright the receipt of funds from foreign sources by any organisation that has been declared 'affected'. Two such organisations cut off from foreign funds are the National Union of South African Students (NUSAS), since 1974 and the UDF, since 1988.

Disclosure of Foreign Funding Act, No. 26 of 1989

This new Act was promulgated on 23 March 1989 and came into operation on 18 August 1989. At least 4 organisations have already been notified that they are under consideration for being declared as Reporting Organisations. The effect of such declaration would be administratively to compel the disclosure of confidential information, such as would be of interest to the security police or other governmental agencies, thereby exposing the organisation or person to such actions as banning or restriction.

5. External repression

It is well known that the tentacles of apartheid repression extend well beyond the borders of South Africa. Its effects are felt in neighbouring and nearby states and have resulted in the destabilisation of the entire Southern African region. On occasion they are felt even further afield.

A recent Commonwealth report describes the destabilisation of Southern Africa over the last 8 years as having reached 'holocaust' proportions. The human cost is estimated at 1.5 million dead through military and economic action, most of them children, while a further 4 million people have been displaced from their homes. Half a million children in Mozambique alone are deprived of education through the destruction of their schools and Angola has per capita the world's largest population of limbless people, some 40 000, as a result of land mines. The economic cost to the 6 frontline states is estimated to exceed 45 billion US dollars (R120 billion) or more than double their combined foreign debt. Considerable development potential and economic growth have been forgone as a result of defence claiming first priority on resources.

The South African government has used, and continues to use, a variety of methods to repress and destabilise its neighbours.

- Armed action, ranging from sporadic commando raids to full-scale invasion and occupation;
- suspected use of under-cover hit squads to abduct and assassinate opponents;

- the encouragement of surrogates or 'contra' forces, through training, logistical support and intelligence;
- political pressures to promote the installation of governments well disposed towards apartheid South Africa;
- economic pressures to create and maintain a dependency on the South African transport, harbour, customs and financial systems.

Conclusion

In reviewing the vast array of weapons of repression in the armoury of the apartheid regime we come inevitably to the conclusion that as at December 1989 virtually all of these weapons are still in place and still in operation. Some forms may have been reduced in use in favour of others, but none has been abandoned. Furthermore, when the inevitable lifting (or modifying) of the State of Emergency comes about, practically the entire range of options will still be available under permanent legislation.

2 THE LEGAL VENEER

The apartheid government always had an obsession with projecting itself to the outside world as a Western-style parliamentary democracy. All public actions taken by it, no matter how reprehensible or abhorrent to the outside world, were always packaged in legislated form as Acts of parliament duly gazetted and followed by regulations where appropriate. Whether it was the denial of fundamental rights of movement, expression, assembly, residence, association and so on; or the forced relocation of millions of dispossessed people, or the creation of 'independent states' recognised by no one, all such actions were clothed in the respectability of formal legislation. Long after apartheid was pronounced a crime against humanity, the South African government still kept up this charade of parliamentary correctness and the 'rule of law'.

Formalised repression was no exception. A long succession of Acts legalising every form of repression imaginable finally culminated in an omnibus piece of legislation known as the Internal Security Act, No. 74 of 1982. A thorough examination and analysis of this Act, its history, application and status as at July 1990 appears in the HRC document, entitled **Internal Security Act**, *published in July 1990.*

There have also been times – during the States of Emergency – when the gloves came off to reveal cold steel. Such States of Emergency were given legal force and standing under the Public Safety Act, No. 3 of 1953 (PSA). The declarations of Emergencies and their consequences are also described in this chapter from material drawn from DPSC and HRC monthly reports from July 1985 to July 1990, and entitled **Public Safety Act and States of Emergency.**

INTERNAL SECURITY ACT
HRC, July 1990

1. Introduction
2. Homelands security legislation
3. Powers of the ISA
   Detention without trial
   Banning of persons
   Listing of persons
   Banning of organisations

Banning of gatherings
Banning of publications
Political trials and imprisonment

1. Introduction

The Internal Security Act, No. 74 of 1982 is the current permanent security legislation of the Republic of South Africa. It came into effect on 2 July 1982, but has a long ancestry stretching back to 1950. Included amongst its progenitors are a whole succession of Acts, starting with the Suppression of Communism Act, and progressing through a series of Internal Security Acts, General Law Amendment Acts, Riotous Assemblies Acts, the Unlawful Organisations Act and the Terrorism Act. In 1979, the Rabie Commission was appointed to streamline and consolidate this plethora of legislation. At the end of its labours a report was tabled before parliament on 3 February 1982, which culminated in the Internal Security Act as we know it today, and in the simultaneous repeal of most of its forerunners. In this sense it can be described as the last word in security legislation, a monument to over 30 years of experience in drafting statutes which could defend apartheid security against its many opponents; a monument to the way in which loopholes and avenues of expression could be closed down one by one, until space for legitimate political opposition vanished altogether.

2. Homelands security legislation

Before examining the Internal Security Act in detail, it is necessary to point out that the so-called independent homelands of Transkei, Bophuthatswana, Venda and Ciskei have their own security legislation as follows:
• Transkei Public Security Act, No. 30 of 1977
• Bophuthatswana Internal Security Act, No. 32 of 1979
• Venda Maintenance of Law and Order Act, No. 13 of 1985
• Ciskei National Security Act, No. 13 of 1982

They are, in effect, carbon copies of the ISA, which comes as no surprise, so that any analysis of the ISA applies equally to the security legislation of the TBVC territories. In the case of the so-called self-governing homelands of Gazankulu, KaNgwane, KwaNdebele, KwaZulu, Lebowa and QwaQwa, these areas fall under the jurisdiction of the ISA.

3. Powers of the Internal Security Act

The powers of the ISA are truly awesome. There is hardly a form of political expression which is not blocked, controlled or threatened by one or other provision of the ISA. This document sets out to analyse these extraordinary powers, to describe briefly the implementation of these powers in the past, and in particular to examine the current status of the way in which they are being applied.

Detention without trial

ISA powers of detention without trial

The ISA provides for detention without trial for 3 different stated purposes:
1. Detention for interrogation (Section 29)
2. Preventive detention (Sections 28, 50 and 50A)
3. Witness detention (Section 31)

1. **Detention for interrogation.** Section 29 allows a detainee to be held in solitary confinement without access to lawyers, family, friends or anyone else other than state officials (interrogators, magistrates, district surgeons, etc.) for the purpose of interrogation. The period of detention is effectively unlimited (a two-year uninterrupted detention is on record) until 'all questions are satisfactorily answered'. The intensely hostile environment of this form of detention has led to innumerable allegations of torture and to a substantial number of deaths. The jurisdiction of the courts over such detention is specifically excluded.
2. **Preventive detention.** Section 28 allows the holding of a person in prison by ministerial order (as opposed to court sentence) if the minister believes that person is likely to commit a security offence. The period of detention is, in effect, unlimited. The wording requires the minister to give reasons for detention, a requirement which has resulted in successful court challenges, and a subsequent abandoning of Section 28 in favour of other means.

    Section 50A provides other means of long-term preventive detention. It allows for detention of up to 180 days (renewable) simply on the basis of the opinion, without giving reasons, of a police officer. This section, introduced as an amendment to the ISA in 1986, can only come into operation when so proclaimed by the state president. So far, this has not been necessary due to the even wider powers of preventive detention that have existed under the States of Emergency.

    Section 50 allows for the holding of a person for a short period of up to 14 days. It has been extensively used when and where no State of Emergency existed and it can be expected that its use will now be resumed.
3. **Witness detention.** Section 31 allows the attorney-general to order the detention of a person in solitary confinement, without any access, and beyond the jurisdiction of any court, if he believes that person could be a material witness in a security trial. Time limit is 6 months, unless the trial has started before then. Almost invariably, Section 31 detention is an extension of Section 29 detention when, as a result of the interrogation process, it is decided that the detainee shall become a state witness (with or without the agreement of the detainee).

Past application of detention without trial under ISA

Records kept over the years show that a minimum of 24 000 detentions have taken place since 1963 when powers of detention under permanent legislation were first introduced (including about 6500 detentions in the TBVC homelands). This figure is aside from the 54 000 detentions which have taken place under State of Emergency powers.

Records kept since 1981 reveal that about 75% to 80% of all detentions end in release without charge in any court of law, attesting to the political nature and purpose of such detention. These records also reveal that only 2% to 4% of detainees are convicted of any offence.

Since 1963, over 70 persons have died in detention, the vast majority of them while being held under ISA and TBVC legislation.

Current application of detention without trial under ISA

During the first half of 1990, detention without trial under the ISA has been going on at a level such that the numbers being held at any one time have fluctuated between 30 and 50. With the lifting of the State of Emergency in all areas except Natal, detentions under ISA can be expected to rise, using Section 29, 31 and 50 and also TBVC homelands legislation. Furthermore, Section 50A could be invoked at any time.

Deaths in detention have continued to occur during 1990, as have reports of torture in detention. Two of the deaths occurred whilst persons were being held under Section 29 of the ISA. Torture and deaths in detention can be expected to continue for as long as detention without trial is permitted to remain on the statute books.

Banning of persons

ISA powers of banning of persons

Sections 18 to 27 of the ISA set forth the manner in which a person may be served with a banning order, and what the stipulations of such a banning order may be:

- Membership of or participation in organisations can be banned under Section 18 by enforcing resignation, prohibiting joining and various other restrictions.
- Confinement to an area can be enforced under Section 19 by specifying the place and times of confinement. This can include house arrest or banishment to a remote area.
- Communication with other people can be barred during area confinement under Section 19 by prohibiting visitors.
- Admission to places or buildings can be prohibited under Section 19; these can include educational institutions, workplaces, etc.
- Attendance at gatherings can be prohibited under Section 20, a gathering being defined as a coming together of 'any number of persons having a common purpose, whether lawful or unlawful'.
- Periodical reporting to a police station can be enforced under Section 21 by specifying the frequency, such as once or twice a day for the duration of the banning order.
- Gagging of the person can be ensured under Section 23 by making it an offence under Section 56(1)(p) to quote that person.
- The duration of the banning order can be unlimited.

Past application of banning of persons under the ISA

Banning of persons under security legislation has been in operation since 1950. Its purpose is similar to that of 'preventive' detention (and in fact frequently has followed it), namely, to neutralise political opponents and withdraw them from the political arena. It provides strict control over the movement, activities, public utterances and association of the person, while interfering severely with the pursuit of a normal life. Since 1950, close on 2000 people have been subjected to this twilight existence under security legislation, apart from those under the States of Emergency. The effective length of each banning order can vary from 1 to 5 years, but, successively applied, orders can extend the period well beyond this. The longest period on record is 26 years.

Current application of banning of persons under ISA

During 1986 a number of court challenges were successfully brought against banning orders on the basis that the reasons which the minister is required to give under Section 25 were invalid. Since that time no banning orders under the ISA have been issued, but use has instead been made of wider powers under State of Emergency regulations. All such SOE restriction orders were withdrawn on 2 February 1990. As a consequence no one is currently under a banning order but the ISA powers still stand.

Listing of persons

ISA powers of listing of persons

Sections 16 and 17 of the ISA instruct the Director of Security Legislation to maintain a list (known as the Consolidated List) of persons' names who are:

- members of unlawful organisations,
- convicted of security offences or treason or sedition,
- banned,
- detained under Section 28.

    The consequences of being listed bar that person from:

- being quoted (an offence under Section 56(1)(p) with a penalty of up to 3 years),
- holding parliamentary office (Section 33),
- practising law (Section 34).

Past application of listing of persons under ISA

The practice of 'listing' dates back to the Suppression of Communism Act of 1950. Many hundreds were labelled as 'communist' in this way over the years and the numbers were swelled by the names of the banned, of the 'preventive' detainees and of the security prisoners. Each year an updated list is gazetted and includes people who are living in exile, resident in South Africa, incarcerated in prisons and those who are deceased.

Current application of listing of persons under ISA

The last annual gazetting of the Consolidated List was on 4 August 1989. A total of 537 names appeared on the list at that time. However, due to the unbanning of organisations on 2 February 1990 and to certain other factors, a substantial number of people have since been de-listed. Nevertheless, over 300 names are still left on the Consolidated List and are subject to the consequences.

Banning of organisations

ISA powers of banning of organisations
Under Section 4 of the ISA, the minister is empowered to declare an organisation to be unlawful. There are a number of consequences of such a declaration and these are enumerated in Sections 13 and 14. Briefly they provide for winding down the organisation by confiscating and liquidating its assets and by prohibiting anyone from furthering its aims in any way. Contravention of such a prohibition becomes an offence under Section 56(1)(a) and is punishable by a sentence of up to 10 years.

Past application of banning of organisations under ISA
The first organisation to be declared unlawful was the South African Communist Party (SACP) in 1950, followed in 1960 by the African National Congress (ANC) and the Pan Africanist Congress (PAC). In all, 24 organisations have suffered this fate, plus a further 42 under homelands security legislation.

Current application of banning of organisations under ISA
All 24 organisations referred to above were unbanned on 2 February 1990. TBVC homelands have since followed suit. As a consequence no organisation is currently under a banning order, but the banning powers remain on the statute books.

Banning of gatherings

ISA powers of banning gatherings
Sections 46 to 53 of the ISA deal with the measures available to prohibit or control various gatherings.

"This is an illegal gathering under the riotous assembly provision of the Internal Security Act. I'm giving you three minutes to disperse!"

Tony Grogan, *Cape Times*, 20 December 1985

- The minister of law and order can, under Section 46, prohibit gatherings of a particular class in any area, at any time and for any period. He can also prohibit specific gatherings.
- Magistrates can, under Section 46, prohibit or impose conditions on specific or all gatherings within their magisterial district, for a period up to 48 hours.
- The police may bar access, under Section 47, to places where a gathering has been prohibited and may, under Sections 48 and 49, disperse prohibited or certain other gatherings with the use of force, including firearms, depending upon certain circumstances.

Past application of banning of gatherings under ISA

Since 1950, literally thousands of gatherings have been banned by ministerial, magisterial and police edict and tens of thousands have appeared in court charged with attending unlawful gatherings. Such gatherings have included public meetings, private meetings, protest marches and demonstrations, rallies, commemorations, conferences and spontaneous gatherings of all kinds.

Since 1976, the minister has imposed a blanket ban, renewed annually, on all outdoor political gatherings for which no permission has been obtained. Since 1986 there has also been a blanket ban on all indoor gatherings at which work stoppages, stayaways or educational boycotts are advocated.

During 1989, the official figure of arrests for attending gatherings banned under the ISA was 2171 persons. During late 1989, as a consequence of the mass support for the Defiance Campaign, permission began to be granted for protest marches and demonstrations to give de jure effect to a de facto situation. There was, however, a high degree of inconsistency, and in August and September alone over 50 marches and demonstrations were broken up by the police, 28 with the application of force resulting in many deaths and injuries.

Current application of banning of gatherings under ISA

The blanket bans on all outdoor political gatherings and certain indoor political gatherings are still in place, having been renewed for another year as from 1 April 1990. Furthermore, the ministerial and magisterial powers to ban specific meetings continue to be exercised. Of particular concern however is the current behaviour of the police in the way that they are exercising their powers of breaking up gatherings. Records show that in the first half of 1990 over 170 persons have lost their lives and more than 1500 have been injured during the course of such police action.

Banning of publications

ISA powers of banning publications

Under Section 5 of the ISA, the minister can close down a newspaper or similar periodical if he deems that the publication expresses views endangering the security of the state, propagates or furthers communism, or propagates views or furthers the aims of banned organisations.

Under Section 15 of the ISA, a newspaper on applying for registration must deposit up to R40 000 if the minister believes it will be a candidate for banning at any stage. In the event of subsequent banning, the deposit is forfeited. Furthermore, registration lapses if the newspaper fails to come out at least once a month.

Under Section 56(1)(b) any person who distributes publications banned under the ISA can be imprisoned for up 10 years while under Section 56(1)(c) possession of such publications can result in a 3-year sentence.

Past application of banning of publications under ISA

During the years 1952 to 1977, 8 newspapers were closed down in terms of Section 5 of the ISA. Although they have long ceased to exist, they were all technically unbanned by a Government Notice dated 3 February 1990 as a consequence of the unbanning of previously unlawful organisations.

In 1988, the deposit requirements of Section 15 forced an Eastern Cape news agency to abandon plans to start a newspaper. More recently, deposits were demanded of *The New African* and *Vrye Weekblad*.

Current application of banning of publications under ISA

No newspapers or other publications are currently banned under the ISA although the powers to do so are still intact. So are the powers to demand a deposit for the registration of a new newspaper. The numerous prosecutions of past years for the distribution or possession of banned publications have tapered off, leaving only one or two trials for such offences allegedly committed before 2 February 1990.

Political trial and imprisonment

ISA powers of political trial

TABLE 2
Summary of the main political offences and penalties

Section	Offence	Penalty
54 (1)	Terrorism	As provided for Treason
54 (2)	Subversion	Up to 25 years
54 (3)	Sabotage	Up to 20 years
54 (4)	Harbouring	As for 54(1)(2) or (3)
55	Furthering communism	Up to 10 years
56	Furthering banned organisations	
	Banned publication	Various
	Breaking banning order	1, 3 or 10 years
	Quoting listed person	
57	Convening or attending a banned gathering	Up to 3 years or R3000
58/59/60	Committing, inciting or funding unlawful acts during a campaign against any law	Various – up to 5 years

Sections 54 to 63 of the ISA define a wide range of political offences, together with the prescribed penalties upon conviction, while Sections 64 to 69 deal with the procedure and jurisdiction of the courts. Section 30 empowers the attorney-general to remove the discretion of the courts to grant bail to a person accused of certain security offences.

Past application of political trial under ISA
The history of political trial and imprisonment goes back to the very beginnings of the ISA and its forerunners. It is impossible to estimate the number of trials, persons charged and persons convicted over the years because of the lack of adequate records. However, an estimate based on records kept by monitoring groups for the last 5-year period shows over 500 such trials involving about 5000 accused and resulting in about 1000 convictions.

The average prison population of 'security' prisoners at any point during this period fluctuated between 300 and 400, with a continuous inflow of new prisoners balancing out the releases at end of sentence.

Current application of political trial under ISA
Political trials under the ISA continue. Some of these trials relate to events before F.W. de Klerk's parliamentary address of 2 February 1990, but others to events after that date. About 30 ISA trials have been completed since that date and as many are still in progress.

About 120 'security' prisoners have, since 2 February, been released before completion of sentence, but about 300 still remain (apart from the much higher number of political prisoners serving sentences for 'unrest'offences).

Summary of the Internal Security Act
DETENTION WITHOUT TRIAL
Powers	S.29 Interrogation
	S.28, 50 Preventive
	S.31 Witness
Past usage	24 000 detentions since 1963.
	75% released without charge. 4% convicted.
	65 deaths in ISA detention.
	Numerous reports of torture.
Present usage (July 1990)	Detentions continue.
	About 80 now held under S.29 or 31.
	Use of S.50 expected to resume.
	TBVC homelands detentions still continue.
	2 deaths in S.29 during 1990.
	Reports of torture continue.

BANNING OF PERSONS
Powers	S.18 to 27
	House arrest, banishment
Past usage	2000 persons banned since 1950 from 1 to 26 years.
	Strict control over movement, activities, utterances, association & severe interference with normal life.

Present usage (July 1990)	Not in use since 1986.
	Powers intact.

LISTING OF PERSONS

Powers	S.16, 17 Consolidated List
Past usage	Since 1950 prohibition quoting of listed persons.
	In 1989 there were 537 named.
Present usage (July 1990)	Still in use. Over 300 names on list.

BANNING OF ORGANISATIONS

Powers	S.4, 13, 14
	'Unlawful' organisations
Past usage	24 organisations banned since 1950. (+42 in homelands.)
	Heavy sentences for furthering aims.
Present usage (July 1990)	All unbanned on 2 February 1990.
	Banning powers intact.

BANNING OF GATHERINGS

Powers	S.46 to 53
	Ministerial, magisterial & police powers.
Past usage	Since 1950, thousands of gatherings banned & tens of thousands arrested (over 2000 in 1989).
	Since 1976, blanket ban on outdoor gatherings.
Present usage (July 1990)	Outdoor ban renewed 1 April 1990.
	Over 170 deaths, 1500 injured during police break-up of gatherings in first half 1990.

BANNING OF PUBLICATIONS

Powers	S.5, 15
Past usage	8 newspapers closed down from 1952 to 1977.
	Hundreds charged with possession or distribution of banned publications
Present usage (July 1990)	No publications banned under ISA.
	Banning powers intact.

POLITICAL TRIAL AND IMPRISONMENT

Powers	S.54 to 63
	Security offences and penalties
Past usage	Tens of thousands charged since 1950, with offences under ISA.
	Thousands convicted and sentenced for terms up to life imprisonment.
	Last 5 years, 500 trials, 5000 accused & 1000 convicted. Between 300 & 400 security prisoners at any point in time.
Present usage (July 1990)	ISA trials continue.
	Over 30 completed this year, further 30 in progress.
	About 300 security prisoners still held.

PUBLIC SAFETY ACT AND STATES OF EMERGENCY
DPSC/HRC, 1985–1990

Legislation

Under the Public Safety Act, No. 3 of 1953, the head of state is empowered to declare a State of Emergency in part or all of South Africa, if in his opinion 'it appears that circumstances have arisen which seriously threaten the safety of the public and the maintenance of public order, and that the ordinary law of the land is inadequate to enable the government to ensure the safety of the Public and to maintain public order'.

Given that the 'ordinary law of the land' is the Internal Security Act with all its awesome powers, there must be very compelling reasons for invoking a State of Emergency. Essentially these are the power to use all security forces (defence force as well as police) on a mass scale, with a minimum of procedural constraint, suitably indemnified against prosecution. Unless withdrawn sooner, a proclamation remains in force for 12 months. However, repeat proclamations can ensure an indefinite State of Emergency. The PSA also provides for the issuing of any regulations deemed necessary for dealing with the state of emergency.

Declarations of States of Emergency

TABLE 3
States of Emergency

Dates declared	Areas affected	Dates lifted/expired
30 March 1960	122 magisterial districts	31 August 1960
21 July 1985	44 magisterial districts	7 March 1986
12 June 1986	All of 'RSA' (not TBVCs)	11 June 1987
11 June 1987	All of 'RSA' (not TBVCs)	10 June 1988
10 June 1988	All of 'RSA' (not TBVCs)	9 June 1989
9 June 1989	All of 'RSA' (not TBVCs)	8 June 1990
8 June 1990	Province of Natal	18 October 1990

The first occasion on which the apartheid government considered that circumstances had arisen which warranted invoking the PSA and declaring a State of Emergency was on 30 March 1960. The relevant circumstances then were the Sharpeville massacre of 21 March 1960, claiming the lives of 67 victims and sending shock waves around the country, and indeed the world; and the banning of the ANC and PAC one week later. The declaration was to affect 122 magisterial districts (out of 265) before being lifted 5 months later on 31 August 1960. Detentions numbered 11 727.

Surprisingly, the Soweto Uprising of June 1976 did not produce a similar reaction on the part of the government, despite the fact that circumstances were hardly any less serious. The reasons why a State of Emergency was not declared on that occasion have never been revealed and remain a mystery to this day.

There could have been little hesitation about the decision to declare a State of Emergency on 21 July 1985. The circumstances then were a rapidly growing and widespread ungovernability arising out of the total rejection by the majority of the population of the tricameral elections in 1984, from which they were excluded, the attempts to foist puppet black local councils on them and the Vaal uprising in September 1984 against the imposition of unaffordable rent increases by the selfsame black local councils. The choice of 21 July 1985 was significant. That was the day on which 60 000 anti-apartheid activists from all over the country flocked to Cradock to attend the funeral of the murdered 'Cradock Four'. Hundreds of buses and other vehicles returning to their home towns that day were intercepted by hordes of Security Police armed with lists of wanted activists and very soon the detention cells were bulging with over 1000 detainees. This State of Emergency was to last for seven and a half months (from 21 July 1985 to 7 March 1986) and was to affect 44 magisterial districts during that time, mainly in PWV (now Gauteng), Eastern Cape and Western Cape. An unintended consequence of the State of Emergency was an almost instantaneous flight of foreign capital and withdrawal of several foreign banks from the country. Lacking the foreign reserves to meet the demand for foreign debt repayment, the government was forced to declare a moratorium on debt repayment, which further compounded the deep crisis of isolation from the international financial system. These essentially were the factors leading to a premature lifting of the Emergency on 7 March 1986, in a desperate bid to restore South Africa's international financial standing, even at a time when the level of ungovernability in the country was by no means declining. In his speech announcing the lifting of the State of Emergency, P.W. Botha said the following: 'To enable the authorities to deal with continued incidents of unrest without subjecting the population to the inconvenience of a state of emergency, existing legislation will be reviewed and amendments proposed.' He was referring to the intention to amend the Public Safety Act whereby Unrest Areas could be declared, in effect mini-States of Emergency without the stigma of the name, but with all the powers. However, he did not reckon with the opposition to this unpalatable device which was to come from the two non-white houses within the tricameral parliament, which, while unable to block the ultimate passage of the legislation, were able to slow it down.

With 16 June (Soweto Day) approaching and a major security crisis looming, the government could no longer wait for the unrest area legislation to save the day, and were forced to opt instead for a full-blown national State of Emergency. This they declared on 12 June 1986, just four days ahead of Soweto Day, and within 2 weeks there were over 10 000 detainees inside the police cells. As a matter of record, the Public Safety Amendment Act, No. 67 of 1986 (the 'Unrest Areas Act') only became law on 26 June 1986, or just 10 days too late to be of use on that occasion; the first time it was to be put into effect was over four years later, on 24 August 1990.

The 12 June 1986 State of Emergency was to be the first of 4 national States of Emergency that ran their full statutory course of twelve months. The other three were declared on 11 June 1987, 10 June 1988 and 9 June 1989, so that as one Emergency expired the next one was activated, complete with new sets of regulations, new detention orders and new restriction orders. It was even reported that as an Emergency was expiring, detainees were cleared out of the cells, taken to the prison gates, served with detention orders under the new Emergency and returned to their cells.

On 8 June, 1990 a State of Emergency was declared in the province of Natal (including the 'self-governing' territory of KwaZulu) thereby taking it into its fifth successive year of Emergency. This was finally lifted on 18 October 1990.

Regulations and orders

The state president is empowered by the PSA to proclaim regulations considered necessary to deal with the state of emergency, and in turn the regulations empower the national commissioner of police and the divisional commissioners of police to issue certain orders.

Since July 1985, these regulations and orders have undergone an evolution as a result of a cat and mouse game with, on the one hand, the defiant communities devising new methods and tactics of resistance and, on the other hand, the authorities responding by introducing new measures of repression to counter the new tactics. In addition, human rights lawyers have continually probed for legal weaknesses or inconsistencies in the proclamations and while many such challenges have met with success, they have in the end simply resulted in amendments designed to close off the exposed legal loopholes.

As time went by the government developed a series of standard regulations which were a product of this cat and mouse game. The series is as follows:
• Security Emergency Regulations

'Happy Birthday!'

Dov Fedler, *The Star*, 14 June 1987

- Prison Emergency Regulations
- Media Emergency Regulations
- Educational Institutions Emergency Regulations

Powers under each set of regulations are described briefly below:

SECURITY EMERGENCY REGULATIONS
    Maintenance of order and use of force
    Arrest and detention of persons without trial
    Entry, search and seizure without a warrant
    Obligation to furnish name and address
    Restriction and banning of organisations
    Restriction and banning of persons
    Prohibition of various activities and campaigns (e.g. release of all detainees)
    Restricting access to specified areas
    Restricting and banning of gatherings
    Imposition of curfews
    Restriction of funeral processions and vigils
    Defining offences and penalties
    Power to act of lowest-ranking security force members
    Immunity from prosecution

PRISON EMERGENCY REGULATIONS
    Segregation of security detainees
    Medical treatment of detainees
    Exercise for detainees
    Detainees in police cells or lock-ups

MEDIA EMERGENCY REGULATIONS
    Prohibition on presence of journalists at unrest or security actions
    Prohibition of dissemination of audio-visual material
    Prohibition on 'subversive' statements, including information on security action, restricted gatherings, strikes, boycotts, detention conditions, political campaigns, blank spaces in newspapers
    Prohibition on photographs of unrest or security actions
    Prohibition of production, importation or publishing of certain periodicals
    Prohibition of systematic or repetitive publishing of 'subversive' propaganda
    Seizure of certain publications or recordings
    Compulsory deposit of periodicals
    Offences and penalties

EDUCATIONAL INSTITUTIONS EMERGENCY REGULATIONS
    Access to school premises
        only during school hours
        only to registered pupils
        only for specified activities

No deviation from approved courses and syllabus

Prohibition on any disruption of school activities (e.g. school boycotts)

Prohibition on outside interference with school activities

Prohibition on possession, display or distribution of banners, posters, T-shirts, pamphlets, etc. supporting specified campaigns or organisations

Regulation of movement and activities during school hours

Consequences and effects of State of Emergency

An effective 5 years of the imposition of a State of Emergency has had devastating consequences on the lives of millions of South Africans, particularly those living in townships subjected to occupation by security forces, curfews, restrictions of every imaginable kind and deaths of men, women and children as almost a daily occurrence.

In later sections of this book, the effects of the State of Emergency in terms of the application of the regulations to all the legalised forms of repression will be described in some detail. However, something needs to be said at this point about the loss of life during the periods of the States of Emergency as a result of the political unrest and the violence of the state in its attempts to contain it. From what can be gleaned from official police unrest reports and from the monitoring of various human rights groups and other sources, the following picture emerges:

TABLE 4
Deaths in political unrest 1984–1989

Year	Number of Deaths
1984	200
1985	900
1986	1 300
1987	700
1988	1 100
1989	1 400
Total	5 600

NOTES

• The numbers of deaths are rounded off approximations, within the spread of the various sources.

• During the earlier years of 1984 to 1986, up to two-thirds of the deaths were accounted for by security force actions.

• During the later years of 1987 to 1989 vigilantism (see Chapter 6), particularly in the Natal region, took over as the predominant cause of deaths.

3 THE DETENTION WEAPON

A number of observers and students of repression around the world have commented that the repression in South Africa during the apartheid era pales into insignificance when compared with some Latin American countries if the numbers of political disappearances and assassinations are used as the criteria for making such judgement. For example, disappearances and assassinations in Argentina were said to total around 30 000 while in South Africa the figure was but a few hundred. However, in South Africa this terminal method of eliminating political opponents has never been the main weapon, but rather the weapon of last resort when all other methods have failed. Apartheid's big gun has been detention without trial and this is where we see the big numbers – conservatively 80 000 people have been subjected to this subtle and sophisticated form of neutralisation. It has the advantages of maintaining the semblance of legality (all detentions are made in terms of legislation); it can be aimed not only at individuals, but at families, groups and organisations and even at whole communities, including women and children; it can be used to extract information to draw others into the net; it can be used to force confessions leading to conviction and permanent incarceration; it can be used to break political activists both physically and psychologically; it can be used to recruit informers and sow suspicion and confusion within communities; it can be followed by a banning order which effectively extends the victim's detention to within his or her own home; and finally it can, if need be, set the stage for permanent removal from society.

The history, powers, application and effects of this insidious and powerful weapon of repression are described in the HRC documents that follow:

Detention without Trial (November 1988)

Torture in Detention (March 1983)

Deaths in Detention (August 1990)

DETENTION WITHOUT TRIAL
HRC, November 1988

1. History of detention without trial in South Africa
2. Current legislation with detention powers
3. Torture and assault in detention
4. Deaths in detention

5. Detention statistics
6. The victims of detention without trial
7. The way out of detention

1. History of detention without trial in South Africa

The government of South Africa has empowered itself to practise detention without trial under two forms of legislation:
1. Security legislation which is permanently in effect, even in 'peacetime';
2. Emergency legislation which functions only when a State of Emergency has been declared, conferring powers usually associated with times of war.

History of detention under security legislation

- **1963.** The General Laws Amendment Act, No. 37 was passed. Section 17 provided for up to 90 days detention, in isolation, without access to the courts, for the purposes of interrogation. Renewable at expiry.
- **1965.** The Criminal Procedures Amendment Act, No. 96 was passed. Section 215bis provided for up to 180 days detention, also in solitary, no access, and renewable. The stated purpose was as a potential witness, but in fact interrogation was the main purpose.
- **1966.** The General Laws Amendment Act, No. 62 came into effect. Section 22 provided for short-term 'preventive' detention up to 14 days, renewable.
- **1967.** The Terrorism Act, No. 83 was introduced with the justification that it was necessary to combat terrorism in South West Africa (Namibia), a response to SWAPO guerrilla action. Within a year it was put to use in charging South Africans. Section 6 provided for indefinite detention without trial for the purposes of interrogation in solitary confinement.
- **1976.** The Internal Security Amendment Act, No. 79 was introduced during the Soweto Uprising for the purpose of withdrawing political activists from the political arena. Section 10(1)(a)bis provided for long-term 'preventive' detention of up to 12 months, renewable. Section 12B provided for up to 6 months detention of potential witnesses, in solitary confinement.
- **1982.** The Internal Security Act, No. 74 was introduced to streamline and supersede all previous security legislation. It is currently on the statute books. Section 28 provides for long-term (12 months) 'preventive' detention. Section 29 provides for indefinite interrogatory detention. Section 31 provides for 6 months 'witness' detention. Section 50 provides for short-term (14 days) 'preventive' detention.
- **1986.** The Internal Security Amendment Act, No. 66 was passed to add a further category of detention without trial. Section 50A provides for 180 days 'preventive' detention and overcomes problems of court challenges experienced with Section 28.
- In addition to the above, it must be mentioned that the four 'independent' homelands have evolved their own respective security legislation modelled exactly on that of their progenitor.

Andy, *Rand Daily Mail*, 7 May 1982

History of detention under Emergency legislation

- **1953.** The Public Safety Act, No. 3 was introduced in response to the defiance campaign of passive resistance to discriminatory laws then being conducted by the ANC (lawful at the time) and other organisations. It empowers the head of state to declare a State of Emergency in certain circumstances, and to make regulations conferring a wide range of powers, including detention of persons without trial for a period limited only to the duration of the State of Emergency.

2. Current legislation with detention powers

Security legislation

The Internal Security Act, No. 74 of 1982, together with the Internal Security Amendment Act, No. 66 of 1986, provides for detention without trial for 3 different stated purposes:

1. Detention for interrogation (Section 29)
2. Preventive detention (Sections 28, 50 and 50A)
3. Witness detention (Section 31)

1. **Detention for interrogation.** Section 29 allows a detainee to be held in solitary confinement without access to lawyers, family, friends or anyone else other than state officials (interrogators, magistrates, district surgeons, etc.) for the purpose of interrogation. The period of detention is effectively unlimited – until 'all questions are satisfactorily answered' or 'no useful purpose will be served by further detention'. The jurisdiction of the courts over such detention is specifically excluded.

45

2. **Preventive detention.** Section 28 allows the holding of a person in prison by ministerial order (as opposed to court sentence) if the minister believes that person is likely to commit a security offence. The period used has been 6 or 12 months and is renewable. The courts have no jurisdiction and access to the detainee is restricted to state officials. Although still on the statute books, this section of the Internal Security Act has fallen into disuse because the wording requires the minister to give reasons for the detention.

Section 50A is similar in effect to Section 28, but does not require any reasons to be given. It is simply dependent upon the opinion of a police officer of the rank of lieutenant-colonel or above and serves to remove the victim from society for up to 180 days, which can then be renewed. This section must be brought into effect by proclamation by the state president, which has not yet been necessary due to the continuing existence of a State of Emergency under which powers of preventive detention are even wider.

Section 50 allows the holding of a person for a short period (up to 14 days) and was very extensively used in the past either when no State of Emergency was in existence or during a partial State of Emergency in magisterial districts not falling under the State of Emergency. It would serve no purpose at the present time but remains on the statute books.

3. **Witness detention.** Section 31 allows the attorney-general to order the detention of a person in solitary confinement, without any access, beyond the jurisdiction of any court, if he believes that person could be a material witness in a security trial. Time limit is 6 months unless the trial has started before then. Almost invariably, Section 31 detention is an extension of Section 29 detention when, as a result of the interrogation process, it is decided that the detainee shall become a state witness (with or without the agreement of the detainee).

'Homelands' legislation

The security legislation in force in the 'independent' homelands mirrors the Internal Security Act very closely, particularly in regard to the detention clauses. The relevant Acts are as follows:

• Venda Terrorism Act (same as Terrorism Act, No. 83 of 1967);
• Transkei Public Security Act, No. 30 of 1977;
• Bophuthatswana Internal Security Act, No. 22 of 1979;
• Ciskei National Security Act, No. 13 of 1982.

Emergency legislation

The Public Safety Act, No. 3 of 1953 empowers the state president to:

(a) Declare a State of Emergency under Section 2, with a time limit of 12 months, if in his opinion circumstances are such that the ordinary laws of the land are inadequate to maintain public order.

(b) Proclaim Emergency regulations under Section 3, such as he deems necessary, including the summary arrest and detention of persons.

At the present time, with effect from 10 June 1988, a State of Emergency is in force under Proclamation R96, 1988. Security Emergency Regulations are in force under Proclamation R97, 1988 (including Section 3 providing for detention powers). Prison Emergency Regulations are in force under Proclamation R98, 1988 (providing for control of detention conditions).

Under Emergency regulations any member of the security force (including the lowest-ranked members of the police, defence force and prison services) has the power to detain and interrogate. An Emergency detainee has no automatic right of access to lawyers, family or friends and may be held for the duration of the Emergency. Since successive States of Emergency can be and are declared, this means that the time of detention is open-ended. Many Emergency detainees are now in their third year of detention, with no end in sight.

3. Torture and assault in detention

Over the years and right up to the present time there has been a continuous stream of allegations of torture and assault in detention. Court proceedings abound with such allegations and these can only be considered the tip of the iceberg. Several major investigations have been undertaken and their findings reported during the last 6 years, which detail the incidence, forms and medical and other consequences of torture, both physical and psychological. In particular the intensely hostile environment of Section 29 interrogatory detention has come under focus, as have the mass detentions of the States of Emergency.

4. Deaths in detention

Ever since detention without trial was introduced as a permanent feature of South African life in 1963, deaths in detention have occurred as a constant by-product of the detention system, particularly during interrogation in solitary confinement. The first death was that of Solwandle Looksmart Ngudle on 3 September 1963, the most recent was that of Alfred Mabake Makaleng on 26 August 1988. During the 25 years of detention without trial, there have been 67 deaths in detention, an average of almost three each year. Only during 1970 and 1972 to 1975 were no deaths recorded, whilst peaks occurred in 1969 (7 deaths), 1976 (13), 1977 (13) and 1986 (4).

5. Detention statistics

Detention under security legislation

The statistics of detentions under security legislation from 1963 to the present time are shown in Table 5. It must be stressed that the figures are conservatively calculated due to the great difficulty in extracting and collating information under a situation in which there has been a great deal of reluctance on the part of the authorities to publish such information. The actual figures must therefore be substantially higher than those shown. It is interesting to note that in the last 5 years there have been more detentions under security legislation than in the previous 20 years, in spite of the heavy incidence of detentions in the year following the Soweto Uprising of June 1976. The figures illustrate a clear correlation between detentions and levels of political resistance.

TABLE 5
Detentions under security legislation

Years	Interro-gation	Witness	Prevent-ive	Sub-total	Home-lands	Total
1963–66	1 095	247	–	1 342	472	1 814
1967–75	800	293	94	1 187	187	1 374
1976–77	2 500	504	350	3 354	120	3 474
1978–81	800	260	1 700	2 760	500	3 260
1982	107	100	3	210	83	293
1983	149	16	38	203	215	418
1984	339	47	191	577	532	1 109
1985	463	41	1 932	2 436	1 953	4 389
1986	477	143	3 512	4 132	520	4 652
1987	532	84	–	616	286	902
1988 (6 mths)	149	1	–	150	28	178
Total	7 411	1 736	7 820	16 967	4 896	21 863

TABLE 6
Detentions under Emergency regulations

Year	Detail	No. of detentions
1960	Partial State of Emergency (29 March 1960–31 August 1960)	11 727 (official)
1985/6	Partial State of Emergency (21 July 1985–7 March 1986)	7 996 (official)
1986/7	Total State of Emergency (12 June 1986–11 June 1987)	25 000 (estimated)
1987/8	Total State of Emergency (11 June 1987–10 June 1988)	5 000 (estimated)
1988/9	Total State of Emergency (10 June 1988 onwards)	2 000 (estimated)

Detentions under Emergency regulations

Details of these detentions are given in Table 6. In total, there have thus far been in the region of 50 000 detentions under Emergency regulations during the 5 States of Emergency since 1960. From the commencement of the first total State of Emergency on 12 June 1986, the authorities have consistently refused to publish figures for all

Emergency detentions but have only revealed the names of those persons detained for longer than 30 days, as required by Section 4 of the Public Safety Act. Fig. 2 shows the official figures and the figures estimated by detention monitoring groups, during this period of secrecy.

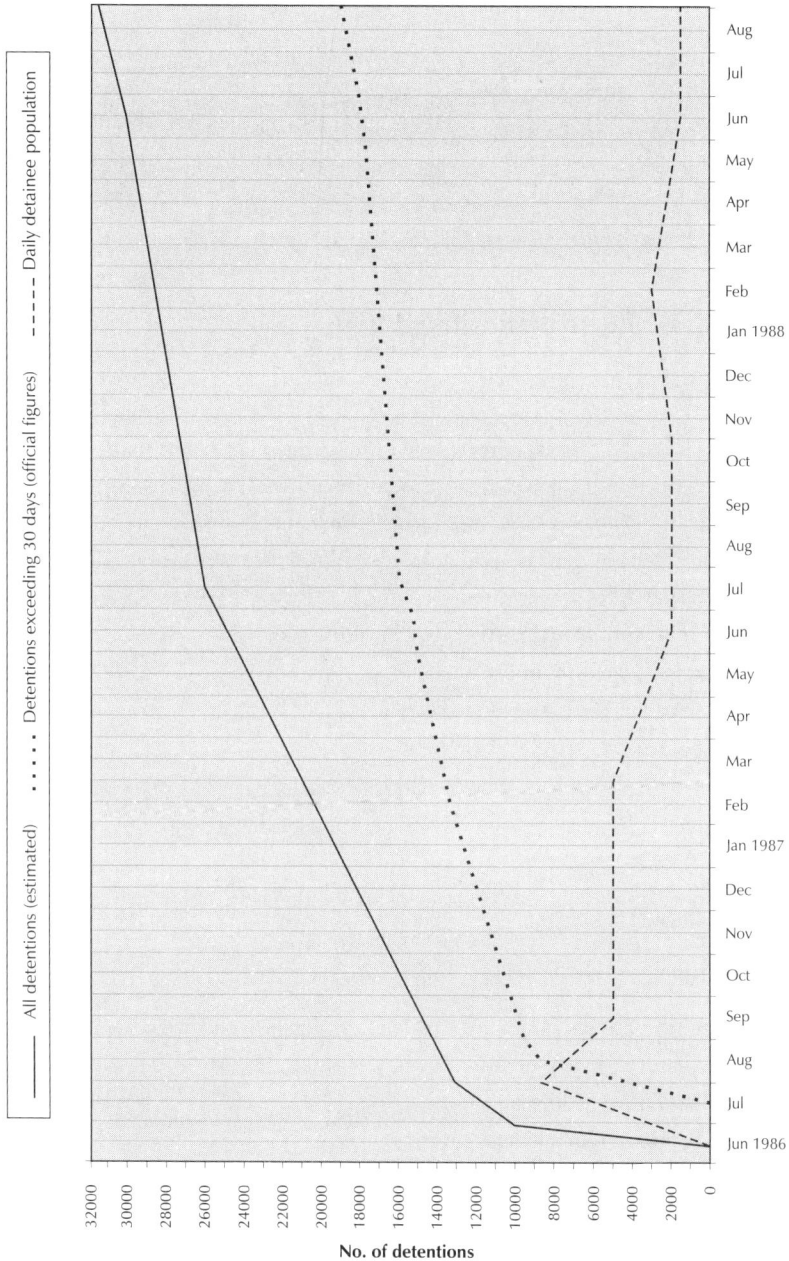

FIGURE 2
Emergency detentions since 12 June 1986

Comments on statistics

The massive total of over 73 000 detainees (certainly an underestimate) since 1960 is a serious indictment of the South African government's attempts to stifle political opposition. These attempts appear to have been self-defeating since, with the passage of time, this opposition has escalated and with it the number of detentions. Periods of major resistance and unrest have produced a rich crop of detentions, as after Sharpeville (11 727 during 1960) and during and after the Soweto Uprising (3474 during 1976/77).

But a totally new dimension has been perceived over the last 4 years starting from the time of the tricameral elections in August 1984. During this period an estimated 51 000 detentions took place, over 70% of all detentions since 1960. Clearly the emphasis has shifted from the detention of political leadership and outspoken critics of apartheid, to include community members at all levels.

6. The victims of detention without trial

Target groups

Ever since the introduction of detention without trial, a consistent pattern has emerged of the groups of persons targeted by the security police; the focus shifting according to circumstances and events. These target groups are as follows:

• Educational: school pupils, teachers, headmasters, inspectors; university students, lecturers, researchers, professors
• Religious: ministers, church officials, church workers
• Cultural: actors, writers, poets
• Health: doctors, nurses, social workers
• Legal: lawyers
• Media: journalists, photographers, editors
• Government: civil servants, members of homeland 'parliaments', party leaders and candidates
• Trade unions: union leaders, organisers, shop stewards, workers

Organisations

In addition to the above target groups, the leadership and members of the following organisations are frequently detained:

• Extra-parliamentary political bodies
• Civic and resident associations
• Women's organisations
• Youth organisations
• Student bodies

There are thus very few areas of human activity which do not produce critics of state policy and thus candidates for detention without trial.

"'Suffer little children' . . . I forget the rest."

Andy, *Rand Daily Mail,* 27 April 1987

Detention of children

The practice of detaining children and youths under South African detention laws is not new. The following figures have been released in parliament in the past by the minister of justice showing numbers of children under 18 years of age detained under security legislation:

- 1977   259 (including as young as 10)
- 1978   252
- 1979   48
- 1980   127
- 1981   49

Official figures released in parliament in early 1986 show the pattern of detentions during the partial State of Emergency which started on 21 July 1985 and ended on 7 March 1986.

- Total no. of detentions   7 996
- No. of juveniles (under 21) 3 681 (46%)
- No. of children under 16   2 016 (25%)

Official figures released in an affidavit to court by the South African Police during April 1987 revealed that of a total of 4224 detainees being held in Emergency detention on 15 April 1987, those aged 18 or less (down to 12) numbered 1424, or 34% of the total. If one accepts the extremely conservative estimate of 20% under 18s for all detentions since

1960, then about 15 000 children under 18 have experienced detention. At the present time, an estimated 100 children (under 18) are still being held in detention, and new detentions of children are being recorded every month. The practice continues.

Detention of women

Women have by no means been exempt from the attention of the security police. Over the years women have represented 10% to 15% of all those detained so that somewhere between 7000 and 10 000 women have been inside police cells during the history of detention without trial. Large numbers have in this way been separated from their children, many of them only babies. Others have been allowed to bring their babies into detention with them and yet others have given birth whilst in detention. Women detainees have undertaken hunger strikes in protest and reports of alleged assault, torture and sexual abuse have persistently emerged. One woman, Elda Bani, died in detention in July 1987 at the age of 56.

7. The way out of detention

Release without charge

Records kept since 1981 reveal that about 75% to 80% of all detentions end in release without any charge in a court of law. The detainee is one day simply advised that he or she is free to go. This can happen within a short time but 6 months is common. Until recently about 2 years was the longest recorded detention. Now, however, even this period is being exceeded, with many Emergency detainees having been held for over 850 days (28 months) with no end in sight. Re-detention is also common, with some persons having been held as many as 10 times. Release is frequently reported to be accompanied by threats not to resume political activity, or by pressure to become an informer.

Release with restrictions

Amongst those who are released without charge, an increasing number are served with banning or restriction orders. Such orders preclude the ex-detainee from engaging in any political activity and frequently place constraints on movement. This action can be said to extend detention beyond the prison walls.

Charging in court

The other 20% to 25% of detainees are charged with various offences ranging from treason, terrorism or subversion, to attending an illegal gathering or possession of banned literature. In most cases, however, charges are eventually withdrawn or the accused is acquitted, leaving only 2% to 4% of all detainees who are convicted of any offence.

Escape from detention

Escape is a very infrequent occurrence. Records show that there have been about 30 reported or known escapes since 1967, with only one reported recapture. Question marks hang over the genuineness of some of the reported 'escapes', where detainees have disappeared without trace. The most well-known case was the disappearance of detainee Stanza Bopape, whose alleged escape has been widely questioned due to the improbability of the police account.

Death in detention

Present records show that 67 detainees did not survive detention. If one is to believe the inquest verdicts, nearly half of these chose the way out of detention by committing suicide.

Sources:
   CALS Human Rights Update, vol. 1 nos. 1–3
   DPSC Monthly Reports, March 1984 to January 1988
   Government Gazettes
   Hansard
   Institute of Race Relations Surveys, 1961 to 1986

REPORT ON TORTURE IN DETENTION
DPSC, March 1983

Ever since the Detainees' Parents Support Committee was formed in late 1981, we have been approached by a steady stream of released detainees asking for assistance and advice, and also relating to us their experiences at the hands of the security police. It soon became clear to us that torture and assault during the interrogation process was commonplace. The more we heard, the more we realised that this abuse is widespread and systematic, not just the work of a handful of sadists. The pattern of torture was much the same in Port Elizabeth, Durban, Soweto, John Vorster Square or Jeffreys Bay.

   When a delegation from the DPSC met the ministers of justice and of law and order in Cape Town during April 1982, we demanded to know what interrogation practices were officially condoned and what limitations are placed upon the methods used by the Security Police in interrogating detainees. To this day we have had no direct reply. Instead we drew an angry reaction, rejecting our allegations of torture and challenging us to prove them. A CID colonel was appointed to investigate our allegations and from a letter to our attorney it looked as though he was going to take his job seriously. To quote:

> It appears from the said memorandum [the memorandum submitted to the ministers and released to the press] that your clients have at their disposal information which can be of cardinal importance for a successful investigation into the allegations of serious misconduct alleged to have been perpetrated by

members of the South African Police, and more particularly members of the Security Branch of the South African Police. Your clients are required to furnish the said information and/or evidence to me as soon as possible to enable me to facilitate the investigation.

The DPSC responded to the challenge by submitting to the CID and to the ministers a considerable number of statements with detailed information regarding the names of the detainees, the abuses to which they were subjected, the dates of occurrence and the names of the perpetrators, where known. In all, 76 statements were submitted, and after waiting for weeks for some reaction, a memorandum was finally prepared which analysed and summarised the DPSC's findings. This memorandum was submitted to the ministers and released to the press.

Recently in parliament, minister Le Grange dismissed our memorandum as 'deliberate poisonous propaganda'. He said that of 43 cases investigated, 11 were unfounded, 1 untraceable, 1 rejected in court (Barbara Hogan) and the remaining 30 cases the attorney-general had refused to prosecute. Le Grange neglected to say why the attorney-general refused to prosecute.

The CID colonel must be a disappointed man. After investigating 43 out of 76 cases, he was unable to bring a single one to a successful conclusion. Not only was he unsuccessful; everyone else before him had failed in their efforts to successfully prosecute the security police in a court of law. It's a no-win situation, because under the detention system there is never a witness sympathetic to the detainee, and the security police are sure in the knowledge that they have the full protection of the state machinery.

Let us spend a short time in describing briefly the nature of the torture and assault that has emerged from our investigation. Firstly, the ambit of these abuses: 18 different locations throughout the country are mentioned with John Vorster Square in Johannesburg, Protea in Soweto and Sanlam Buildings in Port Elizabeth heading the list. Secondly, the perpetrators: the names of 95 security policemen are referred to, with certain individuals cropping up a dozen times or more in our sample of 76 cases. Of the 95, more than 20 are commissioned officers up to the rank of major. Yesterday's interrogators are today's administrators…

The timespan of our sample covers the period 1978 to the end of 1982, with more than half the cases occurring in the last two years. But there is no reason to believe that torture was not taking place before 1978 and we know from reliable sources that it continues.

The common forms of abuse can be divided into physical and psychological but there is a great deal of overlapping. Physical abuse includes the following:

- sleep deprivation, often for several nights and days while being interrogated by successive teams;
- deprivation of food and drink;
- deprivation of toilet facilities;
- enforced standing for long periods, sometimes on bricks;
- enforced exertion (holding up of heavy objects, press ups, running on the spot);
- exposure to cold whilst being kept naked for long periods, sometimes being doused with water;

- suspension from a pole while handcuffed at the ankles and wrists;
- plain assault by hitting, kicking, beating, crushing of toes, etc.;
- suffocation with canvas or plastic hoods, wet towels, etc. to the extent of losing consciousness;
- electric shocks, always while hooded or blindfolded and sometimes while trussed in a canvas strait-jacket.

Psychological abuse takes the following forms:
- solitary confinement for the entire detention period (i.e. up to a year or more); humiliation and degradation, including being denied toilet and washing facilities, verbal abuse and ridicule, racial remarks, etc.;
- intimidation such as being stripped naked, being taken from police cells into the bush and hooding;
- death threats with weapons, etc.;
- threats of torture;
- threats about loved ones, such as threats to kill or detain them;
- threat of indefinite detention and being left alone for long periods (weeks and months) without interrogation.

There can be little doubt that the security police regard their ability to torture detainees with total impunity, as the cornerstone of the detention system. It puts the detainee at complete mercy for the purpose of extracting information, statements and confessions, often regardless of whether true or not, in order to secure a successful prosecution and neutralisation of yet another opponent of the apartheid system. Sometimes torture is used on detainees before they have even been asked their first question in order to soften them up. Other times, torture is used late in the interrogation process when the detainee is being stubborn and difficult.

There is always the danger that the interrogator will go too far. It is in this light that the numerous deaths in detention must be seen as a logical extension and consequence of torture during interrogation. Since the introduction of detention laws in 1963, the latest death of Tembuyise Mndawe brings the number of deaths 54 by our reckoning,. Whether any of these victims were driven to suicide or not is irrelevant. The fact is that the detention situation was responsible for these deaths and torture was a contributing factor.

The incidence of the deaths can be related directly to the intensity of security police action against opposition to government policies. For instance, nearly half of these deaths, 25 in all, occurred in the 18 months following 16 June 1976. It is also significant that deaths in detention decreased sharply in number subsequent to the highly publicised deaths of people like the Imam Haron in 1969, Ahmed Timol in 1971 and Steve Biko in late 1977.

What does the future hold? As long as we have a government which has to suppress the majority of the population in order to maintain power, we cannot expect an end to detentions, torture and deaths in detention. It needs the detention weapon to maintain power and it needs torture to make that detention weapon effective. So, we shall continue to live with detentions and with torture and death in detention. Their frequency will be in proportion to how threatened this government feels from opposition to its policies.

But we must continue to oppose and expose. The DPSC appeals to all detainees when they are released to come forward and submit themselves to medical examination by our panel of doctors and to relate their treatment at the hands of the security police to us. In this way we believe we can build up our records and perform an important watch-dog function.

DEATHS IN DETENTION
HRC, August 1990

1. Introduction
2. Frequency of deaths
3. Ages/gender/occupations of detainees
4. Places of death
5. Length of detention before death
6. Causes of death
    Natural
    Suicide
    Accidental
    Police killing
    Undetermined
7. Strange coincidences
8. Deaths in police custody
9. Conclusion

1. Introduction

Detention without trial in South Africa dates back to the early 1960s. The first State of Emergency, declared in 1960, permitted detention without trial. The year 1963 saw the introduction of detention without trial into the permanent legislation of the land through the General Law Amendment Act, No. 37, one of the forerunners of the modern-day Internal Security Act, No. 74 of 1982, still in daily use. To complete the picture, the so-called independent homelands upon their creation also introduced detention without trial as part of their copy-cat security legislation. All of these powers have served to produce the massive total of an estimated 78 000 detainees over the last 30 years.

The provisions of detention without trial are such as to place the detainee virtually at the mercy of the interrogator, away from any interference from the courts, lawyers, independent doctors, family or friends and for as long as the interrogator wishes. These are the tools with which the law provides the interrogator. It is easy to understand that in these circumstances it might be difficult to resist the temptation to accelerate the process of extracting information by the use of coercion, and that such coercion could become systematised torture. That systematised torture has become widespread during detention over the years is widely recognised as a result of several studies (such as by the Detainees' Parents Support Committee in 1982, the Institute of Criminology at UCT in 1985 and the National Medical and Dental Association in 1987) as well as evidence which has persistently emerged from innumerable trials over the years. Without detailing here the various methods of torture in common use, one method, or group of methods, deserves special mention, namely torture involving strangulation in various forms, because of the high risk of death that is involved.

Along with the recognition of the widespread use of torture there is also a realisation that such methods of interrogation carry with them the ever-present possibility, even inevitability, of the consequence of death, whether as a result of torture going too far or of the victim choosing death as the only relief. The fact is that since monitoring first commenced in 1963, a procession of 73 deaths in detention has been recorded or 1 death for every 1000 detainees. (Details of these deaths are listed in Table 7 overleaf.)

2. Frequency of deaths

Since 1963, when detention without trial was first introduced on a permanent basis, there have been deaths in detention in each and every year with the exceptions of 1970, 1972 to 1975, 1979, and 1989. During the 1960s there was a period of 6 years in which there was a regular occurrence of 2 deaths each year but this jumped to 7 deaths in 1969. After the widely publicised death of Ahmed Timol in 1971, there was a period of 4 years in which no deaths were recorded. Then came the Soweto Uprising of 1976 and within 2 years the mass detentions of that time had produced the horrific total of 26 deaths. The death of Steve Biko near the end of that period resulted in a world outcry and an almost instantaneous halt in the procession of deaths in detention for a while. In the 1980s, the figures started slowly creeping up again and during the years of the States of Emergency (1985–1990) a total of 14 deaths were recorded. The average for the total 27-year period of 2.7 deaths per annum has already been exceeded half way through 1990. For a graphic representation, see Fig. 3 (p. 60).

TABLE 7
List of deaths in detention

Year	Name	Date died	Age	Place	Days held	Official/alleged cause
1963	1. Ngudle, Solwandle	05/09	41	Kompol, Pretoria	17	Suicide by hanging
	2. Mampe, Bellington	??/09	?	Worcester	140	Undisclosed
1964	3. Tyita, James	24/01	?	Port Elizabeth	?	Suicide by hanging
	4. Salojee, Suliman	09/09	28	Johannesburg	65	Suicide, jumped from 7th floor
1965	5. Gaga, Ngeni	09/05	19	Transkei	<1	Natural causes
	6. Hoye, Pongolosha	09/05	?	Transkei	<1	Natural causes
1966	7. Hamakwayo, James	09/10	?	Pretoria Prison	13	Suicide by hanging
	8. Shonyeka, Hangula	09/10	?	Pretoria Prison	40	Suicide
	9. Pin, Leong	19/11	?	Leeuwkop Prison, Pretoria	1	Suicide by hanging
1967	10. Yan, Ah	05/01	63	Silverton Police Sta.	37	Suicide by hanging
	11. Madiba, Alpheus	09/09	?	Namibia	1	Suicide by hanging
1968	12. Tubakwa, Jundea	11/09	?	Pretoria Prison	1	Suicide by hanging
	13. Unknown person	??/??	?	?	?	Reported by min. of police
1969	14. Kgoathe, Nicodemus	04/02	?	Held: Silverton Police Sta. Died: HF Verwoerd Hospital	85	Natural causes: bronchial pneumonia after slipping in the shower
	15. Modipane, Solomon	28/02	?	Held: Silverton Police Sta. Died: HF Vervoerd Hospital	3	Natural causes: after slipping on piece of soap, fatal injuries
	16. Lenkoe, James	10/03	?	Pretoria Prison	5	Suicide by hanging
	17. Mayekiso, Caleb	01/06	?	Port Elizabeth police cells	18	Natural causes: not specified
	18. Shivute, Michael	17/06	?	Ondangwa police cells	<1	Suicide
	19. Monakgotla, Jacob	10/09	?	Pretoria Prison	222	Natural causes: thrombosis
	20. Haroon, Abdullah (Imam)	27/09	45	Maitland Police Sta., CT	122	Natural causes: heart trouble caused by fall down stairs
1971	21. Cuthsela, Mthayeni	21/01	?	Held: Pondoland Died: Transkei Hospital	40	Natural causes: brain haemorrhage
	22. Timol, Ahmed	27/10	30	John Vorster Sq., Jhb	5	Suicide, jumped from 10th floor
1976	23. Mdluli, Joseph	19/03	50	Security HQ, Durban	<1	Injury to neck after falling against chair
	24. Tshwane, William	25/07	?	Modderbee Prison, East Rand	<1	Shot while trying to escape, justifiable homicide
	25. Mohapi, Mapetla	05/08	25	Kei Road Jail, East London	22	Anoxia and suffocation as a result of hanging
	26. Mazwembe, Luke	02/09	32	Caledon Sq., Cape Town	<1	Suicide by hanging
	27. Mbatha, Dumisani	25/09	16	Held: Modderbee Prison Died: Far East Rand Hospital	9	Natural causes: extreme sympathetic system activity with auricular fibrilation of heart
	28. Mogatusi, Fenuel	28/09	22	Johannesburg Fort	70	Natural causes: suffocation during an epileptic fit
	29. Mashabane, Jacob	05/10	22	Johannesburg Fort	4	Suicide by hanging
	30. Unknown man	05/10	?	Carletonville police cells	?	Undisclosed, police said allegation of assault before death involved
	31. Mzolo, Edward	09/10	40	Johannesburg Fort	8	Undisclosed
	32. Mamashila, Ernest	19/11	35	Balfour, Transvaal	3	Suicide by hanging
	33. Mosala, Tbalo	26/11	60	Butterworth, Transkei	87	Natural causes: internal bleeding
	34. Tshazibane, Wellington	11/12	30	John Vorster Sq., Jhb	2	Suicide by hanging
	35. Botha, George	15/12	30	Sanlam Building, Port Elizabeth	5	Suicide, jumped 6 floors down a stairwell
1977	36. Ndzanga, Lawrence	08/01	53	Johannesburg Fort	51	Natural causes: heart failure
	37. Ntshuntsha, Nanaotha (Dr)	09/01	43	Leslie Police Sta.	26	Hanging, probably suicide

Year	Name	Date died	Age	Place	Days held	Official/alleged cause
1977 cont.	38. Malele, Elmon	20/01	61	Held: John Vorster Sq., Johannesburg Died: Nursing home	13	Natural causes: haemorrhage after hitting head against desk during interrogation
	39. Mabelane, Mathews	15/02	23	John Vorster Sq., Jhb	25	Accidental, fell from 10th floor
	40. Joyi, Twasifeni	15/02	?	Idutywa, Transkei	?	Post-mortem result not revealed
	41. Malinga, Samuel	22/02	45	Held: Pietermaritzburg Died: Edendale Hospital	22	Natural causes: heart disease & pneumonia
	42. Khoza, Aaron	26/03	35	Pietermaritzburg Prison	106	Suicide by hanging
	43. Mabija, Phakamile	07/07	27	Tvl Rd Police Sta. Kimberley	10	Suicide, jumped from 6th floor
	44. Loza, Elijah	01/08	59	Held: Verster Prison, Paarl Died: Tygerberg Hospital, Cape Town	65	Natural causes: stroke
	45. Haffejee, Hoosen (Dr)	03/08	26	Brighton Beach Police Sta., Durban	1	Suicide by hanging
	46. Mzizi, Bayempin	13/08	62	Brighton Beach Police Sta., Durban	35	Suicide by hanging
	47. Biko, Steve	12/09	31	Held: Port Elizabeth Died: Pretoria	24	Brain injury during scuffle with police
	48. Malaza, Sipho	16/11	18	Krugersdorp police cells	138	Suicide by hanging
1978	49. Tabalaza, Lungile	10/07	19	Sanlam Building, Port Elizabeth	<1	Suicide, jumped from 5th floor
1980	50. Ndzumo, Saul	10/09	58	Umtata, Transkei	9	Natural causes: heart trouble, diabetes, blood pressure
1981	51. Mgqweto, Manana	17/09	60	Engcobo, Transkei	?	Unknown
	52. Muofhe, Tshifhiwa	12/11	28	Venda	2	Assault by police
1982	53. Aggett, Neil (Dr)	05/02	28	John Vorster Sq., Jhb	70	Suicide by hanging
	54. Dipale, Ernest	08/08	21	John Vorster Sq., Johannesburg	3	Suicide by hanging
1983	55. Mndawe, Simon	08/03	23	Nelspruit Prison	14	Suicide by hanging
	56. Malatji, Paris	05/07	23	Protea Police Sta., Soweto	<1	Culpable homicide: shot in forehead at point-blank range
1984	57. Tshikudo, Samuel	20/01	50	Held: Venda Died: Tshizidzini Hospital	77	Natural causes
	58. Sipele, Mxolisi	??/06	?	Sulenkama Hospital, Transkei	±150	Unknown: police claim he died in hospital month after release
	59. Mthethwa, Ephraim	25/08	22	Durban Central Prison	165	Suicide by hanging
1985	60. Raditsela, Andries	06/05	29	Baragwanath Hospital	2	Fatal head injury; fell from Casspir
	61. Ndondo, Batandwa	24/09	22	Cala, Transkei	<1	Shot by police
1986	62. Kutumela, Makompe	05/04	25	Lebowa	1	Police assault
	63. Nchabaleng, Peter	11/04	59	Lebowa	1	Police assault
	64. Jacobs, Xoliso	22/10	20	Upington	129	Suicide by hanging
	65. Marule, Simon	23/12	20	Held: Modderbee Prison Died: Boksburg/Benoni Hospital	183	Kidney failure
1987	66. Mashoke, Benedict	26/03	20	Burgersfort Police Sta.	215	Suicide by hanging
	67. Mntonga, Eric	24/07	35	Mdantsane Cells, Ciskei	1	Police assault
	68. Bani, Nobandla	29/07	56	North End Cells, Port Elizabeth	333	Natural causes: stroke
1988	69. Zokwe, Sithembele	12/01	36	Butterworth, Transkei	<1	Police shooting
	70. Makaleng, Alfred	26/08	27	Held: Nylstroom Died: Johannesburg Hospital	804	Natural causes: fluid on the brain
1990	71. Sithole, Clayton Sizwe	30/01	20	John Vorster Sq., Jhb	4	Suicide by hanging
	72. Tlhotlhomisang, Lucas	26/03	37	Klerksdorp	7	Police report: meningitis
	73. Madisha, Donald Thabela	01/06	30	Potgietersrus police station	130	Police report: suicide by hanging

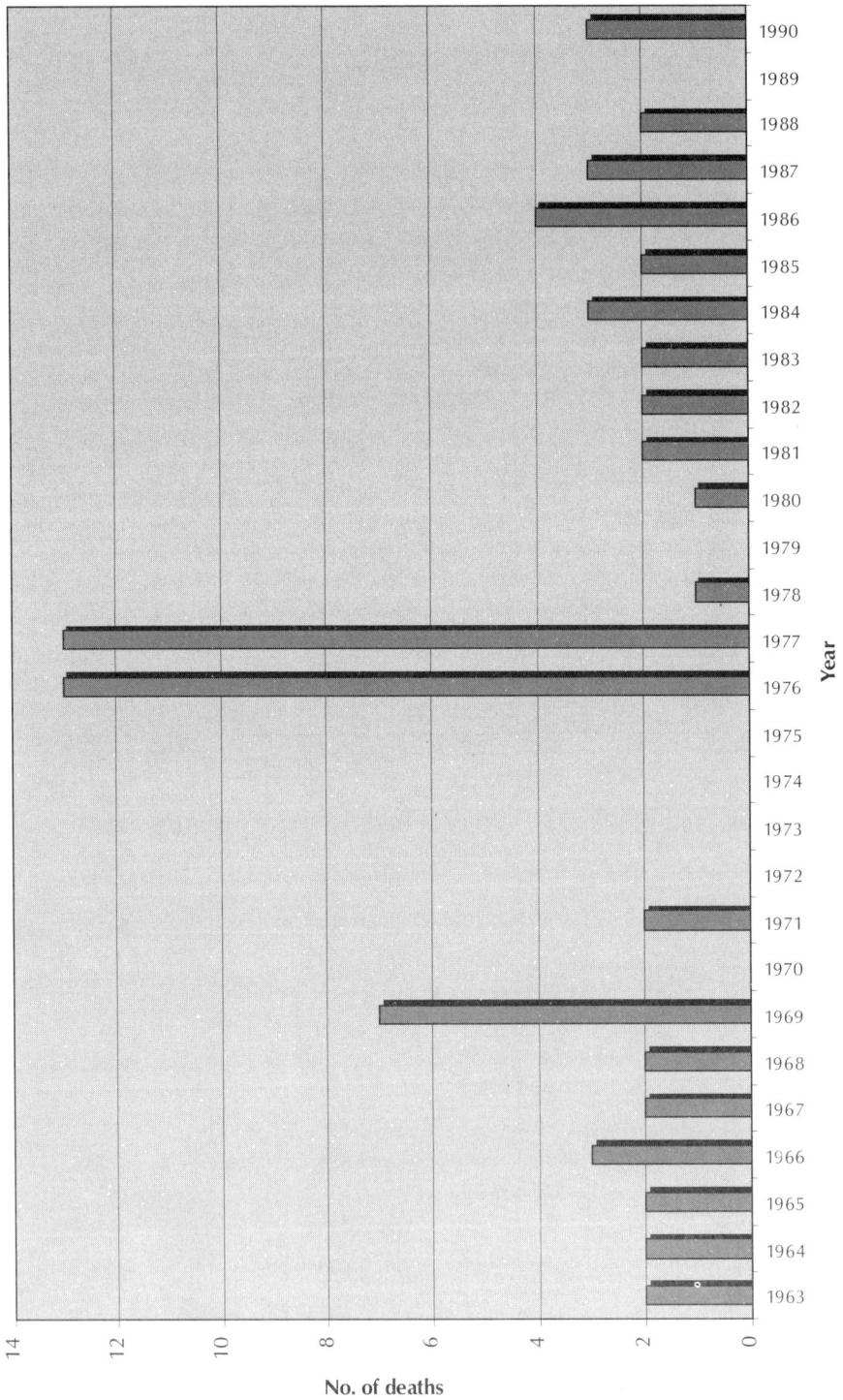

FIGURE 3
Frequency of deaths in detention

3. Details of detainees

Ages of the detainees
The youngest detainee to die in detention was Dumisani Mbatha (no. 27) at the age of 16, while the oldest was Ah Yan (no. 10) at the age of 63.

- 8 detainees were 20 or younger
- 21 detainees were 21 to 30
- 8 detainees were 31 to 40
- 11 detainees were 41 to 59
- 5 detainees were 60 or older.

The ages of 20 detainees are unknown. See Fig. 4.

Gender of the detainees
All detainees to die in detention have been male with one exception, Nobandla Bani (no. 68), who died at the age of 56 after 333 days in Emergency detention.

Occupations of the detainees
Victims have emerged from all sectors of the community, particularly those identified as the usual targets of detention as a result of their opposition to apartheid. They include students, trade unionists, church workers, teachers, doctors and political activists in both township and rural communities.

4. Places of death

Deaths in detention have occurred in virtually all of the main centres where security police headquarters are located, but also in small towns and some rural areas where security

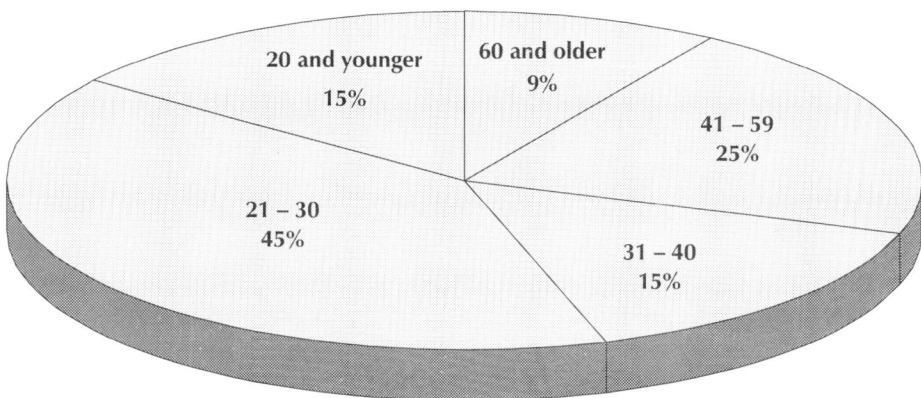

FIGURE 4
Deaths in detention: known ages at death

police operate from police stations. Certain interrogation centres have gained a reputation for being the sites of an unusual number of deaths. These are:

- John Vorster Square in Johannesburg – 7 deaths
- Johannesburg Fort – 4 deaths
- Pretoria Prison – 5 deaths
- Sanlam Buildings in Port Elizabeth – 4 deaths

The following is a geographical breakdown of where the deaths occurred:

TRANSVAAL

Johannesburg	14
Pretoria	10
Modderbee Prison	3
Small towns	8
Lebowa	2
Venda	2

NATAL

Durban	4
Pietermaritzburg	2

BORDER

East London	1
Transkei	10
Ciskei	1

EASTERN CAPE

Port Elizabeth	6

WESTERN CAPE

Cape Town	3
Worcester	1

NORTHERN CAPE

Kimberley	1
Upington	1

OTHER

Free State	1
Namibia	2
Unknown	1

For a graphic representation, see Fig. 5.

5. Length of detention before death

The shortest time in detention before death occurred was 2 hours, in the case of Luke Mazwembe (no. 26), while the longest period spent in detention up to time of death was 804 days, in the case of Alfred Makaleng (no. 70), held over 2 years under State of Emergency detention.

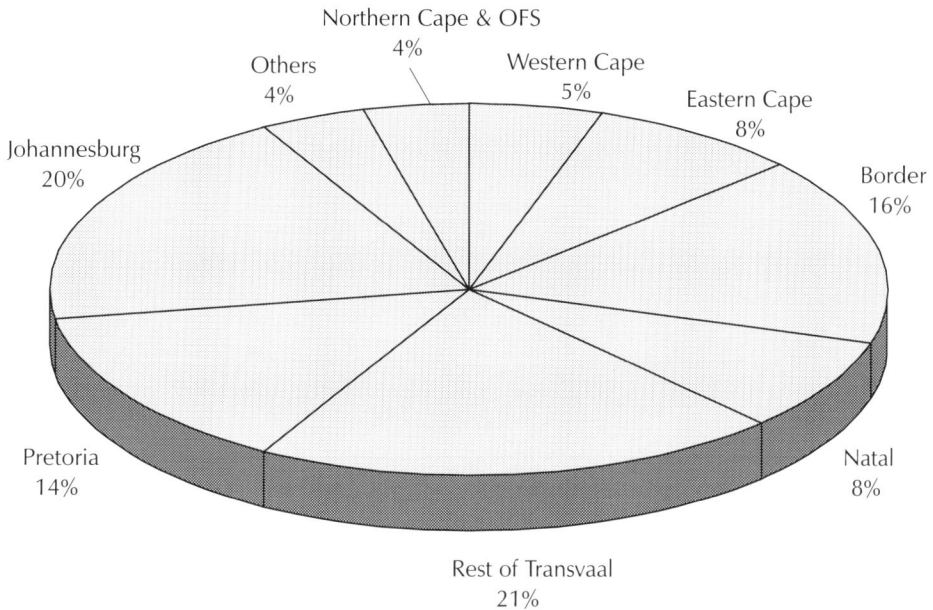

FIGURE 5
Deaths in detention: places of death

A remarkable 28 deaths occurred within the first five days of detention, 17 of them within 1 day.

- Another 15 deaths occurred between 6 and 30 days,
- 12 deaths occurred between 31 and 100 days,
- 9 deaths occurred between 101 and 200 days and
- 4 deaths occurred after 200 days.

The period of detention is unknown in 5 cases. The high incidence of deaths within 1 week of detention (over 40% of known cases) is a cause for serious concern about the intense pressures which detainees must face from the moment of their detention. For a graphic representation, see Fig. 6.

6. Causes of death

The causes of death are normally determined by a post-mortem followed by an inquest in certain circumstances. The post-mortem is conducted by a district surgeon or state pathologist and may be attended by a pathologist appointed by the family of the deceased (usually through their legal representatives) if the family was informed in time and if the family possessed the knowledge and resources to take action. The purpose of a post-mortem is to establish the medical causes of death. An inquest generally follows a post-mortem only if the indicated medical causes point to a death other than from natural

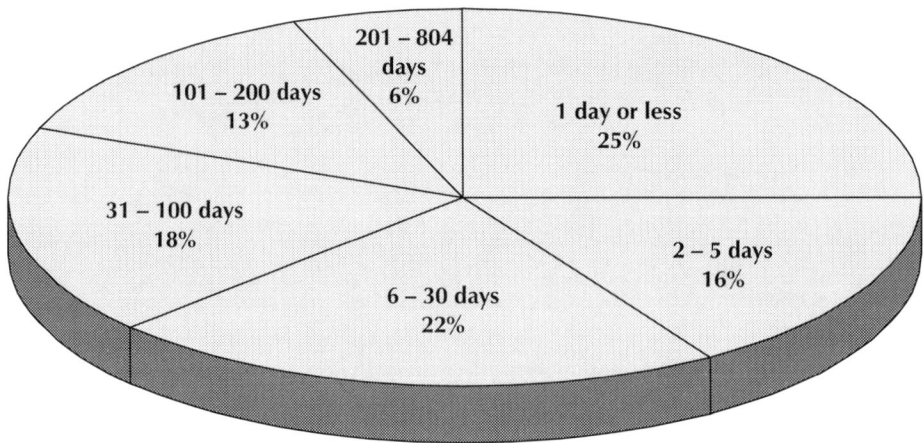

FIGURE 6
Deaths in detention: known length of detentions

causes. It is then the duty of the inquest court to establish the cause and circumstances of the unnatural death and whether any person, through omission or commission, was responsible. Witnesses to a death in detention at an inquest are almost invariably confined to the police themselves since detainees are isolated by detention laws from the outside world.

Death from natural causes
In 21 instances the cause of death was found or declared to be from natural causes. Of these the actual cause was not specified in 5 instances (nos. 5, 6, 15, 17 and 57). Brain damage or ailments was the attributable cause in 4 instances (nos. 21, 38, 70 and 72) and a stroke the attributable cause in 2 instances (nos. 44 and 68). Heart ailments featured in 6 instances (nos. 19, 20, 27, 36, 41 and 50) and pneumonia in 2 instances of death in detention (nos. 14 and 41). Other 'natural' causes were suffocation during an epileptic fit (no. 28), internal bleeding due to gastric ulcer (no. 33) and kidney failure (no. 65). In several instances of death by 'natural causes' the fatal condition was said to have been triggered by unusual circumstances, such as:
• falling while taking a shower (no. 14),
• injuries received when slipping on a piece of soap (no. 15),
• injuries sustained in a fall down some stairs (no. 20),
• fainting and falling against a desk (no. 38).

Furthermore, in several instances reference was made in the post-mortem reports to unexplained wounds, cuts, bruises and abrasions.

Death by suicide
In 33 instances the inquest courts have pronounced the cause of death as suicide by various means. This figure represents exactly 50% of all deaths for which causes have been

declared. The means of committing suicide were declared as follows:
- Suicide by hanging: 26
    (nos. 1, 3, 7, 9, 10, 11, 12, 16, 25, 26, 29, 32, 34, 37, 42, 45, 46, 48, 53, 54, 55, 59, 64, 66, 71, 73)
    N.B. No. 25: Suicide is inferred rather than stated.
    No. 37: Stated as 'probably' suicide.
    No. 73: Police report, no inquest yet.
- Suicide by jumping from buildings: 5
    (nos. 4, 22, 35, 43, 49)
- Suicide by unspecified means: 2
    (nos. 8, 18).

Death by accident

In 4 instances accidents resulting in death occurred whilst the detainees were in the hands of the police but the inquest courts absolved the police of responsibility:
- no. 23 – neck injury sustained in fall against a chair (police claimed there had been a struggle during an escape attempt);
- no. 39 – accidental fall from 10th floor of John Vorster Square while trying to escape;
    no. 47 – brain injury after falling against a wall during a scuffle with the police;
- no. 60 – brain injury sustained in fall from police Casspir.

Death by police killing

Of the 8 instances of police killing, one (no. 24) was adjudged to be justifiable homicide, involving shooting while trying to escape. In the other 7 instances (nos. 52, 56, 61, 62, 63, 67 and 69), policemen were found to be criminally responsible for the deaths, either

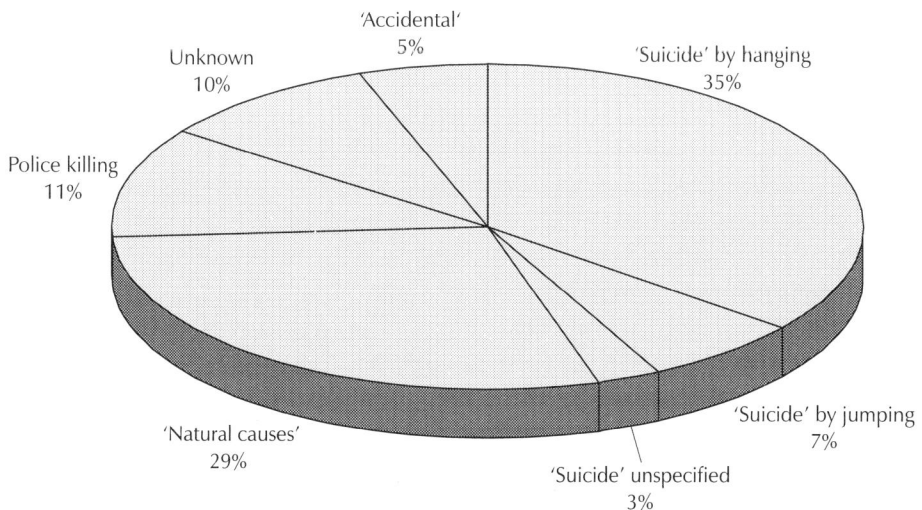

FIGURE 7
Deaths in detention: causes of death

during the course of inquests or during subsequent trials; all 7, with the exception of no. 56, were deaths at the hands of 'homeland' security police (Venda, Ciskei, Transkei, Lebowa).

Death from undetermined causes
In the remaining 7 instances, cause of death is either unknown or undisclosed (nos. 2, 13, 30, 31, 40, 51 and 58).

For a graphic representation of causes of death see Fig. 7.

7. Strange coincidences

A series of unexplained coincidences are to be found within the records of deaths in detention. They are as follows:
- The deaths of Ngeni Gaga (no. 5) and Pongolosha Hoye (no. 6) occurred on the same day (9 May 1965) in the same area (Transkei) both within 24 hours of being detained, both from 'natural causes', neither cause specified.
- The deaths of James Hamakwayo (no. 7) and Hangula Shonyeka (no. 8) occurred on the same day (9 October 1966) at the same place (Pretoria Prison), both said to be suicide. In response to a question in parliament many years later, it was claimed that they were one and the same person, even though records show different detention dates.
- The deaths of Leong Pin (no. 9) and Ah Yan (no. 10) occurred within 2 months of one another, both said to be suicide by hanging. Both had been detained in connection with smuggling illegal immigrants into South Africa from China.
- The deaths of Nicodemus Kgoathe (no. 14) and Solomon Modipane (no. 15) occurred within a 1-month period (February 1969). Both were members of the Bakwena tribe who opposed the appointment of a tribal headman. Both were detained in Silverton police station (near Pretoria) and both died in H.F. Verwoerd Hospital of 'natural causes' said to have been precipitated by falling in the shower (no. 14) and by slipping on a piece of soap (no. 15).
- Of the 4 deaths that have taken place in the Johannesburg Fort, used in the aftermath of the Soweto Uprising, 3 of them occurred within 2 weeks of one another (nos. 28, 29, 31), each from different causes (epileptic fit, suicide by hanging and undisclosed, respectively). The fourth death in Johannesburg Fort took place just 3 months later (no. 36).
- The only 2 deaths to occur in the Pietermaritzburg prison, occurred within 5 weeks of one another (nos. 41 and 42).
- The only 2 deaths to occur in the Brighton Beach police cells in Durban, occurred within 10 days of one another (nos. 45 and 46). Both were declared as suicide by hanging.
- The deaths of Makompe Kutumela (no. 62) and Peter Nchabaleng (no. 63) occurred within the same week in April 1986 in the same area (Lebowa). However, the mystery

was subsequently cleared up when it was established that both had died from assault and torture by their interrogators.

8. Political deaths in police custody

Apart from deaths which have occurred whilst persons are being held in detention without trial under security legislation or Emergency regulations, a substantial number have also died whilst in the custody of the police either under a specific charge or unspecified powers, but clearly in a politically related context such as the unrest situations prevalent since 1984. The vast majority of these deaths are attributable to police action during arrest or subsequent interrogation within a few hours or a few days. In fact, there is often a fine line between deaths which occur during police action and deaths which occur while in custody. Monitoring of such deaths on a systematic basis began only in 1984 and the following numbers have been recorded thus far:

- 1984   6
- 1985   10
- 1986   5
- 1987   4
- 1988   2
- 1989   2
- 1990   3
- Total   32

(See Appendix 1 for details.)

9. Conclusion

Deaths in detention are an inevitable by-product of detention without trial. All attempts by the authorities to eliminate such deaths by safeguards, directives, internal regulations, etc., have met with failure. It should be clear by now that nothing, short of the abolition of the abhorrent practice of detention without trial, will bring an end to these deaths.

Sources:

Institute of Race Relations: Annual Surveys.

Institute of Race Relations: Behind Closed Doors (S. Motala)

Detainees' Parents Support Committee: Monthly Reports

Human Rights Commission: Monthly Updates.

4 POST-DETENTION WEAPONS

As we have seen in Chapter 3, detention without trial, besides serving to withdraw political opponents from circulation, is very often a precursor to further actions designed to extend their removal and even to make it permanent.

Such post-detention measures include:
- banning and restriction orders;
- political imprisonment;
- executions.

These weapons are described in the following HRC documents:
- **Banning and Restriction of Persons** (March 1989)
- **My Home, My Jail** (1989)
- **Political Imprisonment in South Africa** (May 1990)
- **Death Penalty in South Africa** (October 1989)

The repression merry-go-round is well illustrated in Fig. 1, Chapter 1, showing how political activists, once identified, can be drawn into a cycle of detain/release/ban or detain/charge/convict/imprison and even execute, all within the ambit of the law. In some cases the detention step may be leap-frogged. In a later chapter we shall see how, as a last resort, the law may be dispensed with, and abduction and assassination brought into play.

BANNING AND RESTRICTION OF PERSONS
HRC, March 1989

1. Riotous Assemblies Act
2. Suppression of Communism Act
3. General Law Amendment Act
4. Internal Security Act
5. Listing
6. Restrictions

1. Bannings under the Riotous Assemblies Act

The Riotous Assemblies Act of 1930, in a provision introduced by General J.B.M. Hertzog's government, empowered the minister of justice to prohibit any person from being in any area when he is satisfied that such person is 'promoting feelings of hostility between the European inhabitants of the Republic of South Africa on the one hand and any other section of the inhabitants of the Republic of South Africa on the other hand'. A person banished from a particular area under this statute was not entitled to a hearing by the minister before the order was made, nor could he or she appeal against the order.

2. Bannings under the Suppression of Communism Act

When the National Party government came to power in 1948, it preferred to use the wide-ranging provisions of the Suppression of Communism Act (SCA) of 1950 which were more far-reaching. Section 10 of this Act empowered the minister of justice to issue an order imposing severe restrictions on the freedom of movement and expression of any person when he is satisfied that such a person advocates communism or engages in activities that further the aims of communism (which was widely defined). An order of this kind is generally known as a 'banning order' and it confines the person to a particular area as well as obliging him or her to report periodically to a police station. It may go further by restricting the person to his or her residence at all or specified times, in which case the restriction is known as 'house arrest'. In most cases, house arrest is accompanied by a prohibition on having more than a certain number of visitors at home. Banning orders were generally valid for a period of 5 years.

The first banning orders were issued in 1951. The minister of justice said in 1953 that by then 122 people had received such orders. A total of 517 people had received banning orders by 1965. By 1978, a further 841 people had been banned.

3. Bannings under the General Laws Amendment Act

In 1962 the General Law Amendment Act, No. 76 increased police powers to arrest persons who had left the area to which they had been confined in terms of their banning orders and to forcibly return them to the areas concerned. It widened the scope of legal action that could be taken against those people who were listed as being members or active supporters of an organisation that had been declared unlawful (namely the Communist Party) or people who supported the African National Congress (ANC), the Pan Africanist Congress (PAC), Congress of Democrats, Umkhonto weSizwe, Poqo and who supported organisations thought to be acting on their behalf.

The effect of the General Law Amendment Act was to widen the scope of activities that could be restricted and, in so doing, to widen the power of the state to curtail the movements of individuals. The definition of a 'gathering' was widened from being a 'gathering, concourse or procession in, through or along any place, of any number of people having a common purpose, whether such purpose be lawful or unlawful'. This, in effect, meant the minister could ban persons from specified gatherings not having a common purpose, such as social gatherings.

TABLE 8
Bannings of persons 1951–1985

Year	Number of persons banned[a]
1951–1965	517
1966–1978	841
1979	152
1980	24
1981	(not available)
1982	82
1983	61
1984	11
1985	10

[a]These figures are conservative and represent only those reported

4. The Internal Security Act

Political opposition in the 1950s and 1960s had to a large extent been stifled by the extensive police powers of detention and banning. Opposition began to be rekindled around 1968, peaking around 1976. The ideology of black consciousness had become a dominant intellectual influence. The background of an economic recession and consecutive waves of labour unrest sparked off political protest, which was met by intensified state repression in 1976. The targets of this repression were black consciousness leaders, trade unionists and students. The Internal Security Act (ISA) of 1976 amended the SCA of 1950, in terms of which banning orders were issued. Whereas the application of the SCA was confined to those engaged in, or propagating 'communism', the ISA extended the application to those who were deemed to endanger the security of the state or the maintenance of public order. (The powers of banning of persons under the ISA are detailed in Chapter 2.)

5. Listing

The General Law Amendment Act made provision for the minister to publish the names of banned persons in the Government Gazette. If all efforts were made on the part of the state to notify a person of his or her banning order without success, notice could be published in the Gazette, whereupon it was assumed that the person was banned from that date onwards. Another new provision of the Act was the provision to remove the name of a listed person from the consolidated list if 'good cause was shown'. Under section 56 of the

SAK, *The Sowetan,* 17 December 1985

ISA, it is an offence to quote, in a publication, any of the persons whose names appear on the Consolidated List. Doing so carries a prison sentence of up to 3 years. People cannot be quoted if:

- At the time of enactment of the Internal Security Act (ISA) of 1982, people's names were on earlier lists compiled in terms of the Suppression of Communism Act of 1950 or the ISA of 1976. The 1982 law made it possible for some names to be carried forward.
- They have been convicted of specific security offences or of treason.
- The minister is satisfied that a person acts in a way that endangers state security or the maintenance of law and order or that he or she promotes the objects of communism.

6. Restrictions

The revised ISA of 1982 dealt with categories of restricted persons and the requirements of restricted persons and also set up a board of review. However, no bannings took place under the Act from October 1982 and it was speculated that the government might be easing up on banning orders. But the apparent relaxation was short-lived. In 1985, following a renewed upsurge of political resistance in the black townships, a partial State of Emergency was declared in terms of the Public Safety Act of 1953 and this became a new mechanism for serving people with banning orders. Persons detained in terms of the Emergency regulations could be released subject to certain conditions, which amounted to a new form of banning in terms of Section 3(b) of the emergency regulations, imposed by the minister of law and order. The minister was not required to publish the names of the affected individuals. The conditions only expired on the termination of the State of Emergency and contravention of the regulations carried with it a penalty of a fine of up to R20 000 or up to 20 years' imprisonment without the option of a fine.

In November 1986 a new type of restriction order issued in terms of regulation 7(1) was served on persons other than those released from detention. By the end of 1986, 36 persons were known to have been issued with such orders in Johannesburg. Banning and restriction orders have been widely used during 1988 and 1989. The crack-down on 17 organisations in February 1988 was coupled with restriction orders on 12 people that were so severe that they amounted to house arrest. The restrictions were imposed in terms of Section 6(b) of the Emergency regulations.

The banning of an anti-apartheid conference in September 1988 saw restrictions being placed on leaders crucial to the organisation of the conference for periods of less than 2 weeks. This was aimed at specifically preventing them from mobilising their constituencies at the conference without provoking the outcry that would have followed their indefinite restriction. Some of the restriction orders went as far as explicitly prohibiting them from calling for a boycott of the municipal elections. Among those restricted were 3 executive members of the Congress of South African Trade Unions (COSATU), 7 Cape Town activists, 3 members of the black consciousness movement in Bekkersdal, 6 Soweto leaders of affiliates of the United Democratic Front (UDF), a UDF leader from the northern Cape and 2 unionists from Pretoria. The build-up to the municipal elections on 26 October 1988 saw intense state repression. Regulations were promulgated enabling the minister of law and order to place activists under house arrest or to place them under an area restriction simply by placing a notice in the Government Gazette. This was aimed at silencing people who were on the run and who could not be traced by police.

Restriction orders have also been frequently served on former detainees or political prisoners. The ANC leader Govan Mbeki was served with such an order on his release from prison, after having served a 23-year sentence on Robben Island. The order prohibits him from leaving his home town of Port Elizabeth, speaking to journalists and assisting in the publication of any material. In June 1988 he was served with tougher restriction orders preventing him from attending a gathering of more than 10 people.

The restriction orders often have the effect of prohibiting the person from returning to their profession or the conditions of the order are so constraining that they render the person unemployable. Banning orders have also been imposed as the condition of a suspended sentence, as happened in the Delmas treason trial. They are also frequently incorporated as part of the condition of bail. Those involved in the Alexandra treason trial are subject to such restrictions.

Example of a Notice under Regulation 3(8) of the Security Emergency Regulations of 1988:
Under paragraph (8) of the Security Emergency Regulations, 1988, I hereby order that X,

who is being detained in terms of regulation 3 of the said regulations, be released on 5 September 1988 on the conditions set out in the schedule hereto.

Signed: Adriaan Vlok

Schedule: Conditions of release

Under regulation 3(8)(b)(I) of the Security Emergency Regulations, 1988, you are hereby notified that your release from detention in terms of regulation 3 (8)(a) shall be subject to the conditions:

a) that you shall not, as from the date of your release, without the written consent of the Divisional Commander of the Security Branch of the South African Police for the Witwatersrand Division:

1. take part in any manner whatsoever in any of the activities or acts of the following organisations:
   United Democratic Front
   Johannesburg Democratic Action Committee
   National Education Crisis Committee
   National Education Union of South Africa
2. be outside the boundaries of the magisterial district of x at any time;
3. be outside the boundaries of the premises situated at .... in x (X's address) between the hours of 18h00 and 06h00;
4. at any one occasion, receive more than 4 visitors at the above premises;
5. attend or stay present at any meeting consisting of five or more persons (including yourself), convened or otherwise brought about for the purpose of discussing some or other matter;
6. contribute, prepare, compile or transmit in any manner whatsoever any matter for publication in any publication as defined in the Media Emergency Regulations, 1988, or assist in any manner whatsoever in the preparation, compilation or transmission of any matter for publication;
7. take part in any interview with any journalist, news reporter, news commentator or news correspondent;
8. be present on or enter upon any premises occupied by an educational institution which provides formal education as defined in section 1 of the National Policy for General Education Affairs Act, 1984 (Act 76 of 1984);

(b) that you shall, as from the date of your release, report daily to the officer in charge of the Charge Office at the .... Police Station, between 10h00 and 11h00 and between 15h00 and 16h00, subject to such exemptions as the Divisional Commander of the Security Branch of the South African Police for the Witwatersrand Division may at any time authorise in writing.

MY HOME, MY JAIL
The Case of Restrictees in South Africa
HRC, March 1990

1. Consequences and implications of restriction orders

1.1 Social and emotional effects

Although the aim of restrictions was to control an individual's political activity at the individual's rather than at the state's expense, it must be emphasised that an individual's personal and social life were also severely affected.

Restrictions created numerous problems which affected all aspects of the restrictee's everyday life over an indefinite period of time. For restrictees, their homes were their jails and they and their families were the jailers. This entailed a constant need for vigilance. Forgetting to report or failing to notice that an additional person had joined the group of people one was talking to could have resulted in a criminal charge. There was no space for spontaneity or forgetfulness. The restrictees and their families had to be on their guard constantly as police could arrive at any time and any number of times during the night to ensure that restriction orders were being complied with.

Many restrictees were effectively denied a family or social life. Even weddings, funerals, birthday parties and other family get-togethers constituted a contravention of the limit on the number of people with whom restrictees could meet – a limit sometimes as tight as 4.

Between 1984 and 1986, it was common for activists to be visited arbitrarily at all hours of the night at their homes by the police and defence force. Restriction orders made it 'legal' for police to arrive at any time, unannounced, to 'check up' on a restricted detainee. Because of police visits and the vulnerability of the restrictee to right-wing attacks, families stayed at home in order to protect the restrictees. This, in effect, amounted to a curfew on the whole family. The whole family was harassed and intimidated, not just the individual.

1.2 Psychological and physical effects

When one talks about the psychological and emotional effects of restrictions, one is not only dealing with the effects of restrictions but also the after-effects of the detention itself.

The effects of detention fall under the psychological category of post-traumatic stress disorder (PTSD). The symptoms include flashbacks of the violence related to the arrest, period of detention and interrogation; recurring nightmares; difficulties experienced with sleeping, eating and drinking; loss of memory; an inability to concentrate; anxiety, depression, anger, irritability and problems with interpersonal relationships.

Restrictions resulted in a situation where the trauma continued. The restrictee had to cope with ongoing anxiety and stress. Therefore the psychological effects are better described as continuous or ongoing stress. Furthermore, having to deal with undermining and debilitating daily trauma and real threats to freedom and existence, the restrictee was also a victim of cumulative stress. It is difficult, if not impossible, for restrictees to recover from any psychological or physical ailments when they continue to live in a hostile and threatening world. Restrictees were continually exposed and vulnerable to the very real danger of assassination and physical harm to themselves and their families.

Having to report to the police station once or twice per day resulted in the individual having to confront memories of the past on a daily basis. Also, having to expose oneself daily to the police, some of whom might have been involved in the arrest or interrogation, must have certainly undermined self-esteem and confidence. Being unable to secure a job or return to school also weighed heavily on the emotions and self-esteem of the restrictee.

Many restrictees were in poor health, particularly those who embarked on hunger strikes. Many were unable to leave specified townships in order to receive medical treatment for their ailments. The same problem applied to receiving legal assistance. When attorney Dhaya Pillay applied for a relaxation of the restriction orders of former detainee Sandile Thuse (who was on hunger strike for 37 days) so that he could consult a doctor, although she applied 3 weeks in advance, the date for the appointment had passed and there had still not been any word from the police.

Restrictees could not even take a short family holiday to recover from the effects of detention and the hunger strike because most were under house arrest from sunset to sunrise.

1.3 Education and the workplace

Restriction orders often had the effect of prohibiting restrictees from returning to their occupation; for instance, educationalists were forbidden to set foot at any educational institution. Sometimes the conditions of the order were so constraining that they rendered the person unemployable.

Having to report to the police once or twice per day, often at times that cut into worktime, made it very difficult for restrictees to find employment. A reporting restrictee would always arrive late for work and had to leave early to report at the police station. Being limited to a single magisterial district added to this difficulty as employment was almost impossible to come by in the townships.

Having to account for 2 or 3 years of one's life in detention often colours a prospective employee in the eyes of the employer. The employer feels that the applicant is a 'jailbird' and a potential trouble maker. Employers do not want political activists on their staff and in the unions.

Many children who were released from detention with restrictions (and without) are refused admission to school because they are 'too old' or because the headmaster fears that they are trouble makers and will incite other pupils to contravene regulations or rules.

Restricted children generally had to be home at 6p.m. or 7p.m. Those who had to report twice per day, usually had to do so between 4a.m. and 10a.m. and 2p.m. and 6p.m. This prevented them from participating in extramural activities during the day and in the evenings. Many students coming from overcrowded homes were denied their only quiet study time as they were prevented by their restrictions from studying at university libraries in the evenings.

1.4 Financial Costs

Restrictees had to pay their own travelling expenses to report once or twice per day to the police station despite the fact that many of them had no income.

Many, if not most, detainees required medical care on their release. By releasing and restricting people, especially those who were on hunger strike, the state no longer had to pay medical costs. It is more than cruel to refuse a person who needs medical care the ability to earn a living while forcing this person to bear their own medical costs.

1.5 Harassment, attacks and assassination

Restrictees were open to attack and many were continually harassed. Before their detention, many had been attacked in their own homes, yet they were forced to remain in their homes and were prevented from going into hiding as a result of their restriction orders.

Restrictions were clearly associated with harassment and attacks although the identity of the perpetrators of such crimes was not always evident. The harassment included physical and psychological harassment, vigilante attacks, banishment to far-away places, police visits, virtual house arrest, assaults and assassinations. The ex-detainees who were

SAK, *The Sowetan*, 10 February 1988

served with restrictions were particularly vulnerable as their whereabouts were well known since they had to report to a police station once or twice a day. This made them easy targets for intimidatory attacks.

POLITICAL IMPRISONMENT IN SOUTH AFRICA
HRC, May 1990

1. Introduction and definitions
2. Legislation
3. Political trials
4. Political prisoners

1. Introduction and definitions

Within the South African context, the simplest and most essential definition of a political prisoner is a person who is in prison as a direct result of opposition to the system of apartheid. This opposition can take many forms ranging from peaceful protest to participation in political unrest or opting for armed struggle. Acts viewed as normal political opposition in most other countries are criminalised in South Africa. Not only are political activists turned into criminals but legitimate and peaceful acts of opposition are also criminalised.

A definition of political prisoners must include those jailed for their political beliefs and associations. Also those whose deeds are considered a threat to state security and those who acted with political motives in a mass political uprising. Even those whose 'crimes' are simply related to political goals – as opposed to being in pursuit of them – should be included, provided there is a clear political motive. These norms do not judge the validity of the political motivation or of the tactics. Rather, the mere existence of the antagonism between the individual and the government is sufficient to call the person a political offender. Translated into specific statutory categories this definition means all of the following are political prisoners:
- Those convicted under the Internal Security Act 74 of 1982 or its predecessors.
- Those convicted of the common law crimes of treason, sedition and related offences.
- Those convicted of other common law crimes which are politically related, such as public violence.
- Certain persons convicted under the Explosives Act of 1956 and the Arms and Munitions Act of 1969.
- Those convicted under the Emergency regulations.
- Administrative detainees held under the detention provisions of the Internal Security Act or the State of Emergency regulations.

- Prisoners held under the legislation of the Transkei, Ciskei, Venda and Bophuthatswana.

The official figure for what it calls 'security prisoners' was given in parliament as 347, as at 31 March 1989. Using the definition outlined at the start of this report, the HRC estimates that there are between 2500 and 3000 political prisoners in South African prisons.

2. Legislation

There is a plethora of laws and regulations which govern political activity in South Africa. Since 1948, when the National Party imposed apartheid on South Africa, it has consistently used parliament and the law courts to implement this policy and to stifle opposition to it.

One of the first steps that the National Party government took was to introduce the Suppression of Communism Act under which the Communist Party of South Africa, until then a legal political party with members in parliament and in local government, was banned. The Act was so broadly worded that any opposition to apartheid could be branded as 'communist' and therefore unlawful.

Political activists involved in peaceful protest have found themselves in contravention of these laws which criminalise activities that in any democratic country would be considered normal, legitimate and healthy political opposition. Such persons have faced charges for offences ranging from an unlawful gathering or possessing banned literature, to subversion, treason and terrorism. Many have been convicted for public violence, arson, malicious damage to property, incitement and intimidation and some for murder. Convictions and sentences have been heavily dependent upon the interpretation of the courts and often without regard to the causal link between the apartheid system and the circumstances leading to violence.

In most cases it is the opinion of the cabinet minister or other executive official which determines whether a person, organisation or activity needs to be acted against. Once such action has been taken, whether through banning or restriction, and the person or organisation contravenes whatever restrictions have been imposed, the courts are left to decide on their guilt. The decision of the court is not based on the justness of a particular law or statute. It has to decide whether an offence has been committed purely in terms of the law. Thus, what seems a totally legitimate act – for example, that of reading a book espousing the principles and objectives of a political organisation – becomes a crime because the state has passed a law saying so.

The state has in the past consistently argued that 'there are no political prisoners in South Africa. Rather, people have been imprisoned for breaking the law.' The state attempts to legitimise its suppression of opposition by posturing as the upholder of the law. The same state has, however, ignored the law when this has been expedient. In cases where the law did not favour a course that the state wanted to follow, the law was changed. When the courts handed down judgements, in terms of existing law, that overturned actions of the state, amendments were introduced which allowed the state to prevail. This means that the independence of the judiciary in South Africa is an illusion. As new strategies of resistance develop in opposition to apartheid, so they are repressed by laws which are continually being updated.

3.   Political Trials

The South African government sees long political trials as a means of keeping prominent activists out of circulation for extended periods of time, even if many are eventually acquitted. An example of this is the first Delmas treason trial which lasted for 4 years (1985–1988); 22 people were accused and 10 were released on bail after 3 years. The rest were held as awaiting trial prisoners for the full period of the trial. Ultimately 5 people were convicted and sentenced; the rest received suspended sentences or were acquitted.

The ever-increasing number of political trials is an indication of the efforts of the state to criminalise and neutralise legitimate political opposition.

TRIALS DURING 1989:

No. of complete political trials recorded by the HRC	395
No. of accused involved	3183
No. of people convicted	493
No. of people acquitted or charges withdrawn	2690

CONVICTIONS[a]

Treason	154[b]
Terrorism	85
Possession of arms or explosives	28
Furthering the aims of a banned organisation	25
Possession of banned literature	12
Illegal gathering	37
Various other Internal Security Act contraventions	16
Emergency Regulation contraventions	9
Murder and attempted murder	130
Miscellaneous	38
Total	534

[a]In many cases an individual will have been convicted of more than one offence.
[b]Includes 151 involved in the Bophuthatswana 'coup' attempt.

DETAILS OF SENTENCES

Death sentence	42
20 years and over	10
15–19 years	25
10–14 years	36
5–9 years	116
2–4 years	59
Suspended sentences of 2 to 8 years	30
Lesser sentences, fines, cuts etc.	125

It is interesting to compare the 1989 political trial figures with those of previous years:

TABLE 9
Political trials 1986–1989

	1986	1987	1988	1989
No. of trials completed	114	133	141	395
No. of accused	690	792	574	3 183
No. of convictions	195	229	255	493
No. acquitted or whose charges were withdrawn	495	563	319	2 690
Percentage of accused convicted	28.2%	28.9%	44.4%	15.4%

Trials of a political nature still continue in 1990 – 146 trials were completed between January 1990 and April 1990. There are also 184 ongoing political trials

Clearly there has been a huge escalation in the use of the courts. In 1989, there were almost 3 times as many completed trials as there were in 1988, and the number of completed trials for the first 4 months of 1990 is already high. Although the number of accused increased by 5.5 times from 1988 to 1989, the number of convictions did not increase proportionately – in 1989 only 15.4% of the accused were convicted, compared with 44% in 1988.

At a time when the call on all sides is for a cessation of political trials and the release of political prisoners, the courts are working overtime to manufacture a stream of new political prisoners. Nor is there any end in sight – according to HRC records (which are certainly incomplete), at the end of December 1989 there were a further 255 political trials under way or set down for commencement added to which are the 184 ongoing trials as at the end of April 1990.

4. Political prisoners

An estimated 50 000 persons over the last 5 years have found themselves in court as a result of involvement in the violence arising from mass resistance to apartheid. The vast majority has been acquitted or had their charges dropped.

Statistics released in parliament revealed that as at 31 March 1989 there were 347 prisoners serving sentences for 'offences against the state'. Since that date, a number of prisoners were released on completion of their sentences, a handful of high-profile prisoners were released unconditionally before their term, and a number of newly sentenced prisoners were added to the political prisoner population. It is estimated that at the end of 1989 there were about 370 'security' prisoners.

In addition, however, there are between 2500 and 3000 'unrest' prisoners – that is, those caught up in the political violence of the years 1984–1990. Their charges arose out of political protest against apartheid repression. This figure includes 73 on death row (as at the end of April 1990).

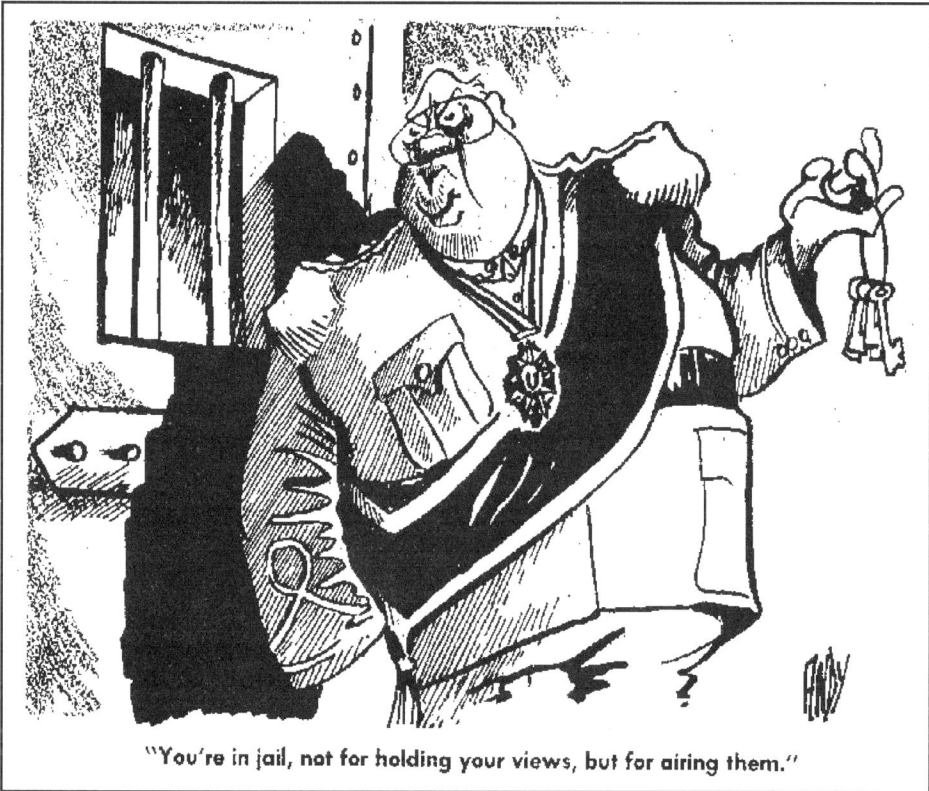

"You're in jail, not for holding your views, but for airing them."

Andy, *The Star*, 11 November 1987

POLITICAL EXECUTIONS
The Death Penalty in South Africa

HRC, October 1989

1. Introduction
2. Statistics (for all hangings)
3. Political trials
4. Prisoner of war status
5. List of political executions

1. Introduction

Officially boasting the second highest execution rate in the world, South Africa is one of 101 countries world-wide which have retained the death penalty on their statute books. In the period mid-1985 to mid-1988, Iran was the only country that executed more people than South Africa. Since 1958 the legislature in this country has added 8 crimes to the original list of 3 capital crimes. It is significant to note that whilst South Africa has been extending the number of capital crimes, the rest of the world has moved away from capital punishment. No less than 16 countries have abolished capital punishment during the past 10 years.

2. Statistics (for all hangings)

From the creation of the Union of South Africa in 1910 until the end of 1988 over 4200 persons have been hanged in South Africa. From 1978 until the end of 1988 a total of 1335 people were executed in South Africa (excluding the nominally independent 'homelands'), the number exceeding 100 each year except for 1981 and 1983. In 1987, 164 people were executed at Pretoria Central prison, the highest annual figure ever in South Africa's history. In one week in December 1987, 21 people were executed in groups of 7 on 3 different days. At the end of June 1989 there were 274 people on death row. In the 5 years between 1983 and 1987, 627 people were executed in South Africa. It took Britain half a century to hang about the same number of people. The 1987 figure of 164 executions was 4 more than Iran with a population of 47 million and 32 more than China with a population of 1 billion. (South Africa, excluding the TBVC states, had a population of just under 30 million at the end of June 1987.) In 1987 there were 25 executions in the whole of the United States, while Western Europe has had no executions since 1985. In the late 1960s Professor Barend van Niekerk of the University of Natal calculated that 47% of all executions in the world take place in South Africa.

3. Political trials

The nation-wide political protests which began in the townships in September 1984 have brought a new category of condemned prisoners to the death-row section of Pretoria Central prison: the political prisoner convicted of offences connected with political conflict. It is estimated that more than 80 people are currently on death row for politically related reasons. They have been convicted for unrest related murders of police officers, black township councillors, suspected police informers or other murders connected with political conflict.

The case that brought the death penalty under renewed public scrutiny was that of the 'Sharpeville Six', who were convicted of the killing in September 1984 of the deputy mayor of Sharpeville, Khuzwayo Dhlamini. Their appeal against the death sentence was rejected by the Appellate Division in December 1987. A legal petition for their clemency was rejected by the state president but the minister of justice granted them an indefinite stay of execution on 14 July 1988 to give them the opportunity to pursue further legal remedies. As international pressure mounted against their sentences, the State President commuted their sentences to life imprisonment in November 1988. The reason for the local and international outcry against their conviction was the basis upon which the 'Six' were convicted, namely the doctrine of common purpose. According to this common law doctrine, an accused can be held liable for a crime (despite the absence of proof that he or she has contributed causally to the commission of the crime) if it can be proved that he or she has made common cause with those who were actually perpetrating the crime. The Appeal Court in the case of the Sharpeville Six acknowledged that it had not been proved that the conduct of the six accused had contributed causally to the death of the deceased, but said that each of the accused 'shared a common purpose to kill the deceased with the mob as a whole, the members of which were intent upon killing the deceased'. The main criticism against the Appeal Court's interpretation of the doctrine of common purpose is that it spreads the net of criminal liability very widely and raises the prospect of many death sentences being imposed in future trials arising out of political conflict. In May 1989, 25 Upington residents were found guilty of murder on the basis of common purpose regarding the death in 1985 of a municipal policeman in Paballelo township. Of the 25, 14 received the death sentence. In June 1989, 12 men were sentenced to death in the Bisho Supreme Court in Ciskei for the murder of 5 youths. In his judgement Mr Justice Heath said that even though only a few of the convicted men had been found to be involved in the actual violence, there was enough evidence to convict them of murder using the common purpose principle. A total of 43 death sentences have been handed down by South African courts in 9 court cases concerning collective violence since 1985.

4. Prisoner of war status

Captured guerrillas are increasingly claiming the status of soldiers entitled to prisoner of war status under the 1977 addenda to the Geneva Conventions. South Africa is not a signatory to the 1977 protocols (which extend the 1949 Conventions beyond declared wars to wars of 'national liberation') but the ANC made a declaration in 1980 to the effect that it would apply the Geneva Conventions and their protocols. This becomes important in cases where the death penalty is an appropriate sentence. According to the Convention on Prisoners of War of 1949, a prisoner of war may not be executed by the detaining power for military activities prior to his or her arrest unless they amount to war crimes. South African courts, however, have not yet taken cognisance of the 1977 protocols. It has been argued that despite the attitude of the courts, the prisoner of war argument can be raised in mitigation of sentence. The fact that the ANC fighter saw himself or herself as being engaged in an international conflict and fighting for a just cause should operate as an extenuating circumstance, reducing the moral blameworthiness of the accused.

5. List of political executions

The following is a list of executions which have taken place in South Africa as a result of offences having a political context. It can only be considered a partial list. We are indebted to the publication *Waiting to Die in Pretoria* by Phyllis Naidoo for much of the information.

TABLE 10 **Political executions**		
Execution date	*Name*	*Remarks*
1963 8 May	May, Zenzile	Poqo members. Killing of Tembu chief G. Gqoboza.
	Mbiso, Modi	
	Mhlaki, Sizwayi	
	Ngalo, Nkosinam	
	Pilapi, Khatazekile	
	Sonamzi, Goli	
14 October	Nyovu, Thembekile Titus	Death of white girl in Paarl riots (1962).
2 November	Damane, Mxolisi	Poqo members. Killings in Paarl.
	Jaza, Felix	
	Madikane, Lennox	
1964 11 February	Bozwana, Notemba	Sabotage in Queenstown (1963).
	Ngcongolo, Bonakele	
May	Bongo, Wellington Mpumelo	
	Mabhongo	
	Mpenze	
6 November	Khayinga, Wilson	Trade union leaders. Killing of state witness, Eastern Cape.
	Mkaba, Zinakele	
	Mnini, Vuyisile	
1965 1 April	Harris, Frederick John	African Resistance Movement (ARM). Bombing of Johannesburg Station.
1979 6 April	Mahlangu, Solomon (21)	ANC guerrilla. Goch Street shooting (1977).
1983 9 June	Mogoerane, Simon (23)	ANC insurgents. Treason/murder/arms.
	Mosololi, Jerry (25)	
	Motaung, Marcus (27)	
1984 August	Lebajoa, Peter	ANC members. Treason/murder of farmer (1978).
	Rivers, Frank Rebane	
	Segoto, Joseph Themba	
1985 18 October	Moloise, Malesella Benjamin (28)	Shooting security policeman (7 November 1982).
1986 9 September	Payi, Clarence Lucky (22)	ANC members. Killing of Benjamin Langa (1984).
	Xulu, Sipho Bridget	
9 September	Zondo, Sibusiso Andrew (24)	ANC member. Bombing of Amanzimtoti shopping centre (9 December 1985).
5 December	Maqwasha, Solomon (20)	Murder of informer in Tzaneen.
	Matsepane, Alex Matshapa (23)	
1987 19 August	Webushe, Welile	Murder in Jansenville, Eastern Cape.
1 September	Jantjies, Mnyanda Moses (21)	Killing of councillor, Uitenhage, Eastern Cape.
	Mielies, Mlamli Wellington (22)	
6 November	Luphondo, Mlungisi (21)	
1988 18 March	Letsoare, Tsepo (22)	Necklace murder of police informer.
25 March	Lucas, Michael (17/18)	Bongolethu Youth Congress. Killing of bus driver (April 1986).
25 March	Gxothiwe, Benjamin (27)	
29 March	Londe, Siphiwo	
	Mohala, Sipho (21)	
	Rewu, Lungile (19)	
5 April	Lloyd, Tobilo Richard	
1989 20 April	Menze, Makhezwana (40)	Addo Youth Congress ('common purpose'). Death of farmer and wife, Southern Cape (June 1985).
	Sephenuka, Ndumiso Silo (25)	
25 May	Mngomezulu, Abraham (23)	Killing of police informer, Johannesburg (1987).
29 September	Boesman, Mangena Jeffrey (35)	Death of informer school teacher in Sterkstroom, eastern Cape (October 1985).
24 November	Dyakala, Kholisile (31)	Killing of security guard in Port Elizabeth (June 1986).
	Mjekula, Zwelidumile (36)	

5 THE STRANGULATION OF ACTIVITY

The classical freedoms of association, assembly and expression did not, of course, escape the apartheid mill. All were comprehensively and ruthlessly repressed, particularly during States of Emergency. Every avenue of political expression was blocked, and as new forms of resistance were devised, these too were stifled, almost at birth. Such attempts to put a stranglehold on all political activity are described below in the following HRC documents:

- *Banning and Restriction of Organisations* (January 1989)
- *Banning of Gatherings* (July 1990)
- *Freedom of the Press* (June 1989)

BANNING AND RESTRICTION OF ORGANISATIONS
HRC, January 1989

1. Chronology of bannings

1950

One of the first restrictions on freedom of opinion and association imposed by the Nationalist government was in 1950 with the Suppression of Communism Act. It declared the Communist Party of South Africa to be unlawful and provided for the 'naming' of communists and for the prohibition of publications expressing the views of the Communist Party. An Amendment to the Act the following year allowed for the listing of any person who had professed to be a communist, or encouraged, supported or furthered the objects of communism before the Act came into law. Thus people could be penalised for breaking laws that were not in force at the time of their actions. The Amendment also tightened the restrictions on the media.

1960

The Unlawful Organisations Act, promulgated on 28 March 1960, gave the governor-general the power to proclaim the banning of the Pan Africanist Congress (PAC) and the African National Congress (ANC). On the 8 April 1960 these organisations were banned. This was one of the measures imposed in a spate of restrictive legislation following the Sharpeville shootings on 21 March, including the first declaration of a State of Emergency on 30 March 1960.

1962

On 14 September 1962, the Congress of Democrats was banned in terms of Proclamation R218. The COD was a white organisation, part of the Congress group which consisted of the ANC, Coloured People's Congress, South African Indian Congress, South African Congress of Trade Unions (SACTU) and the Federation of South African Women (FEDSAW). This was a time of heavy repression by means of house arrests and restrictions on meetings. Nelson Mandela was on trial at the time for incitement and leaving the country unlawfully, and Umkhonto weSizwe was becoming increasingly active.

1963

With the banning of the ANC and PAC, a number of other organisations sprang up which were subsequently declared to be synonymous with the banned organisations and hence banned under the same Act. In May 1963 Umkhonto weSizwe was declared to be the same organisation as the ANC. The organisation Poqo, the military wing of the PAC, was declared to be the same as the PAC, as were the Dance Association, Football Club, Football League and the S.A.A. Football League.

1966

The Defence and Aid Fund was an organisation set up in 1960 to provide legal aid to persons involved in political trials and also to provide assistance to their families. In March 1966 it was declared an unlawful organisation under the Suppression of Communism Act. Although the Fund was a completely separate body, it was accused of being a branch of the London-based Defence and Aid Fund, which was militantly anti-apartheid.

1977

In October 1977 the security police swooped on activists country-wide and banned 18 organisations, mainly black consciousness-related, under the Internal Security Act. Two of the largest black newspapers were also banned, The World and Weekend World. These bannings led to an international outcry from a world still shocked by the death in detention of Steve Biko in September 1977. At the same time many of the leaders of these organisations were held in preventive detention under the Internal Security Act. The banned organisations were:

- Black People's Convention (BPC)
- South African Students' Organisation (SASO)
- South African Students' Movement (SASM)
- Union of Black Journalists
- Black Community Programmes Limited (BCP)
- Black Parents' Association (BPA)
- Border Youth Organisation
- Soweto Students' Representative Council (SSRC)
- African Social Education and Cultural Education (ASSECA)
- Black Women's Federation
- National Youth Organisation
- Eastern Province Youth Organisation

- Medupe Writers' Association
- Natal Youth Organisation
- Transvaal Youth Organisation
- Western Cape Youth Organisation
- Zimele Trust Fund
- Siyazinceda Trust Fund

1978

The Methodist Church of South Africa was banned in the Transkei. This ban was lifted in June 1988 under the military rule of General Bantu Holomisa. The ban had been imposed after the church had spoken out against Transkei independence. Bophuthatswana banned the Human Rights Commission of South Africa in September 1978.

1979

33 organisations were banned in the Transkei again in response to criticism of Transkei independence. Among these were foreign organisations, e.g. the Zimbabwean-based organisation United African National Congress (UANC), some Namibian organisations and some that were even unknown such as the Marxist Front.

1983

The South African Allied Workers' Union (SAAWU) was banned in the Ciskei in September 1983 after it had been instrumental in organising a bus boycott during times of widespread unrest in the Ciskei. This banning was challenged in court in 1987, but the four-year-old ban was upheld.

1984

The United Democratic Front (UDF), Congress of South African Students (COSAS) and the Azanian Students Organisation (AZASO) were banned in the Transkei.

1985

In August 1985, soon after the declaration of the 1985 State of Emergency, COSAS was banned under the Internal Security Act. COSAS, a national student movement, was responsible for the mass mobilisation of students in the period leading up to its banning and it was the largest of the UDF affiliates, building much of the UDF's popular support. The ban was imposed following a secret investigation by an advisory committee appointed by the state president. A challenge to the banning was unsuccessful.

1986

SAAWU, banned in the Ciskei in 1983, was banned in February 1986 in the Transkei.

1988

February

In February 1988 a new mechanism was employed for banning 17 organisations by means of imposing restrictions under the State of Emergency regulations. These restrictions have the effect of banning the organisations until the lifting of the Emergency. If the Internal Security Act had been invoked instead, the organisations would have been entitled to demand that the minister produce a list of reasons for the banning and would have had the right to have the banning order reviewed by the Chief Justice. Thus, by using the Emergency regulations, the courts were entirely circumvented. The organisations (mainly UDF affiliates and the UDF itself) which were prohibited from 'carrying on or performing any activities or acts whatsoever' were:

- Azanian People's Organisation (AZAPO)
- Azanian Youth Organisation (AZAYO)
- Cape Youth Congress (CAYCO)
- Cradock Residents' Association (CRADORA)
- Detainees' Parents Support Committee (DPSC)
- Detainees' Support Committee (DESCOM)
- National Education Crisis Committee (NECC)
- National Education Union of South Africa (NEUSA)
- Port Elizabeth Black Civic Organisation (PEBCO)
- Release Mandela Committee (RMC)
- Soweto Civic Association (SCA)
- Soweto Youth Congress (SOYCO)
- South African National Students' Congress (SANSCO)
- South African Youth Congress (SAYCO)
- United Democratic Front (UDF)
- Vaal Civic Association (VCA)
- Western Cape Civic Association

At the same time as these restrictions, a different set of restrictions were imposed on the Congress of South African Trade Unions (COSATU), which effectively stopped any of their activities not confined to the workplace and narrowly to workers' issues.

March

Following the February restrictions, a new organisation was formed in the Cape – the Committee for the Defence of Democracy. Six days after its launch, it was restricted under the same conditions as the 17 organisations.

June

With the second annual re-imposition of the State of Emergency on 10 June 1988, the restrictions imposed earlier in the year on the 18 organisations (i.e. the original 17 plus the CDD) were renewed.

August

On 10 February 1988 an attempted coup in Bophuthatswana led to the banning, at the beginning of August, of the opposition People's Progressive Party (PPP). The official reason given for the bannings was an allegation that the party leader, Peter Rocky Malebane Metsing, was planning from outside the country to release members of the party who were in jail on charges of high treason in connection with the attempted coup. This

Velk, P, *City Press,* 26 February 1988

ban removed all the opposition in the Bophuthatswana parliament.

After a long build-up of public threats and a concerted campaign in the government-controlled media, the End Conscription Campaign (ECC) was restricted under the same conditions as the 18 silenced organisations.

September
The Prisoners' Welfare Programme (PRIWELPRO) was declared an undesirable organisation in terms of the Public Security Act of the Transkei.

October
The Soweto Students' Congress (SOSCO) and the Azanian Co-ordinating Committee were restricted under the Emergency regulations. AZACCO had been formed in February in response to the restriction of Azanian Peoples' Organisation (AZAPO). SOSCO was formed in 1985 after the banning of COSAS.

November
At the beginning of November, a further 2 organisations were restricted – the Port Elizabeth Youth Congress (PEYCO) and the Transvaal Students' Congress (TRASCO). Later in the month, restrictions were placed for the first time on a right-wing organisation, the extremist Blanke Bevrydingsbeweging (BBB) and at the same time its leader, Johan Schabort, was restricted.

December

During November, the state intimated that a further 5 organisations were being considered for restriction orders. In fact, a further 8 organisations were restricted up to the end of the year, bringing the total to 34 restrictions in 1988. On 8 December, the Black Students Society (BSS) at the University of the Witwatersrand and the Black Students Movement at Rhodes University, Grahamstown, were restricted. On the 13 December, 2 more student organisations were restricted: the Mitchell's Plain Student Congress (MSC) and the Western Cape Students' Council (WCSC). This was followed on 29 December by restrictions on the Democratic Teachers' Union, the National Detainees' Forum, Western Cape Students' Congress and Western Cape Teachers' Union.

2. The number of organisations banned

Table 11 includes organisations which have been restricted from carrying out any activities whatsoever. It excludes the 1988 restrictions on COSATU. The banning of the military wings of the ANC and PAC in 1963 and the bannings of organisations that were considered to be the ANC and PAC under different names, are also excluded for clarity. Some organisations have been banned in more than one area. SAAWU, for example, was banned both in the Ciskei (1983) and the Transkei (1986). COSAS and the UDF have been banned in the Transkei as well as in the rest of the country.

TABLE 11
Bannings of organisations

Year	SA (excluding 'independent' homelands)	Transkei	Ciskei	Bophuthatswana	Total
1950	1				1
1960	2				2
1962	1				1
1966	1				1
1977	18				18
1978		1		1	2
1979		33			33
1983			1		1
1984		3			3
1985	1				1
1986		1			1
1988	32	1		1	34
Total	56	39	1	2	98

3. The types of organisations affected

The organisations have been roughly classified according to their areas of operation and the breakdown is shown in Table 12. Political and student/youth organisations have been by far the worst affected by bannings and restrictions. In the bantustans, the church has paid heavily for criticism of the homeland governments.

TABLE 12
Types of organisations banned

Sector	South Africa (excluding TBVC homelands)	TBVC
Political	11	12
Student and youth	24	4
Civic	7	2
Church	–	8
Human rights	4	3
Others	10	13

4. Legislation used for bannings and restrictions

The Suppression of Communism Act of 1950 was replaced in 1976 by the Internal Security Act which consolidated all security legislation existing at the time. Up to this time, 5 organisations had been banned under the Suppression of Communism Act and these bannings were now subject to the ISA. It was under the ISA. that the 18 organisations were banned in 1977 and also COSAS in 1985. The regulations of the Public Safety Act, under which the State of Emergency exists, allows for the restrictions that are now placed on 33 organisations (including COSATU). The bantustans each have their own security legislation which allow for bannings.

Sources:
    Government Gazettes
    Press clippings
    South African Institute of Race Relations Surveys 1950–1980

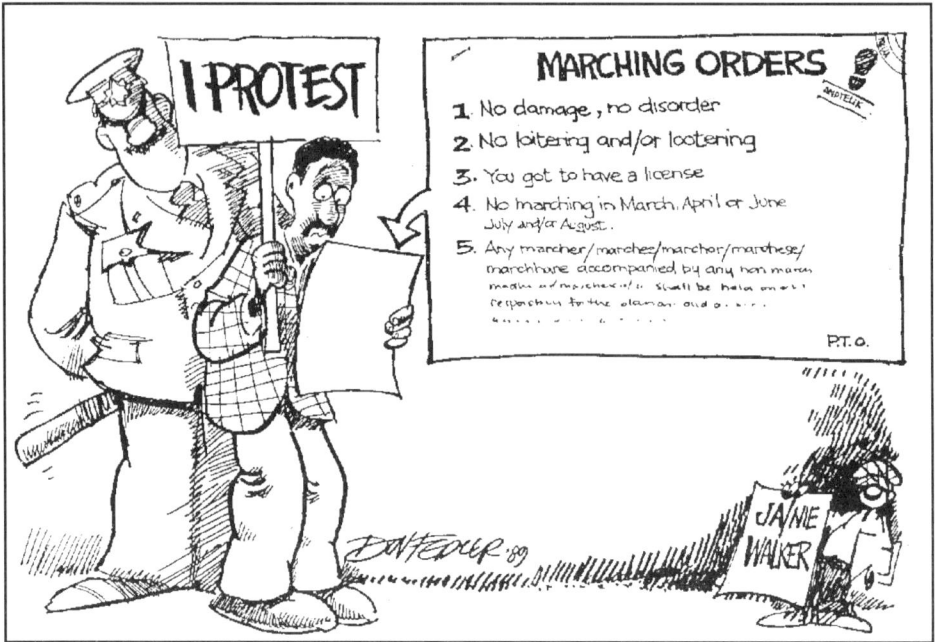

Dov Fedler, *The Star,* 27 September 1989

BANNING AND RESTRICTION OF GATHERINGS
DPSC/HRC, 1982–1990

1. Definition of a gathering

The definition of a gathering in a legal or political sense is a 'gathering, concourse or procession of any number of persons having a common purpose' (Internal Security Act, 1982). This means that 2 or more persons can constitute a gathering, including an illegal gathering. A placard demonstration by 1 person is not a gathering but 2 such demonstrators within sight of one another and having a common purpose do constitute a gathering by this definition.

2. Gatherings legislation

The forerunner of legislation designed to ban, restrict or control gatherings was the Riotous Assembly Act of 1956, subsequently amended in 1974 and then integrated into the Internal Security Act, No. 74 of 1982, described below. Other legislation of a specific nature are the Gatherings and Demonstrations Act of 1973, which prohibits gatherings and demonstrations in the precincts of parliament; and the Demonstrations in or near Court Buildings Prohibition Act, No. 71 of 1982, which prohibits demonstrations or gatherings within a radius of 500 metres of a building in which a court room is situated.

Furthermore, during a State of Emergency, as declared under the Public Safety Act of 1953, regulations and orders may be promulgated which have unfettered powers to restrict gatherings.

Also, the 4 TBVC 'states' have legislation patterned on the ISA.

3. Powers under the Internal Security Act (ISA)

Sections 46 to 53 of the ISA deal with the measures available to prohibit or control various gatherings.

- The minister of law and order can, under Section 46, prohibit gatherings of a particular class in any area, at any time and for any period. The class of gatherings may be outdoor or indoor; the area may be a single building, a town, a district or the whole country; the time may be day or night; the period may be for one day, a weekend, a week, a month, several months or a whole year; and the prohibition may be blanket or specific.

- Magistrates can, under Section 46, prohibit or impose conditions on specific or all gatherings within their magisterial district, for a period up to 48 hours.

- The police may bar access, under Section 47, to places where a gathering has been prohibited and may, under Sections 48 and 49, disperse prohibited or certain other gatherings with the use of force, including firearms, depending upon certain circumstances.

4. Powers under the Public Safety Act (PSA)

The powers to ban and restrict gatherings under a State of Emergency are virtually unlimited, to the extent even of imposing curfews which rule out any right of assembly beyond the hours of daylight. Such powers are assigned to police commissioners or their designates without reference to any higher authority.

5. Application of powers

Since 1976 there has been a blanket ban, renewed annually by the minister under the ISA, on all outdoor political gatherings for which prior permission has not been obtained. Such permission is rarely granted, so that for an uninterrupted period of 15 years outdoor political meetings have for all intents and purposes been prohibited. The latest renewal was on 1 April 1990 for a further year.

Since 1986 there has also been a blanket ban, renewed annually, on all indoor gatherings at which work stoppages, stayaways or educational boycotts are advocated.

Apart from blanket bannings, many thousands of specific gatherings have been banned since 1950 under security legislation and emergency regulations by ministerial, magisterial or police edict. Thousands of 'illegal' gatherings have been broken up by the police with considerable loss of life and injury, while tens of thousands have appeared in court charged with attending unlawful gatherings.

Recent statistics reveal the pattern of police violence in dispersing gatherings:

- In August and September 1989 during the Defiance Campaign, over 50 marches and demonstrations were broken up, more than half with the application of force, including the use of teargas, quirts, birdshot, rubber bullets, water cannon, batons, etc.
- Official figures of arrests for attending gatherings banned under the ISA and PSA during the year of 1989 total 2474 persons.
- HRC records for the first half of 1990 show that over 170 persons lost their lives and more than 1500 were injured during the course of such police action.
- Official figures show that during the one month between 4 June 1990 and 2 July 1990, the security forces acted more than 650 times to disperse gatherings in terms of Section 48 of the ISA.
- A recent innovation in interference with meetings takes the form of 'sitting-in' by the police. As many as 200 police occupy a block of seats in the hall and video-recordings of the proceedings are made in a very prominent manner.

6. Kinds of gatherings affected

An extraordinary range of gatherings have been banned over the years in attempts by the authorities to head off any threat of protest action, expression of solidarity, or, in the words of a typical banning order, 'any gathering at which any form of government or any principle or policy or action of the government of any state or the application or administration of any law is propagated, defended, attacked, criticised or discussed, or which is held in protest against or in support of anything'.

Gatherings which have been perceived to pose such threats have included:

- Protest marches and demonstrations, e.g. against Venda Independence celebrations, Tricameral elections, detentions, forced removals.
- Outdoor rallies, e.g. celebrating Freedom Charter Day.
- Indoor public meetings and conferences, e.g. World Conference on Religion and Peace, Desmond Tutu Peace Lecture, NUSAS annual congress, launch of new organisations, protest meetings against State of Emergency, treason trials and rent increases.
- Private meetings, seminars, e.g. church workshop on rural poverty, innumerable organisation meetings.
- Commemoration services, e.g. death of Steve Biko, Sharpeville Massacre, February 1986 massacre in Alexandra, unrest deaths, prayer service for Benjamin Moloise on death row.
- Funerals of unrest victims.
- Celebrations, e.g. Nelson Mandela's birthday, Steve Tshwete's house warming party after his release from Robben Island.
- Cultural and social events, e.g. concerts, music festivals, carols by candlelight, detainee tea parties, art exhibitions, fun run).
- Meeting of banned persons. Technically a husband and wife, if both banned, were prohibited from being in the same room together, without obtaining special permission.

7. Funerals of unrest victims

Funerals of political unrest victims became a highly charged form of gathering due to the interference of the security forces and inevitably resulted in yet more deaths, ensuring that funerals would take place virtually every weekend from 1985 onwards. At first the authorities attempted to restrict or limit the numbers of mourners at such funerals by banning these funerals from taking place at weekends. Soon, numerous other conditions, first under the ISA and later under Emergency regulations, were added to severely restrict the conduct of funerals and which inevitably aroused the extreme anger of communities at the gross manner in which they were allowed to bury their dead. Special standardised Emergency regulations for funerals have been developed and such blanket restrictions were in force on all funerals in over 70 black townships as at December 1989. Additional conditions include the following:

- to be held weekdays only and between specified hours;
- procession by motor transport only, for both hearse and mourners (nobody permitted on foot);
- route stipulated from undertaker to church to cemetery;
- number of mourners limited (usually 50);
- no freedom songs or political speeches;
- addresses only by ordained local priest and family member (no loudspeakers);
- no banners or placards and no pamphlets or notices to be distributed
- coffin not to be draped in the flags of banned organisations.

Needless to say, such conditions were frequently ignored, providing the security forces with the legal justification for the use of force and thereby stoking the ever increasing spiral of more deaths and more funerals.

FREEDOM OF THE PRESS
HRC, June 1989

1. 1948–1960: The first inroads
2. 1960–1985: The screws tighten
3. The press under the State of Emergency
4. Indirect press controls
   Police-press agreement
   NPU-Defence Force agreement
   Self-censorship
5. Harassment of journalists

Historically, the South African government has been pulled in two directions on the issue

Zapiro, *Vrye Weekblad,* 16 December 1988

of press freedom: it has clearly wanted much tighter control of the press but has stopped short of pre-publication censorship for fear of alienating its Western allies. Instead, it has steadily closed off the areas which the press may freely cover – more than 100 laws now limit what may be reported about key areas of national life, such as the conduct of the army and police. Newspapers have also been subjected to a range of indirect and informal controls, and self-censorship is rife. The result is a newspaper industry increasingly unable to reflect the political realities of South Africa.

1. 1948–1960: The first inroads

Suppression of Communism Act

Before the National Party came to power in 1948, the major press curbs were those under the common law, for example concerning defamation and contempt of court, which are common to most countries. The first statutory attack on press freedom under the new government came with the Suppression of Communism Act of 1950, which empowered the state to close any publication deemed to promote the spread of communism, published by an unlawful organisation or which expresses views propagated by such an organisation. This was later used to ban six newspapers – *The Guardian, New Age, Fighting Talk, The African Communist, World* and *Weekend World.*

Prisons Act

Another law which has become a thorn in the flesh of South African journalists is the Prisons Act of 1959. This makes it an offence to publish a photograph or sketch of a prisoner or the burial of an executed prisoner without official permission with the result that newspapers are not allowed to publish pictures of jailed political leaders such as Nelson Mandela. This law also outlaws the publication of false information about the experience of a prisoner or the administration of a prison without taking 'reasonable' steps to verify its accuracy, and places the onus of showing that reasonable steps have been taken on the accused. The law does not specify what 'reasonable' means, and as a result of a 1967 prosecution of the *Rand Daily Mail* where the judge ruled that the taking of sworn statements was not adequate, almost nothing controversial was published about the prisons for 15 years. There is now an unofficial understanding that newspapers will not be prosecuted under the Prisons Act if they submit reports to the Prisons Service for comment and publish its response in full.

Public Safety Act

The other major statutory inroad into press freedom in the 1950s was the Public Safety Act of 1953 which provided for the declaration of a State of Emergency. The full impact of this would only be felt later.

2. 1960–1985: The screws tighten

On 30 March 1960, days after the Sharpeville Massacre, South Africa's first State of Emergency was declared. Among other things, Emergency regulations made it an offence to publish a 'subversive statement' – defined as a statement likely to subvert the state's authority, inciting others to resist measures taken under the Emergency, bringing about feelings of hostility towards others or causing alarm – and empowered the minister of the interior to close any publication if he considered that it systematically published subversive material. The Emergency was lifted on 31 August the same year but the empowering legislation remained in force. The political upsurge of the early 1960s and the launch of a sabotage campaign by the African National Congress led to ever-tightening restrictions on the press.

Suppression of Communism Act

The Suppression of Communism Act had provided for the listing of people deemed to be communists, and for such people to be served with 'banning orders'. In 1962, it became an offence to quote a banned or listed person. The Suppression of Communism Act has been replaced by the Internal Security Act but the listings mechanism is still in force and serves to silence the leaders of key resistance organisations by preventing the media from quoting them. The Act also makes it an offence to further the aims of an unlawful organisation.

The Defence Act

The Defence Act was amended in 1967 to outlaw the publication of information about the movement or disposition of South Africa's armed forces at any time without government clearance and not only in time of war, as previously. The ban was extended to nursing and transport services, and to statements or rumours relating to the armed forces which might 'alarm or depress the public' or 'prejudice or embarrass' the government in foreign relations. A later amendment made it an offence to promote conscientious objection to military service. The implications of Defence Act restrictions were brought home in 1975 when newspapers across the world reported the SADF invasion of Angola but South Africans were kept in the dark.

The Publications Act

In 1963 the Publication and Entertainment Act established a Publications Control Board with the power to ban any publication other than (mainstream commercial) newspapers of the Newspaper Press Union. The board, which reaches decisions in private without having to hear evidence, and which gives no reasons for its decisions, can declare publications 'undesirable' if it considers them harmful to relations between sections of the population, or prejudicial to the safety of the state, the general welfare or peace and good order.

A 1969 amendment empowered the board to ban all future editions of an offending publication – an effective closure provision – and in 1974 a new Act, the Publications Act, streamlined the censorship procedure. The board (now the Publications Committee) has banned thousands of publications, many of a political nature, and has recently turned its attention to the 'alternative' press. In recent years, some of its decisions have been overturned by a more liberal appeals board.

The Armaments Development and Production Act

The Armaments Development and Production Act of 1968, a response to the United Nations arms boycott against South Africa, made it an offence to publish information about the manufacture and procurement of weapons by South Africa without official permission.

The Newspaper and Imprint Registration Act

The Newspaper and Imprint Registration Act of 1971 requires all newspapers to register and for registration to lapse if a newspaper fails to come out once a month. A black newspaper, *The Post*, was closed in 1981 after a strike by journalists stopped it from publishing for 3 months. In terms of the Internal Security Act, a newspaper must deposit up to R40 000 with the government if the minister of justice believes it may be banned at any stage. This is clearly designed to discourage the registration of small opposition newspapers. In 1988 an Eastern Cape news agency was forced to abandon plans to start a newspaper when the minister demanded a R40 000 deposit and the device was recently used against two other left-wing publications, *The New African* and *Vrye Weekblad*.

The 1970s was the high-water mark of government attempts to subvert the opposition English-language press from within. In 1973, the Department of Information secretly tried to take over the *Natal Mercury* and in 1975, one of the country's major press groups, SA Associated Newspapers. The Erasmus Commission, set up to investigate irregularities in the department's use of public funds, found in 1977 that R30-million from a secret fund had been spent on establishing and financing the *Citizen* newspaper – which, although now privately owned, is still in existence.

After the 1976 student uprising in Soweto and other townships, a major government onslaught was launched against the black press. In October 1977, the *World* and the *Weekend World* were banned under the Internal Security Act on the grounds that it had 'overstepped the limits of press freedom', and their editors placed in preventive detention. At the same time, the Union of Black Journalists was banned under the Internal Security Act. In the same year there was an unprecedented clampdown on the student press. Fifty-one student publications were banned and 5 declared undesirable under the Publications Act.

The Petroleum Products Act and the Nuclear Energy Act
A response to the oil boycott against South Africa, the Petroleum Products Act of 1977, prohibited the publication of information about the procurement and storage of petroleum. The 1982 Nuclear Energy Act introduced similar restrictions with regard to the mining, procurement and treatment of nuclear fuels.

The Police Act
In 1979, the Police Act was amended to outlaw the publication of false information about the actions of the police unless the reporter had reasonable grounds for believing the report to be true, putting the police on much the same footing as the prisons service. The onus of checking the information was placed on the individual reporter, rather than on the newspaper. There have been frequent prosecutions under this provision and it has proved to be one of the most onerous restrictions in the day-to-day work of South African journalists. A 1980 amendment of the Police Act gave the police blanket protection from newspaper coverage of anti-terrorist operations, except for reports based on police information.

The National Key Points Act
Following the escalation of ANC sabotage in the early 1980s, the National Key Points Act was passed, empowering the minister of defence to declare any installation a 'key point', thus prohibiting coverage of the security measures in force there. The Act is silent on how, when or where the minister is to make his declaration and how the press is expected to know whether the power has been exercised.

The Protection of Information Act
In 1982, the Official Secrets Act was replaced by the Protection of Information Act, which places extremely wide and loosely formulated restrictions on the transmission of official information to 'hostile organisations'. In at least 1 case, the Act has been used by the police to refuse to answer press queries on security detainees.

3. The Press under the State of Emergency

The uprising in the townships which began in late 1984 has triggered the toughest press controls in South African history. In July 1985 a partial State of Emergency was declared and Emergency regulations gave the authorities powers to control or ban the publication of news 'in connection with these regulations, or the State of Emergency, or any conduct of a force or member of a force regarding the maintenance of public safety or the termination of the State of Emergency'. A year later, the Emergency became national. On pain of a R20 000 fine or 10-year jail sentence, newspapers have been barred from:

- Filming, photographing or reporting on unrest or security force action in 'unrest', which includes unlawful gatherings and processions, without official permission. Journalists were later prohibited from being on the scene of 'unrest'.
- Publishing a 'subversive statement' – defined as a statement discrediting military service; promoting 'people's courts' and other alternative structures of power; urging illegal strikes and boycott action or assessing the effectiveness of such action or calling for the release of people detained under the emergency. The regulations provide for the summary seizure of publications containing 'subversive' material – a provision that has been used on several occasions, most recently against the mouthpiece of COSATU, South Africa's premier labour federation.
- Reporting on the circumstances or treatment of a detainee or giving information in connection with a detainee's release. In August 1987, the government tightened the emergency media regulations specifically to deal with the 'alternative' press –

Velk, P, *City Press*, 6 November 1988

newspapers outside the commercial mainstream with a strong anti apartheid stance. New regulations empowered the minister of home affairs to warn and then suspend any publication for up to 3 months if it systematically published material 'fanning revolution' or unrest, fomenting hostility towards the security forces, local authorities or any population group, or promoting the image of a banned organisation. The decision to suspend lies entirely within the minister's discretion and cannot be challenged in court, except on narrow, technical grounds. To date, 5 newspapers – the *New Nation*, *South*, the *Weekly Mail*, *Grassroots* and *New Era* – have been suspended for varying periods while others have been warned.

In addition to the above, older legislative curbs continue to be rigidly enforced under the Emergency. For example, in 1987 alone 5 journalists were tried under the Police Act.

4. Indirect press controls

Where possible, the government prefers to encourage self-censorship and the voluntary co-operation of the press. It has tried to achieve this by means of agreements between the security forces and the Newspaper Press Union – the owners of the commercial newspapers – and by constant threats to intensify statutory controls.

Police-Press agreement

In 1981, the NPU reached an agreement with the police providing for police accreditation of selected journalists who would have privileged access to 'confidential and sensitive' information from authorised police sources and to areas closed to the general public. In return, accredited journalists had to undertake not to publish information obtained independently of the police without first consulting the senior officer in the area concerned. Where the information related to 'national security or the combatting of terrorism', the police may request that it should not be published.

NPU-Defence Force agreement

An agreement reached between the SA Defence Force and the NPU in 1967, and updated in 1980, provides for access to military news from the SADF's media liaison section and the minister of defence, on condition that:

- Leaked or unauthorised news relating to the armed forces is suppressed if the authorities request it.
- The minister may refuse to comment on an issue and order that his 'no comment' reply should not be reported. The press must abide by this.
- Reports on the South African military originating abroad may only be published if the minister has been given the opportunity to comment.

Self-censorship

In response to government pressure, the NPU drew up its own voluntary code of conduct in 1962. The code, which provided for the reprimand of offending journalists, required the press to take account 'of the complex racial problems of South Africa' and the 'general good and safety of the country and its peoples'. In 1974, a state press commission recommended the establishment of a statutory press council 'for the self-control and discipline' of the press. This followed a statement by the prime minister, B.J. Vorster, that he had repeatedly warned the press about the need for self-censorship and announcing that legislation providing for the suspension of newspapers was under consideration. The NPU amended its code to require journalists to exercise responsibility in 'matters stirring up feelings of hostility' between the races and 'which can affect the safety and defence of the country'. A board of reference was set up with powers to fine editors and journalists. In 1977, the government introduced a Newspaper Bill providing for a statutory press code and a Press Council with a state-appointed chairman with powers to fine journalists and suspend newspapers. It was withdrawn after negotiations with the NPU which tightened up its code and set up its own Press Council. In 1982, the state-appointed Steyn Commission of Enquiry into the mass media called for the registration of journalists and a statutory Press Council with powers to fine or bar journalists from the profession. The threat of statutory control was once again averted when the NPU promised more rigorous self-regulation through a Media Council, which would sit as a form of court and impose fines of up to R10 000. Journalists' organisations refused to take part in the council saying it had been forced on them. In 1987, the government introduced emergency regulations requiring all freelance journalists and 'alternative' press agencies to register with the government and face de-registration if they angered the authorities. The regulations were withdrawn when it was discovered that they were so loosely framed that they covered even the state's own Bureau for Information.

5. Harassment of journalists

Journalists operating in South Africa have to contend with routine harassment, some of it official, some informal. Such tactics have intensified under the State of Emergency and are primarily directed at the 'alternative' press and foreign journalists. Security legislation has been used to detain many journalists over the years but the practice has intensified under the emergency. In March 1988, 5 journalists were reported to be in detention, including the editor of a leading alternative newspaper, Zwelakhe Sisulu. He was released after 2 years in detention and served with a ferocious restriction order which prevents him from working as a journalist. Journalists are frequently subpoenaed under section 205 of the Criminal Procedures Act to reveal their sources and in some instances have been jailed for refusing to do so. Passports and visas are often refused local journalists wishing to travel abroad. In 1988, for example, a prominent journalist and vice-president of the International Federation of Journalists, Thami Mazwai, was refused a visa to attend an IFJ meeting in Lesotho. Before they were excluded altogether from 'unrest' areas, there were persistent reports of informal security force harassment of journalists covering 'unrest'. Press people were reportedly shot at, tear gassed, sjambokked (whipped), arrested for obstructing police, as well as having film and equipment confiscated. Perhaps the most sinister instance was that of a cameraman for a British television network, George De'Ath, who was hacked to death by vigilantes during 'unrest' in the Western Cape. At his inquest, it was alleged that police and vigilantes had worked closely together, that they had shot at journalists and that there had been a delay before De'Ath had received medical treatment. Police also allegedly obliterated a section of De'Ath's video tape after confiscating his equipment in the wake of the murder. Foreign journalists are frequently deported or have visas refused. Between the start of the emergency and the end of 1987, 12 foreign journalists were expelled, according to official figures. Between July 1986 and June 1987, 238 foreign journalists were refused visas or visa renewals. Among the organisations and papers affected were the *New York Times*, the Australian Broadcasting Corporation, the BBC and Britain's Independent Television News.

The more remote the area in which journalists are based, the worse the harassment. *Saamstaan*, an anti-apartheid newspaper based in the tiny rural town of Oudtshoorn, has suffered arson (on 3 occasions), the breakage of equipment and the theft of an entire issue from a warehouse. One of its staffers has been shot by a 'special constable', another detained, 3 have been restricted and one has been prosecuted under the Police Act. Because local firms will not print the newspaper, it has to be printed in Cape Town – 500 kilometres away.

6 COVERT OPERATIONS

Up to this point attention has been focussed on those forms of apartheid repression which have enjoyed the dubious benefit of the cloak of respectability conferred by legislation emerging from the apartheid parliament. But there is much, much further to travel in order to comprehend the full spectrum of 'total strategy'. The time has come to descend into the murky depths of extra-legal forms of repression, referred to collectively as 'covert operations'.

The repression iceberg

Apartheid repression can be likened to an iceberg, having a visible portion known as formal repression and a submerged portion known as 'informal or extra-legal' repression. The deeper one goes, the murkier the picture becomes and the hazier the statutory links. It is in this netherworld that covert operations are located but they are a part of the whole. Each stratum within this iceberg uses methods less defensible publicly than the previous one and relies therefore on a greater degree of secrecy and covertness (see Figure 8).

The first stratum, based on security legislation, relies on laws passed by the apartheid parliament and on the existence of a massive law enforcement machinery and has been comprehensively covered in Chapters 2 to 5. The second, a security management system, which, while it has no constitutional status, draws on the support of public structures, but also goes much deeper – it can be said to be located on the waterline of the iceberg and extending downwards. The third, vigilantism, relies upon the planting of a 'fifth column' within dissident communities. The fourth, hit squads, is a means of last resort, the elimination of political opponents and the crippling of their structures by faceless assassins and strike groups: they lie at the depths of visibility and legality. There is a fifth component in a special category which deserves attention, namely, external destabilisation, that is, the destabilisation of South Africa's neighbours.

In this chapter we explore the depths of what is known variously as informal repression, counter-revolutionary warfare, low-intensity conflict, or simply – covert operations. Here we shall encounter, not acts of parliament, no laws nor promulgated regulations but centres of control, receiving information, making decisions and issuing instructions – all without any constitutional status but nevertheless supported by secret budgets and resources with no public accountability. For example, within the national budget for 1989/90 over R6 billion was allocated to secret funds about which the public was not entitled to know.

In order to undertake this journey free use is made of the following HRC publications and co-publications:

- *Human Rights and Repression in South Africa*, HRC/SACC/SACBC (May 1989)
- *Children and Repression*, HRC (January 1990)
- *State Violence*, HRC (August 1990)
- *The CCB*, HRC/David Webster Trust (September 1990)

In addition, other sources are drawn upon and acknowledged in the appropriate place.

NATIONAL SECURITY MANAGEMENT SYSTEM

Situated at the waterline from which it could control both the visible and the submerged portions of the iceberg is the security management system known previously as the 'National Security Management System' (NSMS) but more recently renamed the 'National Co-ordinating Mechanism'.

During the days of the NSMS, the nerve centre was the State Security Council which effectively ran the country as a super cabinet over the parliamentary cabinet but without any statutory status. The nerve ends of the system were the approximately 500 regional, district and local Joint Management Centres known as JMCs, forming a complete network around the country and with their fingers on the pulse of every area, township and village.

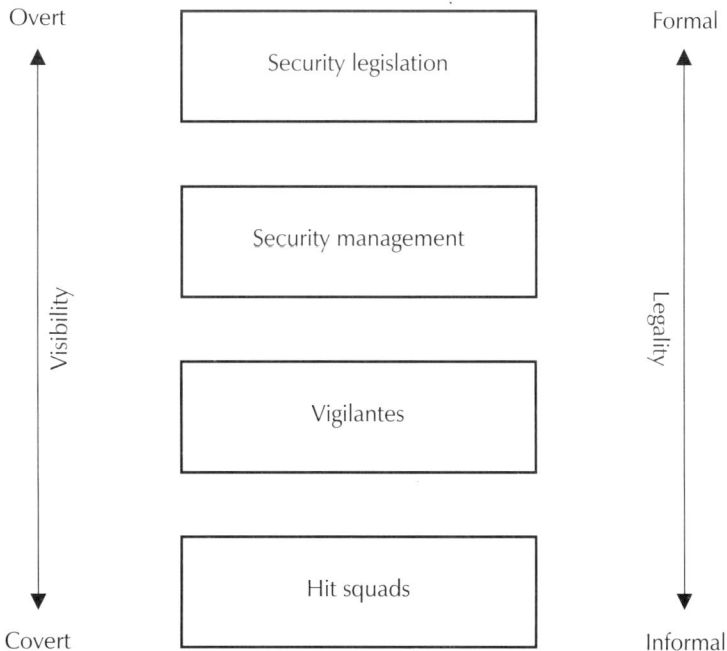

FIGURE 8
The repression iceberg

In this way a constant stream of information was fed to the SSC enabling it to formulate a continuous national security profile and take decisions at both national and local levels. Such decisions could then be implemented by the formal law enforcement structures backed by legislation or by other structures acting covertly. In this way, action could be and was taken at both a macro- and a micro-level. The means existed to react to developing situations with large-scale measures of an overt or covert nature and at the other end of the scale, to remove a troublesome individual like Matthew Goniwe from society, again by either overt or covert measures.

COUNTER-REVOLUTIONARY WARFARE AND THE NATIONAL MANAGEMENT SYSTEM
HRC/SACC/SACBC, May 1989

'There can be no security without reform'. This was the slogan of the P.W. Botha government in the early 1980s and it neatly summed up the intentions of the 'total strategy' reforms of the period. But the failure of those reforms to in any way meet black political aspirations and the threat of the 'people's power' uprising from 1984 to 1986 have led the state to adopt a new set of more thoroughgoing and military informed strategies, known as 'counter-revolutionary warfare'. The essence of the new counter-revolutionary policies has often been expressed by law and order minister

19 September 1996. The trial of Eugene de Kock. Convicted but not yet sentenced, the former head of the Vlakplaas death farm starts talking.

Zapiro, *Mail and Guardian*, 19 September 1996

Adriaan Vlok. To defeat the 'revolution', he says, the state must do 3 things:

- address the security situation (State of Emergency);
- address grievances and bring good government to the ordinary person (upgrading and municipal elections);
- and address the political question (the National Council with limited black representation).

The National Management System and its 500 odd Joint Management Centres (JMCs) are the key co-ordinating structure in the implementation of this new strategy. It is designed, in the words of police counter-insurgency chief Bert Wandrag, to 'nip the revolution in the bud'. But the government's secretive network is struggling to fulfill the intentions of state security planners.

JMCs fall under the jurisdiction of the secretive 'super-cabinet' – the State Security Council – and are the regional, district and local extensions of the National Management System. According to the generals and police chiefs who set them up, they are supposed to co-ordinate the counter-revolutionary warfare strategy of 'eliminating' activists and 'winning hearts and minds' of the masses (WHAM) which has been put into action since 1986. But the growing economic crisis, increasing expenditure on the instruments of repression, the illegitimacy of minority rule and the depth of black political resistance are proving to be insurmountable obstacles to the 'crush – create – co-opt – reform' strategy of the National Party state.

It is in the make-up of a JMC that the overall intentions of the new security managed policies can best be found. A JMC has 5 committees – Intelligence, Security, Welfare, Communications and an Executive Committee which brings together representatives of each of the 4 functional committees. The committees are known by their Afrikaans acronyms, thus GIK (*Gesamentlike Intelligensie Komitee* – intelligence), Veikom (*Veiligheids Komitee* – security), Semkom (*Staatkundige, Ekonomiese en Maatskaplike Komitee* – welfare) and Komkom (*Kommunikasie Komitee* – communications).

The Intelligence Committee is staffed by the National Intelligence Service (NIS), the security branch of the South African Police (SAP) and Military Intelligence. It collects 2 broad kinds of intelligence on communities. The first is 'hard' intelligence on the intentions, plans, activities and problems of activists and their organisations. This intelligence is then channelled to the Security Committee. A second kind of intelligence, so called 'soft' intelligence, encompasses the universe of attitudes, grievances and perspectives which make up a community's overall stance toward the state, its officials and its reform programme. This intelligence is sent to the Welfare Committee.

The functions of the Security Committee and the Welfare Committee encapsulate the overall intentions of state security strategists. These are, to use the words of law and order minister Vlok, to 'take out' activists while 'addressing grievances'. Thereby, it is hoped the conditions will have been laid for eventual political reform through a new accommodating local leadership and the hearts and minds of the masses will be won over to the state instead of the 'revolutionaries'.

The Security Committee, which is staffed by riot police, security police, soldiers and officers of the municipal police and *kitskonstabels* ('instant police') is the repressive arm of the system. It co-ordinates the process of detentions, restrictions, bannings, spying, monitoring and allegedly also violent attacks and harassment which are made on those who are seen to represent an extra-parliamentary threat to the state. The Welfare Committee, on the other hand, takes responsibility for co-ordinating the functions of the civilian administration. In areas identified as important to the counter-revolutionary effort, in particular education and local upgrade programmes, it helps cut red tape and ensures that things get done. Its membership consists of officials of the non-security state departments such as roads, education, welfare, manpower and health as well as local and regional officials of the provincial administrations and Regional Services Councils (RSCs). This overall Security Management strategy is sold to the public via the fourth of the JMC's committees, Komkom. Staffed by local representatives of the Bureau for Information, plus public relations personnel from government departments, Komkom attempts to ensure the maximum publicity for welfare type projects and government supporting 'counter-organisations' (such as counter-youth groups, gospel associations, sports bodies, and local authorities) while explaining the sincerity of state reforms by means of letters, pamphlets, film, radio, television, newspapers, meetings and organised tours.

Business involvement in the JMC strategy comes essentially through its central role in the privatisation and upgrading effort. In addition JMCs have established so-called Community Liaison Forums and Joint Liaison Committees for the purposes of private sector liaison. Many businesses and civic and welfare type organisations which have participated in these bodies have been unaware of the full ramifications of their involvement. Although government ministers have at several times stated in parliament that the system is not secret, they have certainly not gone out of their way to make its workings public. This has led both opposition politicians and academic observers to allege that it has become a 'shadow state' unaccountable to elected officials. What cannot be disputed is that the system – which constitutionally has no status – has effectively appropriated many executive and decision-making powers for itself and is able to lean heavily on departmental officials to implement policies determined within the security dominated JMCs.

STATE STRATEGY
from Children and Repression
HRC, January 1990

Since the imposition of the national State of Emergency in June 1986 up until June 1989, the state adopted various strategies that can be broadly conceptualised and analysed as a 3 phase strategy. The intentions of the state security strategists, in the words of law and order minister Adriaan Vlok, has been to 'take out' and 'eliminate' activists in the first place, while 'addressing grievances' in the second place and thirdly, to find a constitutional dispensation acceptable to the majority of South Africans.

```
┌─────────────────────────────────────────────────────────┐
│              Office of the State President                │
└─────────────────────────────────────────────────────────┘
                            │
┌─────────────────────────────────────────────────────────┐
│              State Security Council (SSC)                 │
│  Chaired by the State President, it includes ministers of │
│  the departments of foreign affairs, defence, law & order,│
│             justice and finance.                          │
└─────────────────────────────────────────────────────────┘
```

Office of the State President

State Security Council (SSC)
Chaired by the State President, it includes ministers of the departments of foreign affairs, defence, law & order, justice and finance.

National joint management centre
Chaired by the deputy minister of law & order, it includes the director-general of all departments.

Working group
Chaired by the deputy minister of law & order, it includes all heads of department.

Joint management centres
Sub committees:
1. Joint intelligence committee
2. Joint operational centre (GOS)
3. Communications committee
4. Constitutional, social and economic
5. Security committee
The jurisdiction of the 11 JMCs corresponds roughly to the development regions.

The secretariat
Four sub-branches
1. Administrative
2. National intelligence
3. Strategic communications
4. Strategy

Joint liaison forums

Sub-joint management centres
Sub committees:
1. Security
2. Political, economic & social
3. Communications
4. Joint operations
5. Intelligence

Inter-departmental committees
Each deals with a specific area of SSC functions that involves more than one department:
1. Manpower 2. Security forces 3. Civil defence 4. Transport 5. Security 6. National supplies & resources 7. Government funding 8. National economy 9. Telecommunications & electrical power supply 10. Science & technology 11. Community services 12. Culture 13. Political affairs

Joint liaison forums

Mini-joint management centres
Sub committees:
1. Security
2. Political, economic & social
3. Communications
4. Intelligence
5. Joint operations. Area of jurisdiction approximates the local municipality

Local management centres
Headed by SAP station commander and SADF company commander, these centres cover the area/jurisdiction of a police station

Community liaison forum
Incorporates churches, youth groups, neighbourhood associations, vigilantes, traders, sports clubs, interest groups, journalists, opinion makers, shebeen owners, cultural groups, moderate political organisations, teachers, etc.

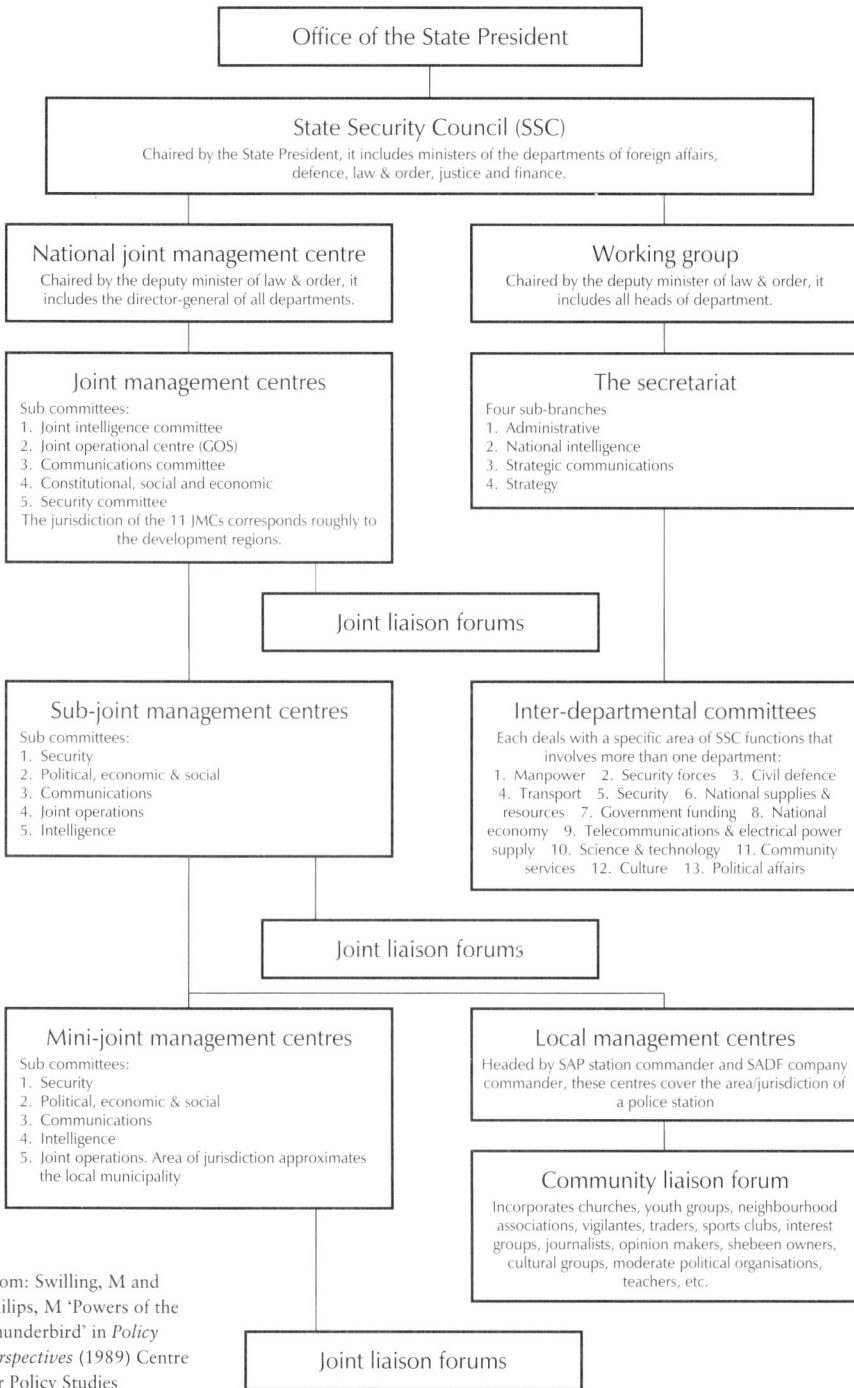

From: Swilling, M and Philips, M 'Powers of the Thunderbird' in *Policy Perspectives* (1989) Centre for Policy Studies

Joint liaison forums

FIGURE 9

The National Security Management System

Phase 1 'Bomb the enemy' (12 June 1986–11 June 1987)

The nature of repression during this period can be summed up as generalised repression. We saw the mass occupation of townships, villages and schools by joint 'security forces'. Particular forms of state repression concentrated on smashing the infrastructure of the mass democratic movement. Areas of community based power and mass mobilisation were closed off. The state's aim was to smash and immobilise community organisations.

From the strategies and forms of repression during this period one can conclude that the main aims of the state were to:

- reverse the 'revolutionary' situation,
- 'pacify' and demoralise the population,
- create a 'political wasteland' by crushing the democratic movement.

Phase 2 'Creating good government' or counter-revolutionary bases (11 June 1987–26 October 1988 and beyond)

In 1987, one of the state's major 'reform' policies was the decentralisation of repressive power to regional and local levels administered by 11 Joint Management Centres (JMCs). The 11 JMCs correspond to the area commands of the SADF. There are 60 sub-JMCs operating at the level of Regional Services Councils (RSC) and almost 500 mini-JMCs at the level of local authorities. (See Fig. 9.)

The immediate task of the JMCs has been to neutralise the power of mass-based democratic organisations, and regain control of the townships. By relying on the JMCs, RSCs and local authorities to maintain 'peace', the state could then reduce the profile of the South African Defence Force and the South African Police. It also increased the role of the municipal police and *kitskonstabels* or instant cops. (The term '*kitskonstabel*' is derived from the fact that they undergo only 6 weeks of training.) At the same time, the level of vigilante action increased and vigilante crimes remain unsolved. The informer network was re-established. Principals and education authorities were co-opted to re-establish control of the schools.

On 24 February 1988, amendments to the Emergency regulations empowered the state to take action against organisations. 17 organisations were restricted, including a number of youth and student organisations. All activities of the democratic movement were effectively banned or restricted. The state also attempted to break the power of the democratic unions by restricting them from participating in politics.

At the same time, in order to make way for the government's so-called reform initiatives, the 'oil spot policy' was instituted in which oil is poured on 'troubled areas'. This is a process of selective upgrading, the purpose being to 'win the hearts and minds' of people by diffusing their grievances. People mobilise and organise around their grievances. By attempting to diffuse grievances, the state is attempting to break organisations. It is the role of the JMCs to co-ordinate, monitor and develop strategies to ensure the implementation of these reformist policies at local and regional level (without addressing the real problems of apartheid). The JMCs have the dual task of carrying out the state's policy of repression and reform. While meeting some of the community's demands for the provision of services and infrastructure, the JMCs simultaneously remove from circulation the leaders who articulate grievances and political aspirations. The leaders are either detained, forced into hiding or subjected to campaigns of intimidation. In Alexandra township, for example, after detaining a large number of Alexandra Youth Congress activists, the state ploughed R90 million into upgrading projects in an attempt to win over a community who for 40 years had been denied electricity, waterborne sewerage, post offices and sufficient schools and homes. Through these 'oil spots' the security forces believed they could 'regain control' over the black population. The state however, does not have the economic resources to upgrade areas on a national scale.

The conclusions that one can reach about the aims of the state during this period, are that the state was attempting to:

1. Internalise and localise the conflict by building up local repressive forces.
2. Re-establish local apartheid structures.
3. Disorganise and diffuse peoples' grievances by selectively upgrading various areas and sectors.
4. Isolate and 'pacify' the areas continuing to resist.
5. Isolate the leaders and organisations of the democratic movement from the masses, and prevent their re-emergence.
6. Isolate the trade unions from the mass democratic movement.
7. Re-establish the building blocks of constitutional 'reform'.

Phase 3: 'Constitutional reform' (late 1988 to mid-1989)

The goal of the state during this period has been the maintenance of relative 'peace' in order to proceed with constitutional reform. During this period the state has aimed to:

1. Consolidate local and regional structures.
2. Create patronage and dependency through the policies of selective upgrading.
3. Divide the mass democratic movement.

VIGILANTES

Vigilantism is an important component of the counter-revolutionary tactic of Low Intensity Conflict (LIC) which first evolved in Algeria and was further developed in South and Central America.

Vigilante groups first made their appearance in South Africa around 1985 and have their origins in the support systems which were built up around the highly unpopular apartheid created structures of homeland authorities and Black Local Authorities (BLAs). They were often recruited from conservative 'traditional' elements, or from the ranks of the desperate unemployed and even from criminal elements. Having a vested interest in these structures that they were called upon or paid to protect, they would intervene, often with extreme violence, in any situation which threatened those structures, such as calls for those authorities to resign. Their growth was actively encouraged or tacitly condoned by the state through thinly disguised support by the security forces, but also by covert support through funding, training and motivating.

Extracts from MANUFACTURING VIOLENT STABILITY
Vigilantes and the Policing of South Africa
N. Haysom, 1989

Introduction

Trade unionists in the Pietermaritzburg area refer to the nearby Edendale Valley as the 'valley of widows'. It has more widows, they claim, than any other valley in South Africa. In 1988 twice as many persons died as a result of vigilante and counter-vigilante violence in the greater Pietermaritzburg area than died in Beirut in the same period. Since vigilante violence erupted in that region over 1200 persons have died, thousands have been subjected to violence on their person or property in one form or another, an estimated 30 000 persons have become internal refugees. Yet in 1988 South African television viewers were exposed only to the human tragedy that is Beirut. They saw little visual footage of the Edendale Valley, if indeed they saw any at all.

By October 1988 over 90% of unrest-related deaths were caused by vigilante and counter-vigilante violence in South Africa. This is a turn-about from the October 1984 figures. It is clear that township residents in South Africa are now far more likely to die as a result of vigilante violence than they are as a result of confrontations with the South African police. For these residents the vigilante phenomenon has become the most terrifying manifestation of a conflict-ridden society. How is it that such extreme violence can be tolerated? How can it occur with such little official concern, such limited local and international media attention?

Low intensity conflict

This paper suggests that the operation of vigilante groups in South Africa's black areas since 1985 is an expression of the militarisation of South Africa, that the prevalence and operation of these groups should be seen as the internal equivalent of the strategy of destabilisation of neighbouring states. It is a low intensity civil war which appears to be conducted an arm's length away from an aggressive state. In fact, however, the state benefits in a variety of ways from the conflict it licenses or sponsors, indeed more so than it would from direct intervention.

As commentators have noted, there is a strong parallel to be drawn between vigilante violence in South Africa, and that in El Salvador and the Philippines. In those countries violence by vigilante and civilian units have become a central component of the mode of repression adopted by the governing regimes. Modern counter-insurgency theory lays stress on 'total war' – which incorporates a 'winning of hearts and minds' (WHAM) component. The necessity of destroying popular movements without appearing to be directly waging war on the populace is the dilemma that has led to the U.S. sanctioned 'low-intensity' civil wars of Central America, the vigilante movements of the Philippines and the destabilisation of states in Southern Africa. The logic of this theory involves the clandestine creation of surrogate armed forces but which organisations appear to emerge 'spontaneously' from the 'people' themselves. It is then claimed that the Contras, UNITA, or the Philippines vigilante groupings are an expression of popular support, or popular rebellion, as the case may be.

Vigilantes

It is necessary to describe the operation and emergence of vigilante groupings in South Africa. This paper records only the patterns and implications of vigilante activities, rather than providing specific details of the various vigilante groupings in South Africa.

The term 'vigilante' is itself a source of confusion. In South Africa the term 'vigilantes' connotes violent, organised and conservative groupings operating within black communities, which, although they receive no official recognition, are politically directed in the sense that they act to neutralise individuals and groupings opposed to the apartheid state and its institutions. These features, and the fact that they are alleged to enjoy varying degrees of police support, is all that links the A-Team, Phakatis, Mabangalala, Amadoda, Witdoeke, Amosolomzi, Amabutho, Mbhokhoto and the Green Berets.

Vigilantes are not an entirely new phenomenon in South Africa. For example, vigilantes supervised by the Ciskeian authorities terrorised the inhabitants of Mdantsane during the course of a bus boycott in that town from June to October 1983. However, 1985 saw a sudden proliferation of such groups as well as the emergence of their more complex urban counterparts.

In 1986 a survey of 13 communities which had experienced vigilante violence revealed a distinct pattern in this new phenomenon. The communities examined in the survey included Crossroads, Ashton and KTC (Western Cape), Queenstown and Fort Beaufort (Eastern Cape), Huhudi (Northern Cape), Thabong (Orange Free State), Umlazi, Inanda and Lamontville (Natal), Leandra, Moutse and Ekangala (Eastern Transvaal) and Soweto (Transvaal).

Zapiro, unpublished, 1987

Firstly, as community leaders from the Cape to the Transvaal reported, nation-wide vigilante activity in the form of violence against members of anti-apartheid organisations commenced in 1985. The intimate connection between the emergence of vigilante activity and the more general political crisis in South Africa is evident from the fact that vigilantes emerged in 1985 as the political crisis in South Africa deepened and, as the crisis of control over black areas extended geographically, so did the incidence of vigilante activity.

Secondly, the composition of both the vigilante leadership and the victim groups were broadly the same in all regions. The target groups were those perceived to be resisting apartheid institutions whether they be students campaigning against 'Bantu education', community leaders creating alternative black municipal structures or communities resisting the jurisdiction of homeland authorities. Vigilante leadership is comprised mostly of functionaries in the homeland governments (including chiefs) and in the urban areas members of the state and local state organs (police and community councillors) or members of an 'embryonic middle-class with an interest in stability and a natural inclination to conservatism'. In the Pietermaritzburg area the warlords appear to come from both homeland functionaries and the members of such an 'embryonic middle class'.

The third feature in the pattern of vigilante violence is such that the vigilantes appear to enjoy police support, operating brazenly as if there are no legal consequences to their extra-legal violence.

It cannot be proven that all vigilante groups have received direct sanction or open support from the security forces – although they allegedly did in areas such as Crossroads, Kwanobuhle and Queenstown. Direct support is not necessary for the generation of vigilante conflict. A mere reluctance to curb vigilante activity or a failure to intervene in conflict in the townships allows one group a substantial advantage over the other. The effect is much the same whether the police actively sanction and support the vigilantes or whether they merely appear incapable of or reluctant to curb vigilante activities, particularly where the vigilante group has access to firearms. The police's passivity while the vigilante gang killed community leader Mayise in Leandra (Transvaal), an impi of Inkatha supporters marched into Lamontville (Natal) or the Mbhokhoto leaders pursued an intensive regional campaign of intimidation in KwaNdebele, must be contrasted to the police's vigorous dispersal of UDF gatherings or their prosecution of members of anti-apartheid organisations or trade unions. When the victim communities or organisations attempt physical contest with the vigilantes, police intervention has supported the vigilantes.

The vigilantes' use of township council facilities (notably in Thabong and Ashton) and resources provided by homeland governments (in KwaNdebele and Ciskei), reveals that support for vigilante activities may take a variety of forms. A copy of minutes of a meeting between a senior police officer and black traders in the Vaal triangle area on 13 November 1985, suggests that police attitudes could have prompted vigilante formation in some areas. At this meeting the police officer offered to arm the traders and encouraged them to form a self-protection organisation. It should be mentioned that it is nearly impossible for a black South African to acquire a gun licence without police approval. In Natal many of the vigilante warlords openly carry firearms and there is evidence to suggest that the police have armed some of these warlords or tolerate others carrying firearms when they knew that the warlord had no permit to carry a firearm.

Finally, a distinctive feature of vigilantism is the extreme and brutal nature of the violence. Thus vigilante violence is associated with the brutalisation of the body of the victims including, the dismemberment or decapitation of the victims. Vigilante violence is extreme and symbolic terror.

Some vigilante incidents

Although the composition and operation of these groupings varies from region to region, the face of the vigilante phenomenon is well illustrated by the following random but representative incidents described in *Mabangalala* (Haysom, 1986) and elsewhere:

- In April/May 1985 a vigilante grouping calling themselves the 'Phakatis' emerged in Thabong township in the Orange Free State. The grouping, openly using the facilities of the municipal authority, embarked on a campaign of indiscriminate assaults on youths whom they believed were involved in a school boycott. One night they apprehended a boy on the streets, David Mabenyane, and whipped him so severely that he died. After whipping the boy and while he was still alive they dropped him at the local police station.

- During August 1985 armed gangs of so-called 'Amabutho' took to searching houses in Umlazi, Natal, claiming they were looking for United Democratic Front (UDF) 'troublemakers'. Mr B.M., a UDF supporter, was at home one night when the Amabutho arrived at his house, surrounded it and set it alight. His brother, Michael, attempted to flee with his infant niece but was shot in the head. His elder sister Florence was also shot as she tried to escape the flames. B.M. recognized 1 of the 3 armed men as a local member of the KwaZulu homeland legislature.

- In 1985 the KwaNdebele homeland leader, Simon Skosana, launched a vigilante organisation called 'Mbhokoto'. On 1 January 1986 a large group of Mbhokoto vigilantes from KwaNdebele abducted over 400 men from the Moutse district, a district resisting the jurisdiction of the KwaNdebele homeland authorities and were taken to a community hall in the capital of KwaNdebele. There they were ordered to strip and were severely beaten for several hours before being released. The prime minister of KwaNdebele supervised the assaults. Some of the victims identified their assailants to the police. Police have not as yet apprehended any of the assailants.

- More recently in Kwanobuhle, a township bordering on Uitenhage in the Eastern Cape, a vigilante group calling itself 'AmaAfrika' emerged in the latter part of 1986. On 4 January 1987 a mob marched through the township destroying the houses of 14 activists and killing 2 persons in a 12 hour attack. The *Monitor* (June 1988, p.46) describes the attack:

  > All the houses they attacked were in the area now known as old Kwanobuhle and in particular in the very oldest section known as Angola. Most of these houses were the homes of members of United Democratic Front-affiliated organisations such as the Uitenhage Youth Congress or area committees ... One of the most disturbing aspects of the day's events was that the Kwanobuhle Municipal Police and the South African Police apparently made little effort to curtail the violence and destruction. It appears to have been pre-arranged by the 2 parties with the understanding that the destruction and

assaults would be perpetrated by the vigilantes with the police monitoring the events to ensure the safety and success of the AmaAfrika ... They also used it as an opportunity to take more detainees.

- In Leandra, a black township on the East Rand, the residents had been involved in a campaign to improve their living conditions and to prevent the forced removal of the inhabitants of the township. To this end they formed an alternative civic structure to the officially approved municipal council. By late 1985 the organisational strength of the alternative Leandra Action Committee (LAC) was such that the authorities were compelled to negotiate with one of its leaders, Chief Ampie Mayise, and not the officially recognised black councillors. Shortly thereafter vigilantes began brazenly attacking members of the Leandra Action Committee. The attacks culminated in a mob assault on Chief Mayise's house on 11 January 1986 during which Mayise was publicly hacked to death. A policeman alerted to the attack by Mayise's call for assistance to the nearby police station was ordered not to intervene. Shortly thereafter youths in the township were forced to flee the area for fear of their lives. The leader of the LAC's house was later attacked and the Leandra Action Committee collapsed. Throughout the period of violence the police are alleged to have openly sided with the vigilantes.
- In January 1986, vigilantes calling themselves 'Witdoeke', emerged in 4 squatter camps referred to here as Crossroads and KTC. The communities numbering nearly 70 000 persons had been engaged for several years in a struggle with the authorities over their right to live in these squatter settlements. They had persisted in their campaign despite detentions, threats and intrigue by the authorities. Vigilantes, with the police allegedly intervening only to assist the Witdoeke, tore through the camps in May and June, destroying and burning the houses and driving the inhabitants out. Inhabitants of the squatter camps have described the attacks which started on 17 May, alleging that police assisted the Witdoeke at the camps by breaking up groups of resisting residents and clearing the way for Witdoeke to penetrate the camp. Police stood by and watched the illegal destruction of property and the assaults. They allegedly intervened whenever the Witdoeke were under attack. During the attack on KTC which commenced on 9 June the police were also alleged to have accompanied the Witdoeke and to have broken the defence line formed by resisting residents. Witdoeke also took 'prisoners' and tortured them without police intervention. In the 2 attacks 53 people were killed and 7000 shacks demolished. In weeks the vigilantes accomplished what the state had failed to do in 10 years. The 70 000 refugees were compelled to seek refuge in other townships including the government designated option – Khayelitsha. The government has denied responsibility for this tragedy but undoubtedly the alliance between vigilantes and security forces made a forced removal possible whereas the authorities were incapable of doing this themselves legally and openly.

From vigilantes to community guards

A national trend which has caused concern amongst human rights activists and victim communities alike, is the induction of vigilantes into the state's formal law and order machinery. The incorporation of many of the Queenstown vigilantes into the Queenstown

Commando is one such example. A more prevalent form of this process is taking place through the appointment of community guards, a form of municipal police under the control of the community councillors. It has already been reported that erstwhile vigilantes in Ashton, Thabong and Mpumalanga have made application to join the community guards. Minister Heunis stated in 1986 that R26 million has been allocated for the training of 5000 guards.

TABLE 13
List of vigilante groups

Region	Town	Name
Northern Transvaal	Ekangala	Mbokodo (Mbhokoto)
(KwaNdebele)	Moutse	Mbokodo
	Leandra	Mbokodo
Eastern Transvaal	Wesselton	Black Cats Gang
PWV (East Rand)	Tembisa	Toaster Gang
KwaZulu/Natal	KwaMashu	Ama Sinyora Gang
	Umlazi	Amabutho
Northern Cape	Huhudi	No name
Western Cape	Ashton	Amasolomzi
	Crossroads	Witdoeke
	Peninsula	Amadoda
Eastern Cape	Cookhouse	Kekanas
	Queenstown	No name
	Fort Beaufort	No name
	Somerset East	Memesi
	Uitenhage, P.E.	Ama Afrika
Orange Free State	Kroonstad (Maokeng)	Three Million Gang
	Parys (Tumahole)	Mabangalala
	Welkom (Thabong)	Pakhatis ('A'-team)

The municipal police ('greenflies') and police auxilliaries (*kitskonstabels*) have indeed, made a special contribution to converting the mood of the townships from protest to fear. Human rights groups from the Eastern Cape to the Transvaal report numerous incidents in which the municipal police have assumed the methods of the vigilantes. Complaints include torture, beatings, thefts and forcible evictions. Their responsibilities have less to do with crime prevention and more to do with pacification. More importantly, the greenflies' increased involvement with the policing of the townships has gone hand in hand with a withdrawal of the security forces from these areas. Thirdly, there has been little or no attempt by the authorities to curb the illegal activities of these forces despite the intense resentment towards them by ordinary residents. The use of municipal police and police auxiliaries is directly in line with a militarisation of ordinary residents and a de-militarisation of the actual government of the townships.

Note: It is appropriate to mention here that vigilantism was destined to play a major role in the post-total strategy era of destabilisation.

HIT SQUADS

Delving further into the murky depths of covert operations we find hit squads. The term 'hit squads' is used rather than 'death squads' since the scope of operations has included activities other than assassinations, such as harassing and threatening individuals to scare them off, destroying facilities of organisations and sowing confusion and dissension through the spread of disinformation. We are now at the lowest depths of the iceberg with zero visibility and zero legality.

STATE VIOLENCE
HRC, August 1990

The existence of hit squads has been felt for many years through assassinations and other acts which have occurred since the mid 1970s and which were clearly of a political nature. In the 1980s, and especially during the years of the Emergency, these incidents escalated sharply in frequency and level of sophistication, both internally and externally. It became clear that such actions were the work, not of individuals acting on the spur of the moment, but of well organised hit squads operating with the advantages of expertise, skills, information, equipment, financial resources and, it seemed, immunity from discovery or prosecution. It also became clear that their purposes were the elimination of anti-apartheid political activists by assassination or their intimidation by harassment of every conceivable kind; and the crippling or disruption of anti-apartheid organisations through destroying their offices by bombing or fire or through burgling or wrecking their equipment and records.

A common denominator for all of these attacks was the access which the perpetrators seemed to have to intimate details and intelligence of the victims movements, habits and activities and the target area's physical layout and accessibility. All the indications pointed in the direction of state-based structures. It then came as no surprise when a now familiar sequence of events commencing in late 1989 led to the revelations that such hit squads were indeed spawned within the structures of the South African Police (specifically the Security Branch) and the South African Defence Force (specifically the Special Forces Division). Nor will it come as a surprise to find that the hit squad concept, as a means of 'last resort', was evolved or at least adopted and expanded by the total strategy proponents, and that it has flourished under the guidance of the State Security Council, as but one of the many strings in its bow. It is inconceivable that the very considerable budgets needed, and approved, for such activities, could have been created without the knowledge and the blessing of those at the very top.

THE EXPOSURE OF STATE HIT SQUADS
HRC, 1989/90

Despite the welter of statistical and circumstantial evidence that the very considerable level of hit squad activity during the 1980s was state sponsored, no hard evidence was forthcoming to penetrate the wall of official denial. None, that is, until in the dying days of the decade, when a remarkable event occurred which threw open the floodgates of hidden information which continues to pour out even today and no doubt will continue to flow for some time yet.

On 20 October 1989, Almond Butana Nofomela was due to be hanged for a non-political murder. The day before, he decided to reveal his involvement in a hitherto unpublicised unit of the South African Police, namely the Vlakplaas C1 assassination unit, as a means of at least temporarily staying his execution. This had the effect not only of revealing the existence of the unit to the public but also of implicating a number of policemen as members of the unit, both past and present. Within 10 days, the current commander of the squad, Brigadier Willem Schoon announced his 'retirement'. Shortly thereafter, on 17 November journalist Jacques Pauw published an interview in the *Vrye Weekblad* with Captain Dirk Coetzee, a previous commander at Vlakplaas who by now had fled the country and who confirmed everything Nofemela had claimed and much more. Two days later another member, David Tshikalanga, added his confirmation, also from outside the country. Besides Vlakplaas, the existence of another base was reported by Coetzee, referred to as 'Daisy', also near Pretoria but intended specifically for launching foreign missions.

It took only another couple of months before the South African Defence Force, on 11 February 1990, admitted that they too had a hit squad called the Civil Cooperation Bureau (CCB). This admission was not voluntary, but came as a result of some more investigative journalism, this time on the part of Kitt Katzin and Steve McQuillan of the *Star* newspaper. They picked up on the fact that police investigations into the political murders of David Webster and Anton Lubowski suggested that certain detained suspects had links with military intelligence. In making the existence of the CCB public for the first time, an SADF spokesman said that the unit was a covert organisation of the Special Forces arm of the SADF, established to gather information about enemies of the state and to conduct 'possible actions against identified aggressors'.

As a postscript to the exposure of operational hit squads within the South African Police and the South African Defence Force, it was inevitable that in time the existence of co-ordinating structures would come to light; we now know that one such structure went by the name of TREWITS, an acronym for *Teenrewolusionêre Inligting Taakspan* (Counter-revolutionary Intelligence Target Centre). Monthly meetings of TREWITS involving members of SAP, SADF and NIS would identify targets, both human and other, for 'taking out', and allocate responsibility for carrying out the tasks either within the country or abroad. The first reference to TREWITS to be noted by the HRC was in a memorandum by General J.V. van der Merwe former Commissioner of Police, submitted to a Parliamentary Portfolio Committee in January 1995 (see p. 8).

The revelations, one after the other, of the existence of Vlakplaas and the CCB hit squads in the 2 wings of the security forces, were but the beginning of a very long journey, continuing today through court cases and the Truth and Reconciliation Commission hearings, to complete the picture. This is not the place to piece together the story thus far; that is more properly the task of the TRC upon completion of its search for the truth. For our purposes, it will suffice to list at the end of this section the names of all State Covert Structures and Covert Projects and Operations known to us; and to list in Appendices 2 and 3 all hit squad abductions, disappearances and assassinations recorded by HRC over years of monitoring.

*We close this section with extracts from **Almond Nofomela's sworn affidavit** of 19 October 1989; and from the HRC/David Webster Trust publication, **The CCB, Origin, Actions and Future of the Civil Co-operation Bureau** (September 1990).*

Zapiro, *Out of Step*, 1987

THE NOFOMELA AFFIDAVIT
19 October 1989

IN THE SUPREME COURT OF SOUTH AFRICA
TRANSVAAL PROVINCIAL DIVISION

IN THE MATTER BETWEEN:

BUTANA ALMOND NOFOMELA   APPLICANT

and

THE MINISTER OF JUSTICE   FIRST RESPONDENT

and

THE SHERIFF, TRANSVAAL   SECOND RESPONDENT

FOUNDING AFFIDAVIT

I, the undersigned

BUTANA ALMOND NOFOMELA

do hereby make oath and state:

1. I am a 32-year old male presently under sentence of death. My execution is scheduled for tomorrow morning, 20 October 1989, at 07h00.

2. The contents hereof, unless otherwise indicated by the context, are true to the best of my personal knowledge and belief.

3. I did not commit the murder for which I stand condemned. I repeat my evidence at the trial which led to my death sentence. I confirm the contentions raised therein by myself and on my behalf by my Counsel.

4. I wish to hereby reveal facts about my past which, I respectfully contend, might very well have had a bearing on my conviction and/or sentence of death had they been known to the Trial Court, Appeal Court and the Honourable First Respondent.

5. I was a member of the Security Branch stationed at headquarters in Pretoria from 1981 until my sentence of death on 21 September 1987.

6. During the period of my service in the Security branch, I served under station commander Brigadier Schoon. In 1981 I was appointed a member of the Security Branch's assassination squad, and I served under Captain Johannes Dirk Coetzee, who was my commanding officer in the field.

7. Some time during late 1981 I was briefed by Brigadier Schoon and Captain Coetzee at Pretoria to eliminate a certain Durban attorney, Griffiths Mxenge. I was told by these superiors that Mxenge was to be eliminated for his activities within the African National Congress. They instructed me to travel to Durban in the company of Brian Justice Nqulunga, David Tshikalange and Joseph Mamasela, colleagues of mine in the assassination squad. I was the leader of this group that was to eliminate Mxenge, and initially I was briefed alone. Thereafter, also in Pretoria, Coetzee briefed the 4 of us together.

There follows a description of how the group drove to Durban where at the CR Swart police station they received further briefing from Coetzee with instructions that only knives be used for killing Mxenge. Poisoned meat was thrown into the Mxenge yard. After monitoring Mxenge's movements for a few days, he was waylaid, forced into a car, driven to a stadium where he was assaulted and stabbed to death. The body was left stripped of items of value in order to simulate a robbery. The group then returned to CR Swart with Mxenge's car where they informed Coetzee of completion of mission. Next Coetzee and Nofomela drove to Piet Retief, taking Mxenge's car with them after fixing on false number plates. There they stripped the car of all removable items such as the radio, before driving it to the Swaziland border where it was doused with petrol and set alight in a plantation. They then returned to Piet Retief and on to Durban.

19. Some days thereafter, Brian, David, Joseph and I returned to Pretoria in the service bakkie in which we had travelled to Durban in, and Coetzee returned in his service bakkie. We drove in convoy.

20. The next day was month end. Usually at month's end we had a week off. Before going off, Coetzee handed Brian, David, Joseph and I R1000 each, which he said was from Brigadier Schoon for successfully eliminating Mxenge.

21. Before we went off for one week, in fact, immediately after our return from Durban, all the items removed from Mxenge's car and placed in Coetzee's service bakkie in Piet Retief were given to Sergeant Schutte by Captain Coetzee in my presence with the instruction that the radio/tape and booster were to be installed in Brigadier Schoon's vehicle. After my return from one weeks leave, Schutte remarked to me informally that the radio/tape had been installed into Brigadier Schoon's service bakkie.

22. After my return from one week's leave, Captain Coetzee informed me that Mxenge's wife is also active in the ANC's activities, and that he might require me to eliminate her as well at some future date. This was the last I heard of this.

23. I was involved in approximately 8 other assassinations during my stint in the assassination squad, also numerous kidnappings. At this stage, I do not recall the names of any of the victims. Some of the assassinations, 4 in fact, took place in Swaziland, one in Botswana, one in Maseru and one in Krugersdorp. The victims were all ANC members, except in Krugersdorp where the victim was the brother of an ANC terrorist. This terrorist had allegedly shot and killed a policeman in De Weldt. The brother had been working in the United Building Society as a security guard (Krugersdorp Branch).

24. All these missions were performed under different officers in the security branch. Another Captain Coetzee, Major de Kock, Lieutenant Vermeulen, Colonel Cronje are these officers. Their superior was at all times Brigadier Schoon, who was at all times aware of these missions.

25. I am instructed that due to a shortage of time, I cannot here furnish details of these other missions.

26. I now wish to explain why I have only revealed all this information at this stage. Major de Kock visited me with Captain Naude after my sentence of death. De Kock told me that Brigadier Schoon asked him to convey to me that I was not to reveal

anything about my activities as a member of the assassination squad, and he further promised that they will help me out of this problem. This visit by De Kock and Naude was 1987. Thereafter other members of the security branch visited me at various intervals. They were Lieutenant Van Dyk, Lieutenant Letsatse, Constable Mofalapitsa, Constable Khumalo, and some whose names I don't know. They all brought messages from Major de Kock that steps are being taken to get me out of the Maximum Prison.

27. Then on 12 October 1989, I received my notice of execution, and on 17 October 1989 Captain Khoza and a certain Lieutenant, both members of the Security Branch visited me and informed me that the instruction from Major de Kock was that I should take the pain. I then realised that I had been betrayed by my superior officers, who had promised to assist me in getting out of the Maximum Prison.

28. It was at this stage that I decided to reveal all of the aforegoing, and I sent a message to the Lawyers for Human Rights to send someone to me to take a statement accordingly and to apply for a stay of my execution.

BUTANA ALMOND NOFOMELA

Signed and sworn to before me at Pretoria on this the 19th day of October 1989, the deponent having acknowledged that he knows and understands the content of this affidavit and that he considers the oath taken by him to be binding on his conscience.

COMMISSIONER OF OATHS

Extracts from THE CCB
Origins, Actions and Future of the Civil Co-operation Bureau
HRC/David Webster Trust, September 1990

Origins and objectives of the CCB

In 1988, the activities and structures which carried out various military assassination functions were consolidated into the vehicle through which the army would operate in future, the Civil Co-operation Bureau. This military organisation has a civil facade. We believe that the reason is the recognition that its covert activities were, and remain, illegal, and the SADF did not want its name tarnished by illegal conduct. The CCB was therefore separate and distinct from the SADF but remained under its command. This organisation would commit acts of arson, intimidation, sabotage and murder.

The CCB's major objective is to disrupt the enemies of the Republic of South Africa to the maximum possible extent. As 'Slang' van Zyl said at the official instruction course:

> We were advised that the disruption of the enemy could, for example, be anything from the breaking of a window to the killing of a person and that this depended on the target's priority classification. The chairman would determine the priority classification for action allocated within these classes, namely the breaking of a window to the killing of a person.

The chain of command

The Civil Co-operation Bureau was a division of the Special Forces which, in turn, is a division of the Operations Section of the SADF. Each of the CCB's 10 regions was run by a co-ordinator and a regional director. And in each region, cells of operators of between 6 and 26 persons, made up the basic task force. These 'guesstimates' are based on evidence before the Harms Commission.

The CCB worked on a so-called 'need-to-know' basis, with operatives and controllers being given only enough information to carry out specific tasks. This meant that CCB 'managing director' Joe Verster, assumed de facto control of the CCB, directing the flow of instructions and information to those both above and below himself. 'Slang' van Zyl has said that often CCB operatives carried out a task with no idea as to its purpose.

Individual operators were provided with basic information regarding the structure and existence of the organisation. They knew only those people with whom it was absolutely essential to co-operate and normally communicated with one another under the guise of assumed names. Ideally, an operator's knowledge would be restricted to the people and activities of his own cell.

The CCB operated in 8 active regions. Those outside South Africa included Swaziland, Lesotho, Namibia, Zimbabwe, Mozambique, Angola, South Africa and Europe. Each region had an area manager and its own co-ordinator who reported to the managing director. Sections 9 and 10 were logistics and administration. Region 6 – the Republic of South Africa – was only activated in 1988, although the CCB blueprint had originally made provision for this area of operation. CCB director, Joe Verster, claimed that this region only gathered specialist information. The evidence indicates that this is untrue. 'Slang' van Zyl and Botha were emphatic that they were told that the CCB's primary task was 'maximum disruption of the enemy'. The nucleus of the Region 6 CCB was formed on 1 June 1988 when Verster hired 4 police officers, Staal Burger, 'Slang' Van Zyl, Chappie Maree and Calla Botha, all previously of the infamous Brixton Murder and Robbery Squad.

The first head of the Civil Co-operation Bureau was General Joubert. He was a member of the general's staff and reported directly to the chief of the SADF, General Jannie Geldenhuys, and/or the chief of staff operations, at least regarding external operations. When reports concerned activities in internal Region 6, certain members of the general's staff were informed, according to evidence given by General Eddie Webb, himself a member of the general's staff and chairman of the CCB since the beginning of 1989.

There is good reason to believe that responsibility for the CCB could have been structured as shown in Figure 10.

Modus operandi

The CCB developed what it termed the 'blue plan', in which CCB members would lead legitimate civilian lives and businesses would be set up or bought to provide civilian business cover for a cell member or his cell. The Matthysen Busvervoer is one such business. In this manner the CCB infiltrated industry, local government and the private sector at various levels. These open activities were referred to as the 'blue plan'.

```
┌─────────────────────────────────────┐
│         Minister of defence          │
│          (Magnus Malan)              │
└─────────────────────────────────────┘
                   │
┌─────────────────────────────────────┐
│       Chief of the defence force     │
│           (J. Geldenhuys)            │
└─────────────────────────────────────┘
                   │
┌─────────────────────────────────────┐
│        Chief of staff, operations    │
│     (Rudolph 'Witkop' Badenhorst)    │
└─────────────────────────────────────┘
                   │
┌─────────────────────────────────────┐
│            Head of the CCB           │
│       (Joep Joubert/Eddie Webb)      │
└─────────────────────────────────────┘
                   │
┌─────────────────────────────────────┐
│          Managing Director           │
│            (Joe Verster)             │
└─────────────────────────────────────┘
                   │
┌─────────────────────────────────────┐
│  Regional manager of the relevant region  │
│       (e.g. Staal Burger, Region 6)  │
└─────────────────────────────────────┘
                   │
┌─────────────────────────────────────┐
│   Co-ordinator of the relevant region │
│         (e.g. 'Christo Brits')       │
└─────────────────────────────────────┘
                   │
┌─────────────────────────────────────┐
│             Cell members             │
│ (e.g. Region 6: Van Zyl, Botha, Maree [Barnard]) │
└─────────────────────────────────────┘
                   │
┌─────────────────────────────────────┐
│         Unconscious members          │
└─────────────────────────────────────┘
```

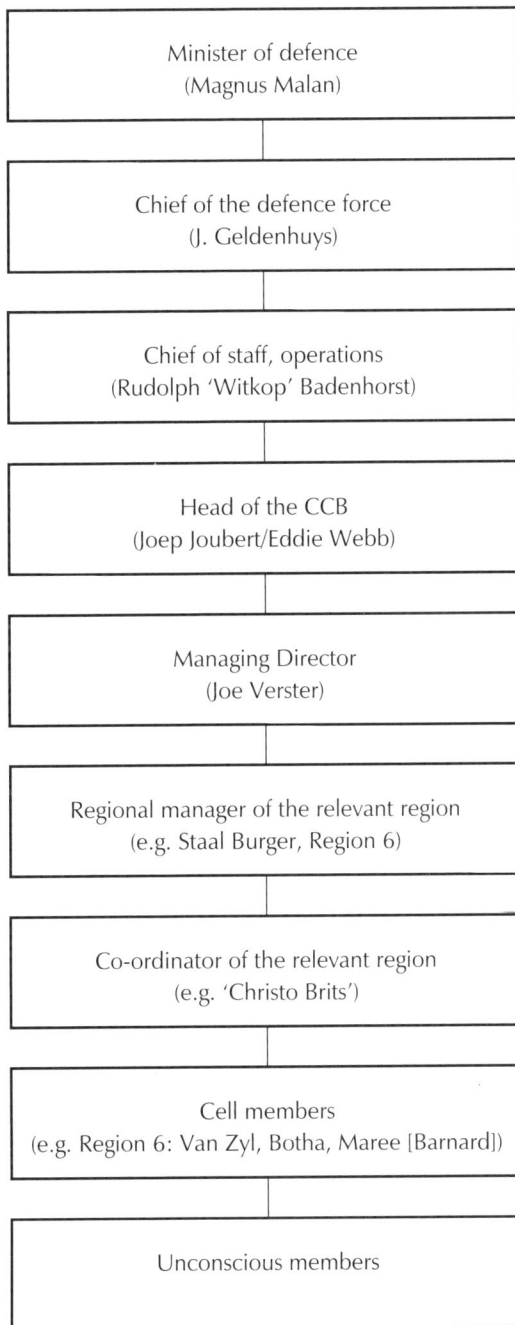

FIGURE 10
CCB chain of command

The 'red plan' targeted victims and detailed action to be taken against them. The scenario was as follows:

Step 1:   A person or a target would be identified as an enemy of the State. A cell member would then be instructed to monitor the 'target'.

Step 2:   A project – i.e. the elimination of a target would be registered with the co-ordinator. The co-ordinator would then have the project authorised by the regional manager and the managing director.

Step 3:   The CCB member would then do a reconnaissance to study the target's movements with a view to eliminating him or her.

Step 4:   The operative would propose the most practical method to the managing director. If the director felt this method was efficient, he would sign the proposal at what was called an 'in-house' meeting. There adjustments could be made to the plan before it was approved. The budget would be considered and finance would be made available for the project. The finance would come from the budget the Defence Force allocated to CCB activities. Indications are that money was always paid in cash.

Step 5:   The co-ordinator would be requested to make available the necessary arms and ammunition such as limpet mines, poison and/or live ammunition or other logistical support such as transport, etc.

Step 6:   The project would be carried out and the target would be eliminated. To do this the cell member could engage the assistance of what were termed 'unconscious members'. These were essentially underworld criminals who would, for money, kill as instructed. These 'unconscious' members were never told of the motive or the SADF connection – a false motive was usually supplied.

Dov Fedler, *The Star*, 16 April 1991

LISTING OF STATE COVERT STRUCTURES
HRC files, 1990–1996

The following is a partial listing of State covert units and activities compiled by the HRC from various sources. By the very nature of the subject matter the listing is very far from being complete and likely to contain inaccuracies.

SAP units

1. Combating of terrorism unit C1 (later known as C10)

   National headquarters – Wachthuis Building, Pretoria.

   Operational facility – Vlakplaas (near Pretoria).

   Regional facilities:

   > Natal: Mount Edgecombe/Phoenix (north coast), Elandskop (midlands), Camperdown, Bulwer

   > Northern Transvaal

   > Others yet to be identified

   Special facility: 'Daisy' Farm

2. Security Branch covert units

   Covert intelligence

   Covert Strategic Communications (Stratcom)

3. Counter-revolutionary intelligence unit C3 ('TREWITS')

   With representation from Military Intelligence (MI) and National Intelligence Service (NIS), TREWITS identified targets for neutralisation internally and externally.

   (TREWITS = *Teen Rewolusionêre Inligtings Taakspan*)

4. 'Koevoet' Counter-insurgency unit

   Established in Namibia in 1978.

SADF units

1. Directorate: covert collection (DCC)

   Wing of military intelligence.

   Reported to have been involved in the arming and training of Renamo, Ciskei Security Forces and Inkatha.

2. Directorate: special tasks (DST)

   Wing of military intelligence (?).

   Planning of support for RENAMO and UNITA.

   Planning of activities of 'Recce' regiments.

3. Civil Co-operation Bureau (CCB)

4. Special force operational units

   32 Battalion.

   No. 1 and no. 5 Reconnaisance Regiments ('Recces').

'Hammer' unit (Eastern Cape elimination squad).

5. Seventh Medical Battalion.

Involved in the development of chemical and biological warfare.

6. Front organisations

Adult Education Consultants (AEC)

Front for DCC.

Responsible for numerous 'counter-mobilisation' projects.

Creed Consultants

Subsidiary of AEC; coordinator of Caprivi training.

Wisdom Group

Chemical and biological weapons development.

Privatised companies include:

Delta G

Protechnics

Roodeplaat Navorsings laboratorium

Roodeplaat Teelonderneming

State covert projects/operations

1. Counter-mobilisation projects

Designed to establish alternative structures within township communities to counter the growing popularity of the United Democratic Front (UDF); and to promote 'black-on- black' violence within communities.

Project Orange

Project Ancor

Project Kampong

Numerous subsidiary projects.

Under the control of Adult Education Consultants (AEC)

2 . Counter-revolutionary operations

Designed to develop or support militant anti-liberation movement groupings, or promote destabilisation:

Operation Milia; support for RENAMO

Operation Marion; support for Inkatha

Operation Katzen; foster Xhosa Resistance Movement

Operation Pastoor; stoke East Rand violence

Operation Longreach

Project Henry; foster AmaAfrika National Front

Project B

3. Chemical weapons projects

Operation Coast

Project Jota

Note: For list of hit squad abductions/disappearances see Appendix 3; for a list of hit squad assassinations see Appendix 2.

EXTERNAL DESTABILISATION

Finally, within the pattern of informal repression and covert operations, something needs to be said about operations carried out by the apartheid state against its neighbours which resulted in the destabilisation of the entire Southern African region. In a Commonwealth report of 1989 entitled **Apartheid Terrorism***, this destabilisation during the 1980s is described as having reached 'holocaust' proportions. The report estimated that at that time the human cost was 1 million dead through military and economic action, most of them children, while a further 4 million people had been displaced from their homes. The economic cost to the 6 Frontline States was estimated to exceed 45 billion US dollars, not to mention the destruction of agriculture, industry, education and health care in countries like Mozambique and Angola.*

Amongst the destabilisation methods resorted to by the apartheid state were:

• *Armed action, ranging from sporadic commando raids into several neighbouring countries to full-scale invasion and occupation as occurred in Angola.*

• *Hit squad raids to abduct or assassinate political opponents.*

• *The encouragement or even the creation of surrogate anti-government forces through logistical support, intelligence and training as in Mozambique and Angola.*

• *Political pressures to promote the installation of governments well-disposed towards apartheid South Africa as in Malawi, Swaziland, Lesotho and Namibia.*

• *Economic pressures to create and maintain a dependency on the South African transport, harbour, customs and financial systems.*

One of the by-products of these activities is that we have inherited the remnants of the

Zapiro, *Out of Step*, 1987

mercenaries involved in all the colonial wars of Southern Africa, such as the Selous Scouts of Rhodesia, Koevoet from Namibia, RENAMO elements from Mozambique and UNITA elements from Angola. Large numbers of these 'Dogs of War' have found their way into the Special Forces and other Security Force structures, there to play a role in internal covert operations.

Extracts from APARTHEID TERRORISM
Destabilisation report by the Commonwealth Secretariat, 1989

Evolution of political events in the Southern African region

South Africa remained apart from the 'wind of change' that swept most of the rest of the continent to majority rule in the 1960s. Protected by a ring of colonial buffer states, Pretoria concentrated its regional policy on strengthening economic and military ties with those states and on thwarting the activities of liberation movements in the region. The *coup d'état* in Portugal on 25 April 1974, caused by military opposition to the far-off African wars, changed the face of the region virtually overnight, bringing independence to Mozambique and Angola in 1975.

Attempts at *'detente'* and 'dialogue' by the South African prime minister, B.J. Vorster, collapsed with the invasion of Angola by the South African Defence Force (SADF) in 1975, Pretoria's first large-scale military intervention in the region.

Perceiving the threat to its safety in terms of an externally organised 'total onslaught' conceived by the Soviet Union, rather than in terms of democratic opposition to apartheid, South Africa's response was drawn from the ideas of a French General, Andre Baufre, who developed a theory of 'total strategy' based on his experiences in wars in Europe, Algeria and Indo-China. The South African concept of 'total strategy', detailed in a defence white paper in 1977, encompasses economic, military, political and diplomatic tactics toward the region and uses military means to achieve economic ends.

During the period from mid-1980 to 1982, South Africa launched a concerted offensive against the region involving direct incursions as well as sabotage, assassinations, kidnappings, bombing and espionage, particularly against the newly independent state of Zimbabwe. In Mozambique, captured documentation revealed the extent of redeployment of MNR, their source of supply and their instructions to destroy or disrupt economic targets. There was also evidence of direct sabotage by the SADF, and an open commando attack in Maputo. In Angola, the SADF reoccupied part of southern Angola in an invasion in August 1981 and remained for the next 4 years. Sabotage of the Benguela railway closed it to all traffic. Two brazen commando attacks against regional capitals, Maputo and Maseru, in this period killed 33 South African exiles, 12 nationals of Lesotho and a Portuguese technician. Further afield in the region, a South African initiated *coup d'état* failed in the Seychelles in late 1981.

The period between 1983 and 1985 saw an escalation of this activity in a more systematic implementation of 'total strategy' but using a more subtle tactical approach. Beginning with a period of heightened military activity followed by the diplomatic offensive of 1984 and then a rapid return to the former posture, these changes characterised in the South African press as 'thump and talk'.

The sabotage of a main pumping station on the pipeline in the Beira corridor in 1982 had brought the Zimbabwe National Army into Mozambique to protect its lifeline to the sea and the escalation in 1985 brought Zimbabwean combat troops into Mozambique. The Cahora Bassa power lines were put out of operation through sabotage in 1983 and the Limpopo and Nacala railways were similarly halted in 1984. Two attacks in Maputo in 1983 killed 3 ANC officials and 6 others, only one of whom had ANC connections, and damaged a jam factory. In Angola, the SADF launched 'Operation Askari' in December 1983 and were surprised by new and sophisticated Soviet weaponry.

This period saw the conclusion of a military agreement for the withdrawal of troops from Angola, and a security agreement with Mozambique called the 'Nkomati Accord', both in early 1984. It was revealed that Swaziland had signed a similar agreement 2 years earlier. South African troops withdrew and then re-entered southern Angola in 1985 and, in Mozambique, the capture of the main MNR base at Gorongosa revealed massive violations of the Nkomati Accord by South Africa.

Economic and military pressure against Botswana escalated in this phase in the form of bombings and raids as well as withholding of SACU revenue payments and border congestion. In a massive SADF attack into Gaberone in June 1985, 10 houses and an office block were destroyed and 12 people killed, only 4 of whom had any connection with the ANC. Despite the pressure, Botswana has refused to sign a security agreement saying its territory is not used for aggression against its neighbours.

The period between 1986 and 1988 saw a massive escalation of military action across the region, directly and through surrogates. 1986 began with the economic blockade of Lesotho that prevented movement of migrant labour, food and other essential supplies and led to the *coup d'état* on 19 January; the year ended with the death of President Samora Machel of Mozambique in a still unexplained plane crash in South Africa. In between those events were the 19 May raids on 3 Commonwealth capitals in the region, an increase in economic pressure on Mozambique, Zambia and Zimbabwe, and a massive invasion of the centre-north of Mozambique aimed at taking and holding towns and cutting the country into two. Tanzania committed a brigade of combat troops to northern Mozambique, as well as its earlier offer of military training facilities, and Britain increased its training of Mozambican military units in eastern Zimbabwe.

A further escalation through 1987 was signalled with the 25 April SADF commando attack on Livingstone, Zambia, 11 days before the South African election showing, as is often the case, that these events are timed for internal consumption. Cross-border attacks into eastern Zimbabwe and Zambia began in mid-1987 and escalated through 1988, killing and kidnapping nationals and destroying property. Commando attacks and bombings in Maputo and Harare killed and wounded nationals and Botswana continued to be a target for bombings and cross-border raids. In May, on the Botswana border, South Africa staged 'Iron Eagle', its largest ever airborne commando exercise, delivering a message of military power not dissimilar to that of a year later, in September 1988, when it staged its largest ever naval exercise off the coast of Walvis Bay.

South African-trained forces continued their economic destruction in northern Mozambique and, following a massive infiltration from South Africa of men and equipment in April and May, a new wave of terror began in the south. There were several large massacres, including one of over 400 people at Homoine and another of over 100 people, as well as vicious attacks on civilian convoys. As 1987 drew to a close, attacks on the main roads around Maputo increased, isolating the capital by making its main access roads unsafe to normal commercial traffic.

Malawian troops entered Mozambique in this period to protect railway workers repairing the Nacala line, the country's shortest and cheapest route to the sea and out of operation since 1984. Mozambicans continued to flee into southern Malawi swelling the ranks of the displaced to well over 600 000 by late 1988.

A South African offensive in south-eastern Angola in late 1987 led to the siege of Cuito Cuanavale; the commitment of Cubans to the fighting in the south for the first time since 1976; the subsequent agreement a year later on South African and Cuban troop withdrawal and Namibian independence.

South African car bombings, assassinations and kidnappings escalated sharply in 1988, particularly in Botswana, Zimbabwe, Mozambique, Zambia, Swaziland and Lesotho, as well as against ANC representatives in Europe. In the diplomatic offensive, P.W. Botha visited Songo near Cahora Bassa but the military situation deteriorated after the meeting. Having destabilised the region, however, South Africa, now claimed to be the 'stabiliser'. The deputy minister of defence, delivering 'non-lethal' equipment to Mozambique for the rehabilitation of Cahora Bassa power lines, said: 'South Africa is the stabiliser of the region and would like to expand this role.'

However, lest the region forget South Africa's military might and its 'superpower' aspirations, a new intermediate-range ballistic missile – capable of delivering a nuclear warhead as far north as Angola and Tanzania – was test launched in early July 1989. The missile is a modified version of Israel's Jericho II IR BM and has been developed, with assistance from Israel, since 1987.

CROSS-BORDER OPERATIONS
compiled by HRC, 1989

1. Commando raids

1975	August	Invasion of Angola.
1978	4 May	Air and ground strike on SWAPO refugee camp at Kassinga inside Angola; over 600 deaths.
1981	30 January	Matola, Mozambique; 12 killed, 3 abducted.

1982	9 December	Maseru, Lesotho; 42 deaths.
1983	23 May	Air attack on Maputo, Mozambique; 6 deaths.
	17 October	Maputo, Mozambique; no deaths.
1984	?	Botswana; 3 deaths, execution style.
1985	14 June	Gaborone, Botswana; 12 deaths.
	20 December	Maseru, Lesotho; 9 deaths (followed by coup against Chief Leabua Jonathan).
1986	19 May	Simultaneous air and ground strikes on Botswana, Zambia and Zimbabwe during Commonwealth EPG mission to South Africa; 3 deaths.
1987	?	Livingstone, Zambia; 4 deaths.
	May	Mozambique; 3 deaths.
1988	28 March	Gaborone, Botswana; 4 deaths.
	June	Gaborone; 2 SADF members captured.

2. Bomb attacks

1974	?	Botswana; parcel bomb kills student leader Abraham Tiro.
	?	Zambia; parcel bomb kills John Dube.
1981	1 August	Harare, Zimbabwe; car bomb kills chief ANC representative Joe Gqabi.
		Gaborone, Botswana; car bomb kills ANC executive member.
1982	March	London (UK); ANC headquarters bombed.
	June	Mbabane, Swaziland; car bomb kills 2 ANC representatives.
	August	Lesotho; car bomb kills 1 person; ANC representative Chris Hani survives.
	17 August	Maputo, Mozambique; parcel bomb kills ANC member Ruth First.
1984	28 June	Lubango (Angola); letter bomb kills SACTU member Jeanette Schoon and daughter.
1985	13 February	Botswana; house of exile Nat Serache blown up.
	14 May	Gaborone, Botswana; car bomb kills exile Vernon Nkadimeng.
	1 July	Lusaka, Zambia; ANC headquarters bombed.
	16 November	Gaborone, Botswana; car bomb kills 4 exiles (including 2 children).
	7 December	Lusaka, Zambia; parcel bomb injures ANC member.
1986	April	Maputo, Mozambique; car bomb injures 50, extensive damage.
	8 September	Stockholm (Sweden); ANC offices bombed.
1987	8 April	Gaborone, Botswana; car bomb kills 3, injures 2.
	14 May	Harare, Zimbabwe; booby-trapped TV set kills wife of ANC official.
	17 May	Harare, Zimbabwe; ANC offices bombed.

	October	Harare; car bomb, survived by activists Joan and Jeremy Brickhill.
1988	January	Harare, Zimbabwe; grenade attack on ANC offices.
	January	Harare; car bomb injures exile Paul Brickfield.
	January	Bulawayo, Zimbabwe; car bomb kills 2 ANC members.
	20 January	Lusaka, Zambia; ANC offices bombed, 4 Zambians injured.
	27 March	Brussels (Belgium); unexploded bomb found outside ANC offices.
	17 April	Maputo, Mozambique; car bomb severely injures ANC member Albie Sachs.
	December	Livingstone, Zambia; car bomb kills 2 and injures 13 others.
1989	January	Zambia; 2 deaths in 2 bomb blasts.

3. Cross-border abductions

1970's		Nduli, Joseph (Exile)	Abducted from
		Ndhlovu, Cleopas (Exile)	Botswana/Swaziland.
		Ramotse, B.S. (Exile)	
1981	30 January	3 persons	Abducted from Mozambique during Matola raid.
1984	2 May	4 ANC members	From Swaziland.
1986	July	Msibi, Sidney	From Manzini, Swaziland; returned November.
	August	Seme, Lucas (ANC)	From Swazi police cells.
	11 December	Schneider, Daniel (Swiss)	From Mbabane,
		Bischoff, Corinne (Swiss)	Swaziland; released 2 days later after interrogation in South Africa by security police.
	11/12 December	Mzeni, Shadrack (ANC)	From Mbabane, Swaziland.
		Cele, Grace	
		Nyoni, Danger	
	15 December	Ebrahim, Ebrahim (ANC)	From Swaziland; tried and convicted in South Africa court under ISA.
1987	May	Nyanda, Sheila (ANC)	From Mbabane; released November 1988.
1989	March	Molapo, Sekhonyana	From Lesotho; released 9 days later after interrogation and attempts to recruit him as an agent.

(For cross-border assassinations, see Appendix 2)

PART B
THE CRACKS APPEAR
1988–1990

Introduction '

From its inception in 1948 and right up to the mid-1980s the apartheid fortress seemed impregnable. But during the 1980s cracks began to appear, almost imperceptibly at first, then widening towards the end of the decade until the disintegration of apartheid power was clear for all to see.

The seeds of its own destruction were sown by the apartheid government when in 1984 it rammed through the tricameral system of government, excluding the black African majority, coupled with the puppet structures of Black Local Councils. This, in effect, triggered a national uprising of such proportions that the government was obliged to resort to the declaration of a State of Emergency in 1985.

This declaration, in turn, was to result in a major flight of capital from South Africa, the depletion of the country's foreign reserves and in due course a strangulation of the economy to the point of imminent collapse.

Even with the awesome tools of the State of Emergency, the government was unable to win its war against the liberation struggle waged by the majority population and by early 1989 the Emergency measures were failing in the face of a national detainee hunger strike, followed by a national defiance campaign to which the authorities had no effective answer.

On another front, namely the military intervention in Angola and the military occupation of Namibia, the escalating costs were contributing heavily to the looming economic crisis and withdrawal from 1988 onwards became inevitable.

In the meantime, international initiatives were taking place to hasten the capitulation of apartheid power. Apart from almost total isolation of apartheid South Africa at all levels, proposals began to emerge urging the government to begin negotiations with the liberation movements for a peaceful settlement and transfer of power to a democratic government. These proposals found expression in the Harare Declaration of August 1989 and the UN Declaration of December 1989.

Driven by these inexorable pressures, both internal and external, the regime responded tentatively at first by holding secret talks with liberation movement leaders in prison and in exile; then by releasing a few high profile political prisoners; and finally by agreeing to unban all liberation movements and commence talks about a process for terminating apartheid power.

In Part B of this book, an analysis is given of the factors and events leading up to the demise of apartheid power with particular reference to the role of repression even at a time when a negotiated settlement was becoming a possibility.

Calendar of major events on the road to the disintegration of apartheid power ·

Year	Internal events	External events
1984	Tricameral constitution adopted (Act 110 of 1983). Military occupation of Vaal townships (September).	
1985	Partial State of Emergency declared (21 July). Rubicon speech by P.W. Botha (15 August).	Withdrawal of foreign banks from South Africa. Moratorium on foreign debt repayment.
1986	National State of Emergency declared (12 June).	USA adopts CAAA (Comprehensive Anti-apartheid Act).
1987	Intense national resistance.	
1988	Release of Govan Mbeki.	Battle of Cuito Cuanavale. Withdrawal from Angola. Withdrawal from Namibia.
1989	National detainees hunger strike commences (23 January). National defiance campaign launched (26 July). Last all-white election (6 September). Release of Walter Sisulu and 7 other high profile prisoners (10 October). 'Downgrading' of NSMS (29 November).	Harare Declaration adopted by OAU (21 August). UN Declaration on apartheid adopted by consensus (14 December).
1990	De Klerk unbans liberation movements (2 February). Release of Nelson Mandela (11 February). Signing of Groote Schuur Minute (2 May). Signing of Pretoria Minute (August).	Namibia achieves independence.

7 APARTHEID POWER IN CRISIS

The year 1989 will go down as a watershed year in the struggle for a non-racial democracy in South Africa. If there is one event which could be said to have ushered in this new phase of our history, it was the detainees' hunger strike.

Starting on 23 January 1989, nearly 1000 detainees, detained from one State of Emergency to another, took matters into their own hands and by their determined action forced open the detention cells. But they did more than that. They opened the floodgates to the resistance of the masses of South Africa after 4 years of oppression under Emergency rule.

The success of the hunger strike unleashed a new mood, a mood of open rejection of detentions, bannings, restrictions and other forms of state repression. A mood of open defiance against apartheid laws and the apartheid government.

While internal resistance must always be the engine for change in South Africa, it took the hunger strike to get that engine running again. Change took place in South Africa not because of any change of heart on the part of the state but because of the cumulative effect of both internal pressure and pressure from the international community.

The crisis within the structures of apartheid power which came into sharp focus during

Tony Grogan, *Sunday Times*, 28 February 1988

1989 and which held great promise for a negotiated transformation of South African society to a democratic order, are described in extracts from the following HRC publications:

- *HRC Review of 1989*
- *Days of Defiance* (September 1989)
- *Apartheid under Pressure* (May 1990)

In the first part we consider 2 crucial events from the watershed year of 1989. We begin with a brief description of the national detainees hunger strike before examining the period immediately prior to the last all-white elections of 1989, which brought De Klerk to power. We then examine the defiance campaign and the repressive response of the state.

In the second part we extract a segment from a document written in May 1990 in which 3 questions are posed and answered. We asked whether repression was on the way out, whether apartheid was really being dismantled and finally what possibilities existed for a peaceful resolution of the conflict.

THE GREAT HUNGER STRIKE
from HRC Review of 1989

The largest ever protest by detainees against their detention began on 23 January 1989 when 20 State of Emergency detainees at Diepkloof prison began an 'indefinite' hunger strike demanding the immediate and unconditional release of all detainees. The action sparked off a national wave of hunger strike protests by detainees, and solidarity action by people and organisations in South Africa and around the world.

By the end of March over 700 detainees had participated in the hunger strike protests. This was not the first time detainees had embarked on hunger strikes to demand their release. State of Emergency detainees in particular, increasingly frustrated by their seemingly endless detention, had embarked on numerous hunger strikes in the last few years. Between 23 January and 22 December 1989, the Human Rights Commission had recorded 53 hunger strikes involving 1429 State of Emergency detainees, 24 Section 29 detainees and 34 who were held under homeland legislation.

Most of the hunger strikes of previous years were sporadic, relatively short in duration and localised. The 1989 hunger strike wave, on the other hand, affected every part of the country, continued over many weeks and showed no signs of abating until the detainees demands for their release were met.

The initial response of the minister of law and order was to dismiss the demands of hunger strikers and a refusal to be blackmailed. However, when it became apparent that the hunger strikes were turning into a crisis with major local and international implications for the South African government, minister Vlok's attitude changed. The growing pressure for the release of detainees, the rapid spread of the hunger strike action and the deteriorating health of the hunger strikers forced the minister to act to defuse the situation. As a result of the pressure, the minister undertook to release a 'substantial number of detainees' over the following 2 weeks. By the end of the period the release of only 202 had been recorded by the Human Rights Commission and other monitoring groups.

In the storm of protest which followed these limited releases, and with the intensification of the hunger strike by detainees, the minister was forced to accelerate the releases. By 31 March the minister claimed to have signed release orders for 650 detainees, while the HRC had records of under 500 releases. This process was still relatively slow, however, and some detainees who were becoming increasingly frustrated decided to take their fate into their own hands. The result was a spate of escapes by detainees from hospitals and subsequent taking of refuge in international embassies and consulates. This resulted in further world attention being focussed on the plight of the hunger strikers. At the same time, the hunger strike action had spread beyond the State of Emergency detainees and was now also focussing attention on the plight of Internal Security Act detainees. Despite stringent security measures and under conditions of great secrecy, a number of section 29 detainees added their voices to the action by joining the hunger strike.

Clearly the determination of the detainees, combined with outside pressure forced the minister to retreat somewhat from his original position, resulting in a major victory for detainees.

THE 1989 DEFIANCE CAMPAIGN
from Days of Defiance, HRC, September 1989

1. The last all-white elections

On Wednesday 6 September 1989, the majority of South Africans will once again witness the election of a national government in which it has no say. This election takes place under a State of Emergency which has been in force for over 3 years; which prohibits freedom of speech, assembly and association and under which arbitrary detention without trial awaits anyone stepping over an invisible line drawn anywhere at any time by any member of the security forces.

In a move to put forward the real issues concerning the majority, the Mass Democratic Movement embarked on a defiance campaign launched at the beginning of August. The campaign has gathered momentum and has spread across the whole country embracing a wide range of issues.

The ingredients of the bitterness of the election and of the strong spirit of the defiance campaign have fed into the existing repression making the pre-election period a time of escalating detentions of activists, bannings of meetings, violent police action and attacks on people and property. Until Article 21 of the UN Declaration of Human Rights is implemented in South Africa and free and fair democratic elections are held, repression of the disenfranchised will always be part of an election which excludes them.

2. Background

There are 2 new factors on the South African political scene which have had a major influence on events in the pre-election period. Firstly, there is the defiance campaign spearheaded by the Mass Democratic Movement (MDM). Secondly, there is the crisis of the Nationalist government caught between appealing to the white electorate and its growing sensitivity to the opinion of the international community.

3. The defiance campaign

The MDM represents a broad front encompassing the United Democratic Front, the COSATU-affiliated unions and the church drawn together in their demands for the lifting of the State of Emergency, the unbanning of organisations and individuals and the formation of a non-racial democratic and unitary South Africa, amongst others. Its strategy has been to place the real issues facing the country in the foreground during this period to show to both South Africans and the world the irrelevance of the elections.

The campaign has essentially been two-pronged: to highlight the segregation of amenities and services, and to highlight the continuing restrictions on organisations and individuals which make normal political activity impossible.

In respect of amenities and services, the campaign has reached into many spheres such as health, education and transport. There have been a series of organised public events to 'declare' facilities open to all races. For example, doctors sent black patients to white hospitals for treatment, black patients arrived at white hospitals for treatment and racially-mixed groups of people boarded buses and used beaches. To protest against the restrictions, public meetings have been held where both organisations and individuals have declared themselves unrestricted. People have appeared in public wearing T-shirts proclaiming restricted organisations and people under restriction orders have attended functions openly in defiance of those restrictions.

There have also been public protests around the country on a variety of other issues, for example the curbs on the media, the detention of children, detentions generally and the Labour Relations Amendment Act (LRA).

At the beginning of August the first acts of defiance began with the action around health facilities. The events were peaceful. They were followed by protests at white schools, some of which were broken up by riot police. The first significant act of repression against the campaign came in the run- up to the sixth anniversary of the United Democratic Front on 20 August, at which restricted organisations were scheduled to declare themselves unbanned. The anniversary meeting was banned and on Friday 18 August, Mohammed Valli Moosa, the acting general secretary of the UDF, was detained from his office in Braamfontein. From this time onwards violent police action has been reported on a daily basis.

The defiance campaign has been particularly strong in the Western Cape. It has also been the hardest hit in terms of brutal police repression. This must be seen in the light of the schools crisis that has been simmering in the Western Cape for the past 18 months. The crisis had begun to escalate approximately 6 weeks before the defiance campaign and has fed into the campaign in a series of disciplined and consistent demonstrations and protests. The severity of police repression in this area also indicates that police are acting not just against the campaign but also in an attempt to smash the well organised and highly motivated student organisation (Western Cape Students' Congress) which has been re-building itself despite being restricted.

4. Arrests and prosecutions

The state has responded to defiance actions in 2 ways: through police force and through arresting protesters and charging many of them. At least 1569 people have been arrested since the beginning of August.

Many people have been arrested and then released a few hours later without being charged. This has been an intimidatory tactic on the part of the police. Others were arrested for a few hours and interrogated about friends or planned actions. However, the majority of arrests have led to a clogging up of courts as people are charged with various offences. In some instances special courts have sat until midnight in order to process all the people who have been charged that day.

5. Banning of meetings

Throughout the period under review, many gatherings were not defined as meetings as such and were not therefore banned, but rather declared 'illegal gatherings' and were approached as such by the authorities. Fourteen specific meetings were banned, 5 prohibitions of meetings in certain magisterial districts or under the auspices of certain specified organisations were issued, 2 meetings were restricted and interdicts were issued against the bannings in 2 instances.

6. Media harassment

The Emergency regulations prevent journalists from:
- Filming, photographing or reporting on unrest or security force action in 'unrest', which includes unlawful gatherings and processions, without official permission.
- Publishing a 'subversive statement' – defined as a statement discrediting military service, promoting 'people's courts' and other alternative structures of power, urging illegal strikes and boycott actions, or assessing the effectiveness of such actions, or calling for the release of people detained under the Emergency.
- Reporting on the circumstances or treatment of an Emergency detainee, or giving information in connection with a detainee's release.

- Direct powers of censorship under the Emergency have been placed in the hands of state officials whose actions are effectively immune from judicial control. These powers have been exercised to seize and temporarily close down newspapers. Newspapers and publications exist under the constant threat of closure. Recently the state charged a number of newspapers of contravening the Internal Security Act and Emergency regulations.

On 1 September 1989 the South African Police issued an 'early warning' to the media to strictly comply with all media Emergency regulations. The warning follows on from frequent and continued harassment of journalists during this period. To date, 74 journalists have been arrested at different events throughout the country. Some of them face charges. They were all released after questioning. Some video cassettes, equipment and material have been confiscated. In one incident a journalist was attacked by a police dog during his arrest.

On 30 August journalists in Johannesburg and Cape Town held placard demonstrations to protest against the media regulations. There were no incidents reported from Johannesburg but 12 of the journalists mentioned above were arrested in Cape Town. On 2 September 50 journalists covering the protest march in Cape Town were arrested.

7. Police action against protesters

Against the background of threats by both the acting state president F.W. de Klerk and law and order minister Adriaan Vlok that police would not hesitate to take firm action against anti-government protesters, activists and organisations have been hard hit by heavy-handed police action against peaceful protests.

A. Findlay, *City Press,* 17 September 1989

Police have made free use of teargas to quell the wave of protests. Other weapons used on occasions include shotguns, stun grenades, batons and water cannons. Ammunition used included buckshot, birdshot and rubber bullets. There is no discernible policy as to when the police are armed with what weapons and there appears to be no policy of 'minimum force'. On one occasion, policewomen were used to halt a march. This was held up by the authorities as proof of their commitment to avoiding violent confrontation but the exercise was not repeated. Reports were received of 46 meetings and protests which were broken up by the security forces. In 2 instances kitskonstabels were sent in and in Vereeniging, where black mineworkers had occupied white married quarters, the SADF was called in to remove them.

APARTHEID UNDER PRESSURE
A current analysis of repression, apartheid law and structures, and prospects for a negotiated settlement
HRC, May 1990

Three questions are uppermost in the minds of those concerned with the situation in South Africa today. Is repression finally on the way out? Is apartheid really being dismantled? And what are the prospects for a peaceful resolution of the conflict? They are questions which are closely interrelated and which require an integrated answer. The central issue in addressing these questions is the demise of apartheid (not its reform) and its replacement with a new democratic order. Let us look at each question in turn.

1. The current level of repression

Detention without trial for interrogation or 'preventive' purposes, barring access to the courts, lawyers, family or friends has been practised on a wide scale for 30 years. Over 75 000 victims have experienced the detention cells in that time, some for as long as 3 years. Over 50 000 of that number have been detained during the last 5 years, attesting to the extreme level of repression exercised during the State of Emergency. Today, detention without trial continues on a daily basis, it is happening as we speak. The numbers are in the hundreds rather than the thousands of the recent past and the current detainee population stands at between 400 and 500, including children under the age of 18. The long history of torture in detention has not ended as reports continue to come in.

Banning and restriction of persons (house arrest in its extreme form) is, since F.W. de Klerk's address to parliament on 2 February 1990, something of the past. However, the powers under the legislation are still intact and could be invoked at any time.

Political trials and imprisonment are at a level which can only be described as frenzied. During 1989, a record number of 395 known political trials were completed involving over 3000 accused, with 42 death sentences and 237 prison sentences of between 5 and 20 years. The year 1990 started off with over 250 political trials under way and looks set to exceed last year's record. The current political prisoner population is estimated at around 3000, of whom about 12% are 'security law' prisoners and the balance are 'unrest' prisoners convicted of such offences as public violence.

The government denies it conducts political trials or holds political prisoners but nevertheless announced through F.W. de Klerk's address of 2 February that those serving sentences simply for membership of previously banned organisations would be considered for release. Since that announcement there have been about 80 releases (including that of Nelson Mandela) only some of which complied with the stated condition and in many cases release was imminent anyway. This out-flow has also been partly nullified by the inflow from ongoing trials.

Political executions have since 2 February been suspended along with all other executions, pending a judicial reassessment of capital punishment legislation. The outcome of this reassessment is presently emerging but still leaves about 80 political prisoners on death row, uncertain of their fate.

Other repressive acts against persons have included denial or withdrawal of passports, banishment to remote areas and withdrawal of citizenship followed by deportation to a homeland. Most prevalent at the present time however is the 'listing' of persons under the ISA making it an offence, punishable by up to 3 years imprisonment, to quote any utterance, past or present, of any person on the list. There are over 300 persons currently gagged in this way, some deceased, some in exile, some in prison.

Organisations are no longer banned or restricted since the address of 2 February. The unbanning of the ANC, PAC and SACP was certainly the most dramatic aspect of that address. However, the powers to ban or restrict organisations are still intact and could be brought into play at any time. Furthermore the United Democratic Front and the National Union of South African Students are prohibited in terms of proclamations issued under the Affected Organisations Act from receiving any foreign funding.

Freedom of assembly continues to be severely restricted, constituting a major source of conflict at the present time. On 1 April, the annual blanket ban on all outdoor political gatherings without permission was renewed for the fifteenth consecutive year under the ISA. During late 1989 permission for protest marches, rallies, etc., began to be granted fairly readily and police seemed to be acting with restraint at such gatherings.

However, attitudes seem to have hardened again, permission for gatherings is frequently refused and in some areas the security forces have returned to their former use of extreme force in breaking up peaceful marches and demonstrations, resulting at times in heavy and unnecessary loss of life. A recent estimate is that 139 people have been killed and 1429 injured directly or indirectly by police action since the De Klerk address of 2 February. Such heavy-handed and irresponsible action carries the danger that communities (and particularly the youth) struggling to articulate their grievances and aspirations will conclude that peaceful methods lead nowhere.

Media restrictions, reminiscent of wartime conditions, which were imposed under the SOE over the last few years, were relaxed to some extent on February 2. No longer is it forbidden to report on unrest situations or actions of the security forces by way of the printed or spoken word, but visual reporting is still prohibited. Furthermore, in practice, journalists are frequently ordered or removed from the scene of unrest under SOE regulations. No newspapers are currently banned or under the threat of suspension but the powers to act under the ISA are nevertheless still in place.

Political activity has escalated considerably since the highly successful detainee hunger strike and defiance campaign of 1989. Laws and regulations which ban or restrict political campaigns, boycotts, stayaways and 'alternative' structures, have been largely disregarded. Security force response, as mentioned previously, has blown hot and cold but for some time now has returned decisively to its former brutality.

Having surveyed the scene of formal repression, we need to spend a short time looking at its ever present and more sinister accomplice, informal repression – the extension of repression into the realms of the semi-legal and the non-legal.

Informal repression in the South African context is not new but received a tremendous boost during the P.W. Botha era of 'total strategy' devised to combat what was perceived as the 'total onslaught' against the bastions of apartheid. Army generals and police chiefs of the security establishment developed the National Security Management System, with the National Security Council at its head. In security matters the Council became more powerful than the cabinet itself. Its tentacles reached every level of society through Joint Management Centres by co-opting local councils, local industry, local business, etc. In this way anti-apartheid activists and organisations were identified, monitored, harassed and neutralised in various ways. Since the departure from the political arena of P.W. Botha, the role of the National Security Council has been downgraded and subordinated to the cabinet but the essential components of the National Security Management System are nevertheless still intact, even if in modified form.

Vigilante groups have their origins in the support systems which have been built up around the unpopular apartheid-created structures of homeland authorities and of black local authorities. Their growth has been actively encouraged or tacitly condoned through thinly disguised support of the security forces and local police. The impression of so-called 'black-on-black' violence is easily created by such means. There is currently a high level of rejection amongst the black community of homelands and black municipal councils which is generating a flurry of disruptive activity on the part of vigilante groups. The violent situation in Natal must be seen in this context.

Hit squads have now clearly emerged as an essential component of the 'total strategy'. There can be few who still doubt the existence of hit squads within the structures of the South African Police and of the South African Defence Force and that these squads have perpetrated a full spectrum of atrocities in the name of defending apartheid. If anything is still in doubt, it is the question of how high up the line command originates. Evidence emerging from the Harms Commission of Inquiry suggests the involvement of cabinet ministers, so that it will not come as a surprise to find that the State Security Council has guided and promoted this form of unconventional warfare. In the meantime, in spite of commissions of inquiry, hit squads continue their activities.

In summary, it must be said that all the powers of repression available to the apartheid regime are still intact and most of them continue to be exercised. The lifting of the State of Emergency alone will not signal the end of repression since virtually all of its awesome powers are available through the permanent legislation of the Internal Security Act.

2. The current status of apartheid laws and structures

Let us now turn to the question of whether apartheid is really being dismantled. We need to examine which racially discriminatory laws are still on the statute books and which administrative structures still exist to implement those laws.

The law basic to the entire system of apartheid, and from which all other laws derive, is the Population Registration Act of 1950. This act presumes to identify and classify from birth each and every person as belonging to one of 4 distinct races. Racial classification then determines each individual's destiny from the cradle to the grave in terms of franchise, mobility, residential rights and social benefits and services provided by the state. It is a law built into the constitution and today stands firm as the foundation stone of the system of government.

The first consequence of racial classification is the specific exclusion of the black racial group from the vote for central government as provided for in the Republic of South Africa Constitution Act of 1983, in the latest form. To reinforce this exclusion, the Homeland Citizenship Act was introduced in 1970 to create so-called independent homelands, whereby many millions of blacks were declared citizens of these homelands and simultaneously deprived of their South African citizenship, such as it was. The absence of franchise for South Africa's 27 million blacks is still very much the situation today and is of course the most fundamental issue of all to be addressed if lasting peace is to become a reality.

Access to land by the black population group is strictly limited by the Native Land Act of 1913 and the Development Trust and Land Act of 1936. This legislation allocates 13.6% of the country's land area for 75% of the population and denies them ownership of land outside these allocated territories. During recent years these statutes have been frayed at the edges due to the refusal of millions of blacks to be herded into overcrowded homelands and due to their settling into urban areas against all odds.

In recognition of the permanence of this urban black population, limited freehold housing rights have been permitted. Nevertheless the laws governing land ownership rights are intact to this day. Similarly, regarding rights of ownership, the rights of residential occupation within any area is strictly controlled by the notorious Group Areas Act of 1966 (first promulgated in 1950) and reinforced by the Prevention of Illegal Squatting Act of 1989 (first promulgated in 1951). This legislation is designed to effect a total social and residential separation of the 4 classified race groups. It, too, is suffering a measure of disarray as a result of the huge pressure of overcrowded urban populations spilling over into areas designated exclusively for white occupation. In an effort to manipulate legislation to accord with the realities of the situation, the South African government has been dabbling with such concepts as free settlement areas which raise more problems and contradictions than they solve. In spite of this fancy footwork, the Group Areas Act reigns supreme and prosecutions for its infringement continue apace.

The quality of services and social benefits provided by the state is determined according to racial group by a complex web of legislation at first and second tier level. In the areas of education, health care and social welfare, facilities are segregated and grossly unequal, services are administered through separate state departments, and budgetary allocations are highly discriminatory. As a result, there is a chronic state of crisis in all of these areas, never worse than at the present time.

The Reservation of Separate Amenities Act of 1953 is a law which has come under considerable pressure and defiance in many of its aspects and seems due for repealing in the near future. It provides for the racial segregation of such public amenities as public transport, parks, beaches, swimming baths, resorts, caravan parks, hospitals, clinics, railway stations, post offices, banks and virtually any public area except a public road or street. Many of the provisions have fallen into disuse by default or executive decree within the main centres but many smaller towns continue to enforce them rigorously, protected and encouraged by the knowledge that the Act is still on the statute books. As the custodian of petty apartheid, the Separate Amenities Act represents the softest target for the proponents of reform strategy. Nevertheless, when state president De Klerk announced in late 1989 that the government had decided to repeal the Act at some time in the future, he qualified this announcement by saying that 'there are a few sensitive areas where the institution of fitting measures will be necessary when the Act is repealed'. Apartheid does not give up easily.

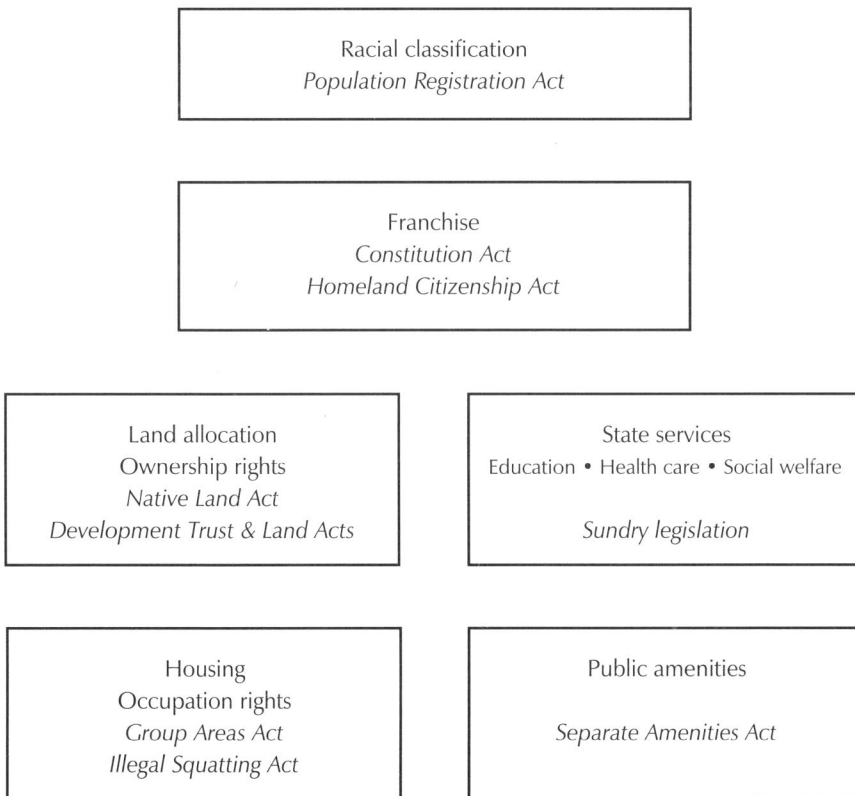

FIGURE 11
Apartheid law and constitution

Having briefly outlined the racial laws still in place on the statute books, we can look at the government structures which make and implement these laws and judge whether such structures are serving to perpetuate the apartheid system.

Central power is vested in the tricameral parliament, a structure which gives token representation to those classified as 'coloured' and 'Indian' but retains effective control in the hands of the white group. The population group classified as 'black' is totally excluded. This structure which came into existence in 1984 amidst widespread protest leading to a State of Emergency, is essentially apartheid in concept in several senses. Firstly, it excludes three quarters of the population on racial grounds; secondly it is composed of 3 separate houses, each a different race group; and thirdly, effective control lies in the hands of the white minority representing less than 15% of the total population. One can say therefore that its legitimacy rating is 15% at best.

Black local authorities were introduced about the same time as the tricameral parliament and were intended to serve as a sop to the urban black population for their exclusion from central government by offering some form of representation at local government level. Elections to black councils have been virtually totally boycotted and those who accepted office regarded as sell-outs and collaborators, bent on lining their own pockets. The imposition of black councils without consulting the communities they purported to serve was the major factor, alongside the introduction of the tricameral parliament, in triggering off mass protest throughout South Africa, starting in 1984 and continuing to this day. Great pressure has been placed upon black councillors to resign and for the councils to be dismantled. In spite of councils being propped up by official security forces and unofficial vigilante groups, wholesale resignations and collapse of councils have taken place. At the present there is a strong resurgence of popular feeling against what are perceived as puppet structures and resignations are again on the increase.

The homelands are monuments to apartheid political and social engineering. The rationale for their creation was to provide the black population group with a means of expressing their political aspirations since this was forever to be denied them within 'white' South Africa at central government level. In fact, the homelands concept, besides attempting to address the issue of black political representation, also is intended to perpetuate the existence of docile labour reservoirs, control the flow of labour to the mines, industry and farms, and limit access of the black population to urban areas. Much has been written about the destruction of home life, the uprooting of whole communities, the impoverishment and overcrowding and many other consequences of this experiment in social engineering in which some 13 million people have been compressed into the patchwork of land pieces which make up the 10 homelands – 6 of them 'self-governing' and 4 of them 'independent'. Much has also been written about the way in which forced removals of the earlier years of some 3.5 million people, has given way more recently to forced incorporation by redrawing boundaries and also of the loss of South African citizenship by 8 million homeland citizens. Suffice it to say at this point that the homeland system is in a state of disintegration in the face of mass rejection by the inhabitants of the homelands themselves who have wearied of the corrupt, inefficient and repressive administrations of these puppet structures. There is now a widespread call for the reincorporation of these territories into a unitary South Africa, with some of the homeland leaders now even supporting this call, while others continue to resist it.

Returning to the original question of whether apartheid is really being dismantled, it is clear that the laws that underpin apartheid remain on the statute book and are still being implemented. That they are under considerable attack is apparent and if any dismantling is taking place it is as a result of the struggles and resistance by the victims themselves making both the laws and structures of apartheid unworkable.

It should, however, be borne in mind that apartheid must not be examined simply in terms of its statutory provisions. Apartheid has infected the very heart of our country through a complex web of institutions and structures. It is going to take a major effort by the people of South Africa, supported by the international community, to reverse this.

3. Prospects for a negotiated settlement

In spite of the stubborn persistence of repression and of apartheid laws and structures, there can be no doubt that a spirit of change is in the air and that very real possibilities exist for a negotiating process to get under way. Why, after so many years of turning a deaf ear to the voice of black demands, is there now an apparent willingness on the part of the white minority regime to come to the negotiating table? Does that willingness stem from a change of heart? Or does it come from pressures which the regime is unable to resist? Two sources of intense pressure are easily discernible and undoubtedly account for the shift away from the deeply repressive 'total strategy' era dominated by the 'securocrats' towards an era of outreach determined by the politicians

The first, and more fundamental source of pressure, is the mass resistance of the majority population to apartheid, resistance which reached boiling point at the imposition of the tricameral parliament and black local authorities, resistance which has survived the intensely repressive years of State of Emergency, resistance which expressed itself through the mass hunger strike of detainees and the defiance campaign of 1989, resistance which simply won't take no for an answer.

The second source, which arose out of the first, is the isolation which descended upon the apartheid regime from the international community and in particular the deep economic crisis which resulted from that isolation. It is that economic crisis which needs to be understood if the new strategy of outreach which slowly began to emerge 2 years ago with the withdrawal from Angola, is to be seen in its proper context.

The declaration of the first State of Emergency on 21 July 1985 precipitated a crisis of confidence on the part of foreign investors and particularly foreign bankers who were exposed to the tune of 24 billion US dollars, most of it short term loans. Their anxiety turned to panic when the South African government unilaterally declared a moratorium or 'standstill' on foreign debt repayment shortly thereafter in an attempt to stem the flood of capital pouring out of the country. In spite of negotiating a series of 3 favourable foreign debt repayment agreements with creditor banks since 1986 (the most recent in October 1989), the South African government has had to watch the huge capital sum of 12 billion US dollars flow out of the country during the past 5 years, and faces the prospect of a similar net outflow of capital during the next 4 to 5 years as the world's bankers demand repayment of their existing loans and decline to consider making any new loans until they perceive political and economic stability in the country. In addition to repayment of foreign loans, a considerable proportion of the capital outflow to date has been due to a flight of capital on the part not only of foreign investors but also and more especially on the part of South African businessmen who have devised ways, both legal and illegal, of transferring their assets abroad.

Can the apartheid economy survive such a huge capital haemorrhage? Clearly it cannot. The foreign exchange which the capital outflow draws upon can only come from 2 sources, namely balance of payments surpluses or from foreign reserves. South Africa has since 1985 been forced to run its economy on the basis of a surplus on its balance of payments which means driving up exports (not an easy task in the face of trade sanctions) and driving down imports which, in turn, has a depressing effect on an economy highly dependant upon imported technology and capital equipment. Surpluses over the last 5 years totalled a little over 10 billion US dollars, somewhat short of the outflow of 12 billion dollars. The shortfall obviously had to come out of foreign reserves held by the South African Reserve Bank in the form of gold and foreign currency (some foreign currency is also held by commercial banks). Figures released by the South African Reserve Bank reflect a drop in the value of foreign reserves over the last 2 to 3 years from about $3 billion to around $2 billion. This latter figure represents about 6 weeks import cover, regarded as a dangerously low level. But the official figures mask the full story. It is known that the South African Reserve Bank has access to short term bridging loans, probably against the security of pledging future gold production which, if deducted from the declared reserves, would show the nett foreign reserves to be negative for much of the time. In international terms the South African economy is in fact bankrupt and living from hand to mouth.

Nor are future prospects any brighter. In spite of the massive foreign capital bleeding that has taken place over the last 5 years, there has only been an effective reduction in the foreign debt of about 4 billion dollars. The total debt still stands at 20 billion dollars, of which 8 to 9 billion fall due during the 4 year period of 1990 to 1993, in spite of the apparently easy terms of the Third Interim Debt Arrangement of October last. The major hump occurs in this year, 1990, with as much as 2.5 billion dollars falling due in the months of May and June alone. Add to this daunting prospect the fact that flight of capital (other than debt repayments) still continues, although at a lower level than the avalanche of 1985/6.

The looming economic crisis must long have dawned upon the apartheid government as incapable of solution by any means other than a political one. That realisation led them out of Angola, out of Namibia and in the direction of negotiations with those whom they had subjugated or persecuted for so many years. In shifting direction, the politicians within the government must have prevailed over the securocrats and convinced them of the absolute necessity, in the interests of their own survival, of abandoning the doctrine of 'total strategy' and of seeking political solutions. Whether the securocrats remain convinced and will stick to the agreement is now in some doubt with the security forces again reverting to type and acting with great force against peaceful protest marches and demonstrations. This ideological tussle has still to run its course. In the meantime, as

Balance of payments surplus	Foreign reserves (declared)
1985 – R5,9B ($2,4B)	May 1988 – R6,2B ($2,8B)
1986 – R7,2B ($2,9B)	May 1989 – R5,2B ($2,0B)
1987 – R6,1B ($2,4B)	May 1990 – R5,5B ($2,1B)
1988 – R2,9B ($1,1B)	
1989 – R4,1B ($1,6B)	(6 weeks import cover)

Capital outflow
1985–89 actual:
R30B ($12B)
1990–93 expected (minimum)
R21B ($8,4B)

Flight of capital	Foreign debt repayments
Withdrawal of foreign investment	Inside and outside standstill 'net'
Export of capital by South Africans	
(legal and illegal)	

Foreign debt
Aug 1985 –$24B (R61B)
Jan 1990 – $20B (R52B)
Reduction – $4B (R9B)

Repayment schedule
1990– $2.5B to $3B
1991/3– $6B
Balance –$11B

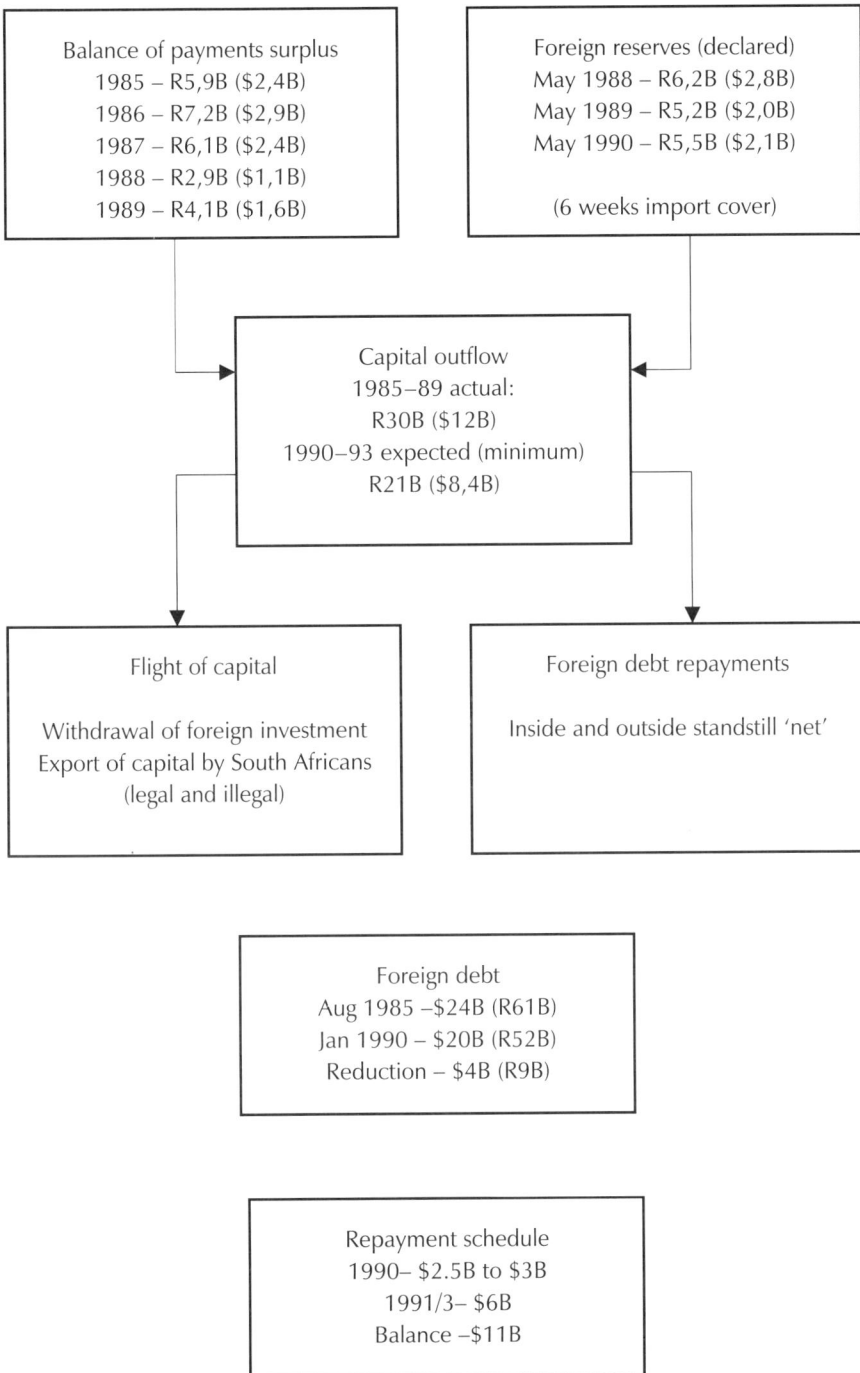

FIGURE 12
South Africa's foreign debt crisis

crunch point approaches, desperate efforts are being made by the government to gain international acceptance and in particular access to the international financial system.

As negotiation with the black majority becomes an imperative for the apartheid regime, what will the substance of the negotiations likely to be and, in particular, how is the regime likely to respond to the demands which are being made? Both the demands and a process are set out in the Harare Declaration drawn up and adopted by the OAU ad-hoc Committee on 21 August 1989 and widely endorsed both nationally and internationally. Strong support for the Harare Declaration was effectively given by the United Nations General Assembly which, at a Special Session on 14 December 1989, adopted by consensus a resolution entitled 'Declaration on apartheid and its destructive consequences in Southern Africa'.

The Harare Declaration, after enunciating some of the principles on which a democratic order in South Africa could be based, proposes a process for a political settlement which involves 4 distinct stages.

1. Creating a climate in which negotiations can take place. This involves the halting of repression and clearly the responsibility for this step lies with the government. The requirements are inseparable since it makes no sense to release political prisoners while continuing to hold political trials and generate new political prisoners. Nor can political trials be stopped without repealing the laws and measures which give rise to such trials.

2. Ceasefire talks between the 2 conflicting sides to achieve a suspension of hostilities.

3. Actual negotiations could now commence and these would address the principles and mechanisms for dismantling apartheid and for creating a new, democratic order.

'My next trick takes a little longer'

Dov Fedler, *The Star,* 1 December 1989

4. The transition process to be put into effect under the supervision of an interim administration and involving the holding of elections.

Only after the adoption of the new constitution does the Harare Declaration call for the lifting of sanctions by the international community. It says, in effect, that the pressures which were responsible for making negotiations a possibility should not be relaxed until their objective has been attained.

What of the apartheid government's responses to the demands for the lifting of political repression and the dismantling of apartheid? While there is undoubtedly a genuine commitment to change on the part of state president F.W. de Klerk and at least some of his government, is that change the same as the change demanded by the opponents of apartheid everywhere? So far, it seems that it is something substantially less which gives the uncomfortable feeling that a game is being played – a game to see how little can be given up while still securing a relaxation of pressure, both internal and international.

In the area of repression, the apartheid regime has very little room in which to manoeuvre, since without meeting very specific demands, negotiations will not even begin. The February 2 address to Parliament met the demands for the unbanning of organisations and people, temporarily suspended political executions and released a very limited number of political prisoners, but left all the other demands virtually untouched. However the Groote Schuur meeting between the government and the ANC on 2–4 May produced an agreement to address all of the remaining issues as a matter of urgency. So in the area of repression the signs are promising, but we must wait and see. Certainly, however, this is where the pressures are producing results.

In the area of apartheid laws and structures the situation is not so encouraging. The foundation stone of apartheid, the Population Registration Act, is in no immediate danger of being repealed, the argument being that it is central to the present constitution and can only disappear with the arrival of a new constitution. On the issue of the franchise, president De Klerk has very recently categorically rejected majority rule as an option, and his ministers still grope for phrases such as 'minority protection' to cover the entrenchment of group rights. Votes of equal value are talked about, but 2 parliamentary chambers are hinted at, with the upper chamber consisting of ethnic groups with power of veto. It is clear that any insistence by the regime on the question of group rights will bedevil the prospects for successful negotiations.

No direct response is forthcoming on the issue of the Land Act or the redistribution of land but on the issue of the Group Areas Act, president De Klerk stated on 19 April 1990 that it will be replaced 'possibly next year [by] something ... generally acceptable' to the 3 houses of parliament (which excludes the opinion of the black majority). The provision of state services and public amenities on racially discriminatory lines continues to crack under pressure such as authorising white hospitals to accept black patients because there is an over capacity of 11 000 beds in white hospitals and a shortage 7 000 beds in black hospitals. Henceforth, superintendents of these hospitals will decide whether or not to admit black patients to white hospitals. In this way the government is attempting to shift its responsibility. Insofar as government structures are concerned, the tricameral parliament, the black councils and the homelands administration are all being maintained in the face of fierce rejection but because of their unpopularity they are no longer being promoted with any enthusiasm. For example, the so-called self-governing homelands are no longer to be urged to take their 'independence'.

All in all, one is left with the impression that the apartheid government is moving forward under pressure but constantly looking for ways to maintain apartheid power under some new guise. Any let-up in pressure at this time would encourage that tendency.

PART C
THE ERA OF
DESTABILISATION
1990–1994

Introduction

The 1990s got off to a promising and auspicious start with the announcement in parliament on 2 February 1990 by the then state president F.W. de Klerk that all hitherto banned organisations were immediately unbanned and that further measures were being taken to set the stage for talks aimed at reaching a negotiated political settlement in South Africa. This dramatic announcement was followed a few days later, on 11 February, by the release of Nelson Mandela from prison after 27 years of incarceration. In the months that followed, further steps to lift repressive measures were taken, if somewhat hesitantly and grudgingly, and talks were indeed held, the first at Groote Schuur in Cape Town from 2 to 4 May and the second at Pretoria on 6 August. Each meeting produced minutes of agreement on the measures needed to arrive at a climate conducive to the commencement of substantive negotiations for a political settlement. Of particular significance in the Pretoria Minute was an agreement by the ANC to suspend the armed struggle as their contribution towards creating such a climate.

The ink on the Pretoria Minute was not yet dry before a wave of violence of unprecedented proportions emerged from the migrant workers hostels in the PWV (Gauteng) area to engulf the adjacent black townships. It took some time before a pattern could be discerned of an orchestrated campaign of destabilisation of the communities forming the support base of the liberation movement. Vigilantism became rampant, collusion by the security forces was thinly disguised and the hidden hand of hit squads was manifest by its results. Thus, at the very moment of the apparent capitulation of apartheid, South Africa was being cruelly plunged into a period of destabilisation from which it is yet to fully emerge. Destabilisation by whom? With what motives? These are the questions which are addressed in Part C of this book.

There follows, as with Parts A and B, a chronology of political events during this period. But in addition, for easy reference, there is a statistical summary and a graphical calendar (Fig. 13) which illustrate the levels of political violence and destabilisation during the period from July 1990 to April 1994, a period of 46 months.

The political calendar during the era of destabilisation

Date	Events	Deaths in political violence Highs*		Lows**	
1990					
July	Formation and launch of IFP Sebokeng massacre			July	144
August	Pretoria Accord. ANC suspension of armed struggle.	August September	709 369		
October	President de Klerk's first visit to Europe.			October	106
1991				January	140
February	ANC/IFP peace accord.	March	314	February	105
April	ANC threatens to withdraw from talks if the violence is not addressed.				
May	Mass protest regarding political prisoners, ongoing violence, education crisis, anti-Republic Day.	May	336		
June	Government sponsored conference on violence.			June	171
July	'Inkathagate' revelations.			July August	142 170
September	National Peace Accord signed.	September	316		
November	National anti-VAT strike.				
December	Convention for a Democratic South Africa (CODESA) talks begin.			December	167
1992				January	110
March	White referendum on negotiations (70% in favour of change).	March April	437 356		
May	CODESA II commences.				
June	Boipatong Massacre. ANC suspends talks with the Government and withdraws from CODESA	June July August	373 329 348		
September	Bisho Massacre. ANC/government Record of Understanding signed.	October	299	December	175

1993				January	175
				February	178
April	Multi-party talks resume. Chris Hani assassination/funeral.	May	343		
June	AWB invades World Trade Centre.				
July	Election date announced.	July	604		
		August	562		
		September	489		
		October	475		
		November	447		
December	Drafting of Interim Constitution completed.	December	404		
1994					
March	Bophuthatswana uprising. IFP march through Johannesburg.	March	552		
April	Right wing bombings. IFP enters elections. Elections.	April	487		
May	ANC victory. Mandela becomes president. Government of National Unity installed.				

* 300 deaths or more
** 180 deaths or less

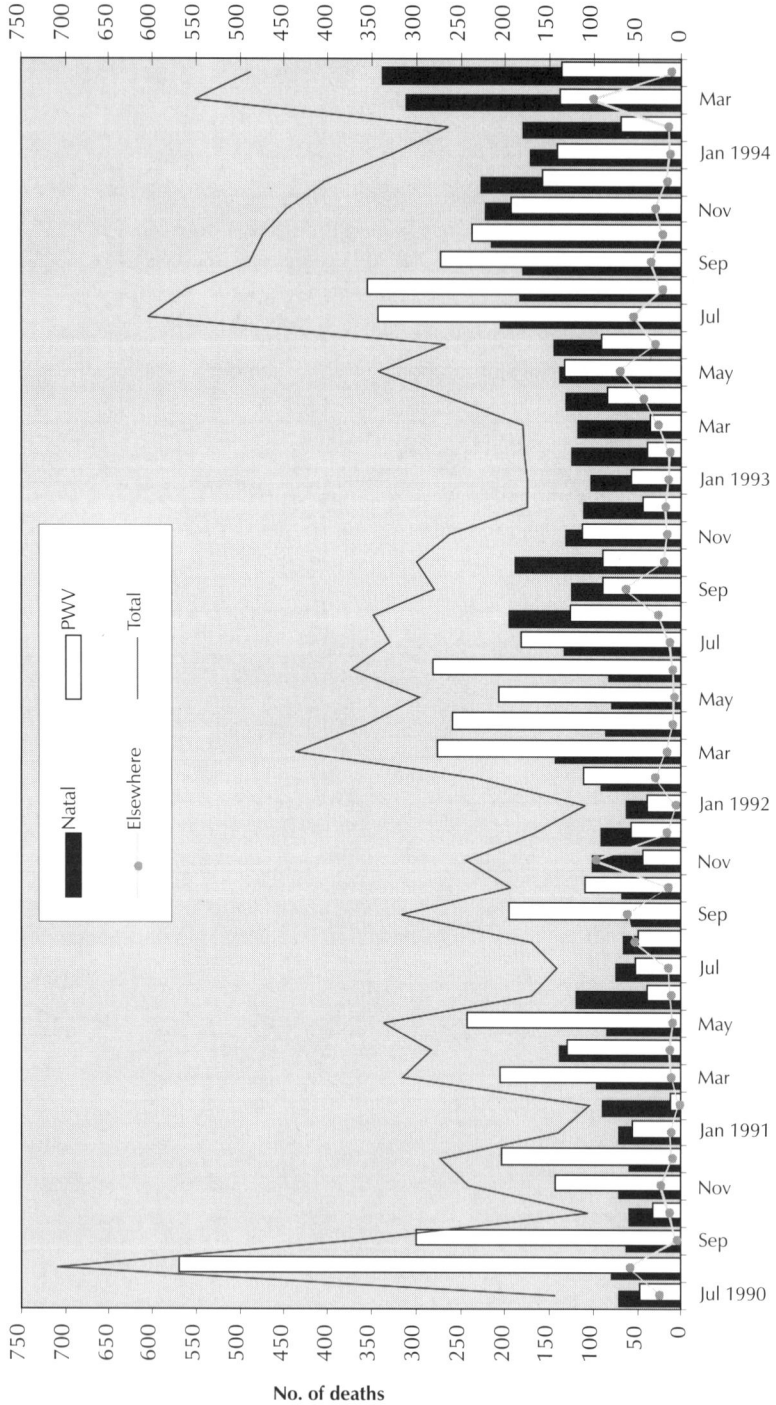

FIGURE 13
Deaths in political violence (July 1990–April 1994)

Destabilisation 1990–1994: a statistical summary

	July 1990 – June 1991	July 1991 – June 1992	July 1992 – June 1993	July 1993 – April 1994	Total	Monthly Average
National statistics						
Incident count	2 166	3 534	4 178	5 541	**15 419**	335
Death count	3 190	3 039	3 096	4 608	**13 933**	303
Injury count	6 855	5 033	5 085	5 257	**22 230**	483
Major massacres	36	15	12	28	**91**	2,0
Political arrests	8 211	8 725	9 137	3 310	**29 383**	639
Regional death statistics						
KwaZulu Natal	1 004	1 004	1 645	2 232	**5 885**	128
Gauteng (PWV)	1 982	1 688	1 086	2 047	**6 803**	148
Other regions	204	347	365	329	**1 245**	27
Sources of death						
General incidents	2 903	2 806	2 871	4 477	**13 057**	284
Security forces	238	114	166	83	**601**	13
Hit squads	28	96	49	nil	**173**	3.8
Right wing	21	23	10	48	**102**	2.2
Victims						
Train commuters	67	227	107	94	**495**	10.8
Bus & taxi commuters	55	119	84	130	**388**	8.4
Women	46	189	253	371	**859**	18.7
Children	56	106	58	209	**429**	9.3
Security force members		68	200	112	**380**	8.3
White civilians			34	33	**67**	1.5

8 A NEW TOTAL STRATEGY EMERGES   July 1990–June 1991

The unbanning of the liberation movements on 2 February presented them not only with their most important milestone to date in the struggle for liberation but also with an altogether new challenge, namely, how to begin their transformation from underground movements into open party political structures, organising their constituencies in a climate of free political activity. The creation of such a climate was what the talks at Groote Schuur and Pretoria were all about. With the apartheid government seemingly moving towards the removal of repressive measures during these talks it appeared as if apartheid power was capitulating and that a free political climate was around the corner. The explosion of violence which was to erupt in the Reef/Vaal complex within a few days of the signing of the Pretoria Minute on 6 August 1990, soon dispelled such notions. The hoped-for normalisation of free political activity did not materialise and the creation and organisation of party structures at branch and regional level had to give way to fire-fighting and emergency response to the slaughter of communities. In the year from July 1990 to June 1991, over 2000 violent incidents were to result in the loss of over 3000 lives and in the injury of nearly 7000.

The violence of that year was characterised by undisguised high-profile mass attacks by hostel dwellers from their hostel fortresses on township communities, particularly those in the Vaal/Reef complex – 34 major massacres were counted between July 1990 and June 1991. The complicity of the security forces in these actions became a matter of common knowledge.

Clearly, a new total strategy was emerging, a strategy of destabilisation and paralysis designed to strangle the growth of the liberation movements into fully fledged party organs.

The events and nature of this first year of destabilisation are described in the following publication from which this chapter is drawn:

The New Total Strategy (August 1991)

THE NEW TOTAL STRATEGY

twelve months of community repression, July 1990 – June 1991

HRC, August 1991

Introduction

Since July 1990, the Human Rights Commission has been monitoring the actions of 4 groups involved in the repression of township communities and has published its findings through the medium of monthly Area Repression Reports. A full year has now run its course, a critical year in terms of the explosion of violence that has taken place and the threat it imposes to peaceful negotiations. This report attempts to analyse the effects of the twelve months of repression on the community, to place in context the origins and purpose of that repression and to address the question of whether this repression is a key to a new and unfolding total strategy.

Part 1. Acts of repression

Security forces
Vigilantes
Hit squads
The right wing
Summary of the toll

Part 2. Haphazard or orchestrated?

Allegations of collusion
The new total strategy
Conclusion

Part 1. Acts of Repression

Security forces

By security forces we refer primarily to the South African Police (SAP) and the South African Defence Force (SADF) but include also such entities as municipal or council police and homelands police and army. In monitoring the actions of the security forces the HRC has become aware of 2 major effects. Firstly, death and injury caused to the community primarily in the course of breaking up demonstrations, protest marches and other gatherings declared as illegal under various laws such as the Internal Security Act. Secondly, the arrest and charging of persons for taking part in unlawful gatherings and, to a much lesser extent, for other political activities. In essence, these actions of the security forces are the state's response to popular mass protest action. We also briefly examine allegations of security force complicity in activities falling outside the parameters of the law.

Death and injuries

There was a total of 238 deaths recorded, an average of 20 per month. During the same period about 10 times that number of injuries were recorded but the ratio is probably much higher than that since many injuries go unreported.

Arrests

The powers of arrest as a response by the security forces to mass protest action are obvious from the figures. Over 8000 arrests were recorded during the period at an average monthly rate of 684.

Other security force actions

Apart from the 'legitimate' actions of the security forces as described above, the record abounds with allegations of unlawful actions perpetrated by the security forces during the 12-month period. Such unlawful actions run the full spectrum from acts of omission to acts of commission; from neglecting to act in performance of their proper and expected duties, to engaging in activities falling outside the law

Vigilantes

Vigilantism in the South African context is a phenomenon born directly out of the creation of apartheid-motivated structures of government and administration. The structures concerned are the homelands (both the 'independent' and 'self-governing' varieties) and the black urban councils. Both structures are strongly rejected by the vast majority of the black population and strong pressures have built up for their dismantling. In response to these pressures, private 'armies' of vigilantes were developed to support and defend these unpopular structures and came to receive the tacit and then the active encouragement of the state as an element which fitted in well with their 'total strategy' of the Emergency years. It was an element that helped to promote the image of 'black-on-black violence' at no political cost to the government.

Vigilante groups have been active at least since 1986 in many parts of the country, always in association with homeland governments and black councils. Their actions have been characterised by extreme violence calculated to bring terror and chaos into the local community and to disrupt normal life and organisation.

Loss of life has been extremely high. During the 12-month period monitored by HRC, the horrific total of 2640 vigilante-related deaths was recorded. This represents 83% of all politically related deaths for the period and illustrates how devastating the vigilante component is in relation to the overall violence directed at township communities. It should be pointed out that not all of the 2640 deaths were suffered by township dwellers. A certain proportion was inflicted on the attacking vigilante groups by way of defensive action, pre-emptive action or revenge killings. In many cases it has been impossible to identify the dead in terms of their political affiliation (or lack of it) but several monitors

167

estimate a preponderance of township victims of up to 90%. HRC has recorded all deaths attributable to a vigilante initiated situation as 'vigilante-related'. It must be emphasised that while elements associated with Inkatha bear the primary responsibility for the spread of vigilantism in Natal for the last 6 years or so and in the Transvaal over the last 12 months, the organisation of Inkatha itself cannot simply be characterised as a vigilante grouping given its long standing origins of a cultural organisation and its recent transformation into a political party.

Fig. 14 illustrates the month-by-month death toll wrought by vigilante-related actions, with political deaths from all sources shown for comparison. No attempt will be made here to catalogue the individual events and massacres which took place during this period; these have been recorded in the monthly HRC Area Repression Reports and elsewhere. But attention needs to be drawn to significant events which may have had a bearing on the pattern which has emerged. For example, the explosion of violence in August/September was preceded by the launch of Inkatha as a political party in July, and erupted in earnest within days of the ANC suspending the armed struggle on 6 August. Thereafter the pattern conveys the impression of a tap being turned off and on, off and on, and off again.

The trough in October coincides with the final lifting of the State of Emergency, at that time still in effect in Natal, and also with F.W. de Klerk's visit to Europe. The trough in January/February coincides with the opening of parliament and the peace accord reached between Inkatha and ANC on the 29 January, and the trough in June with the government-sponsored peace summit.

The on/off pattern of township killings comes even more sharply into focus if death statistics for the period are analysed per area. The tap-turning has taken place mainly in the PWV area (or more precisely, the Reef/Vaal complex). By contrast the picture in Natal shows a remarkable steadiness at an average of close to 100 deaths every month, confirming that the carnage there continues virtually uninfluenced by recent events in the rest of the country and has a momentum of its own.

The advent of vigilante violence into the Reef/Vaal complex from July 1990 seems to have been launched primarily from East Rand bases, with 61.4% of the area's deaths in the first 3 months. Soweto with 21.2% was not unscathed, nor was the Vaal with 8.0%.

Subsequently the target areas shifted, with the first vigilante-related death in Alexandra occurring in March, after being totally free of any such incidents for 8 months of the Reef township violence. Thereafter Alexandra became a prime target and also a sinister forerunner of a link-up between supporters of a black council and supporters of a homeland.

The general impression gained is that vigilante attacks in the Reef/Vaal complex are far from being haphazard or spontaneous. There is a distinct appearance of planning and control with the ability to move forces around the area and mount attacks at predetermined times.

Hit squads

Evidence for the existence of professionally organised and trained hit squads stretches back to the 1970s but it was only in the dying days of the 1980s that hard evidence came to

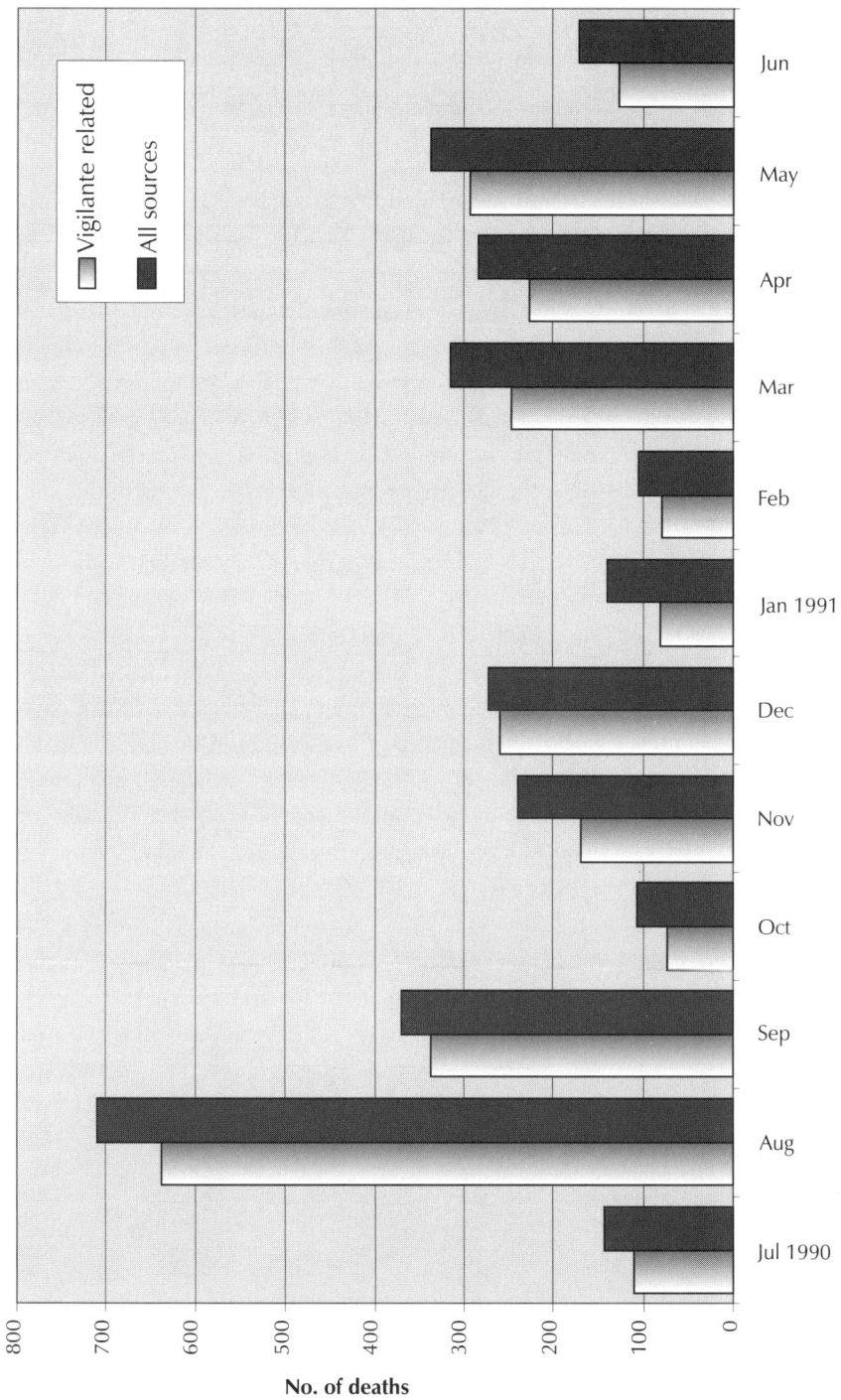

FIGURE 14
Deaths: vigilante-related and all sources

169

light to confirm what had been suspected for a long time, namely, that these hit squads were the creation of the state, located within, trained by, and financed by the state structures of the South African Defence Force, Police and National Intelligence Service. Before and during the States of Emergency, the state-based hit squads performed a designated role within the total strategy guided by the National Security Management System under the control of the State Security Council. Their activities encompassed South Africa, the Southern African Region and the world beyond. Numerous hit squad entities have been identified and exposed thus far and doubtless there are others yet to be exposed.

Hit squads are characterised by the clear possession of expertise in the use of weapons, explosives, chemicals, etc. and their ease of access to resources such as information, equipment, bases and funding. In contrast to the use by vigilante groups of widespread and indiscriminate terror to achieve their ends, hit squads are highly focussed in their objectives which are to eliminate or intimidate identified and designated political opponents and to cripple or disrupt targeted organisations. The record of the 12-month period July 1990 to June 1991 shows the manner in which these 2 specific objectives are currently being pursued by hit squads in their present role of contributing to the onslaught on township communities.

However, before analysing the method and effect of these strikes, it must be emphasised that this is not the whole story. It is not possible, for instance, to quantify the way in which hit squads have acted as provocateurs in sparking off conflict, exploiting sectional divisions and in supporting vigilante groups. Running through the records of township violence is a trail of references to the involvement of whites, sometimes with blackened faces, in situations which at first sight appear to be simply vigilante or even security force related but which on closer scrutiny reveal a hidden hand.

Hit squad actions against individuals
The ultimate neutralisation of the political opponents of apartheid lies in their assassination. Well over 100 political activists, both inside and outside the country, have suffered this fate at the hands of hit squads during the 1980s. Assassinations and attempted assassinations of this kind continue on almost a daily basis. During the 12-month period, HRC recorded the following:

- Assassinations   28
- Attempted assassinations   40
- Disappearances   1

In addition, the following actions, designed to intimidate, were recorded:
- Death threats against activists   14
- Abductions   6
- Harassment   5

Of the 94 targeted individuals listed above, 51 are or were members and office bearers of the ANC, 19 active in civic/residents associations and 10 trade unionists.

Hit squad actions against organisations
The other classical target of hit squads – anti-apartheid organisations – also continues to come under attack. For the 12-month period, HRC recorded the following:

- Attacks on buildings and offices   7
- Burglaries   3
- Smear campaigns   3

Of the 13 attacks, the ANC was the target6 times, and COSATU or its affiliates 5 times.

The right wing

The 'right wing' in the present South African context can be described as the residue of apartheid-supporting whites left over after the National Party and government opted for a reformist strategy. It consists of the Conservative Party and a proliferation of extra-parliamentary groups bitterly opposed to the abandonment of legalised apartheid and comprises about one third of the white population or about 5% of the total population. Within this residue there are militant elements, perhaps amounting to 1% or less of the total population, which are prepared to resort to violence to express their opposition. While some of this violence is directed at white groups supporting reform, the vast majority of actions are targeted on the black community.

In general there are 2 categories of right wing violence, the one involving semi-spontaneous and indiscriminate acts by individuals or small groups driven by emotional anger and the other organisationally based and involving planning and marshalling of resources.

During the 12-month period July 1990 to June 1991, HRC has compiled records of the militant right wing's involvement in 93 incidents, in the course of which they managed to bomb 14 targets, kill 24 people and injure a further 246. A wide range of targets have attracted the vitriolic attention of the right wing:

- political organisations, including NP, DP, ANC, SACP;
- workers, including trade unions;
- media, including newspapers, journalists, photographers;
- black users of amenities, including hospitals, parks, beaches, swimming pools, hotels, cinemas, shops;
- black 'invaders' of 'white' areas such as housing, schools, farms.

In addition, naked racial hatred and prejudice has been manifested in indiscriminate attacks of terror on individual blacks, railway stations, taxi-ranks and a synagogue.

Summary of the toll

The toll on the life of township communities over the 12-month period has been devastating. Over 3000 lives have been lost; nearly 7000 injuries have been recorded, but the real figure is certainly in excess of 10 000; no one can say how many are maimed for life; and over 8 000 have been arrested. In addition, tens of thousands have lost their homes and have become internal refugees.

Part 2. Haphazard or orchestrated?

Allegations of collusion

The records of the twelve months of Area Repression Reports abound with allegations of collusion between the 4 actors responsible for the unprecedented onslaught on township communities. Collusion between the security forces and vigilante groups, particularly elements of Inkatha, emerge with great frequency and in many different forms as outlined above. The latest revelations of police funding of Inkatha and its trade union wing UWUSA are added confirmation of the complicity which has long been suspected. Regarding hit squads, there must be very few who now doubt their existence or their organisational base within the security forces. Their highly focussed role of striking specific targets complements the broad terror role of vigilante groups but there are also frequent allegations of direct collusion in training, arming and supporting vigilante activities and even in sparking off or participating in incidents. Right wing activities can best be described as individualistic and opportunistic, although the possibilities of collusion with vigilante groups cannot be ruled out, and there is evidence of security force personnel in their individual capacities taking part in right wing actions and making use of security force resources.

The picture that emerges is that there is a high degree of co-ordination between the activities of the security forces, vigilantes and hit squads; a conclusion that has been drawn by many for some time now and a conclusion that is re-inforced almost daily as new revelations come to the surface. The patterns of township destabilisation, in terms of location, timing and methods, strongly indicate the existence of an orchestrated strategy, the origins and motivation for which must be sought inside South African government circles.

What may still be in question is the level at which orchestration is taking place but all indications are that a new total strategy has emerged from the ashes of the old total strategy of the P.W. Botha era. Why did the old fail and how does the new hope to succeed?

The new total strategy

The apartheid government now stands precariously poised between 2 divergent and probably irreconcilable threats to its future survival. On the one hand the threat of economic collapse and, on the other, the threat of the loss of power.

To avert the threat of economic collapse it is absolutely imperative for the government to break the stranglehold of isolation from the international financial system and to this end it has embarked upon a major diplomatic and propaganda offensive to create the impression that repression and the structures of apartheid have been dismantled, that sanctions (which 'never worked anyway') are crumbling on all sides and that South Africa is now a safe area into which to pour capital, either by way of loans or investment. However, the measures which have had to be taken in order to convey this impression, namely the withdrawal or modification of oppressive and apartheid legislation and measures, have raised the spectre of the second threat, the threat of the loss of power.

```
┌─────────────────┐         ┌─────────────────────┐         ┌─────────────────┐
│ Internal        │ ──────► │ Apartheid government│ ◄────── │ International   │
│ resistance      │         │ 1948–1984           │         │ rejection       │
└─────────────────┘         └─────────────────────┘         └─────────────────┘
                                      │
                                      ▼
┌─────────────────┐         ┌─────────────────────┐         ┌─────────────────┐
│ Liberation      │ ──────► │ Total strategy      │ ◄────── │ International   │
│ struggle        │         │ States of Emergency │         │ financial       │
│                 │         │ 1985–1990           │         │ isolation       │
└─────────────────┘         └─────────────────────┘         └─────────────────┘
                                      │
                                      ▼
                            ┌─────────────────────┐
                            │ Reform              │
                            │ 1989–1991           │
                            └─────────────────────┘
                                      │
┌─────────────────┐                   │              ┌─────────────────┐
│ Loss of power   │                   │              │ Economic collapse│
└─────────────────┘                   │              └─────────────────┘
                                      ▼
                            ┌─────────────────────┐
                            │ New total strategy  │
                            │ 1990–               │
                            │ Destabilisation/    │
                            │ negotiation         │
                            └─────────────────────┘
                                      │
                                      ▼
                            ┌─────────────────────┐
                            │ Christian democratic│
                            │ alliance            │
                            │ Elections           │
                            │ ?                   │
                            └─────────────────────┘
```

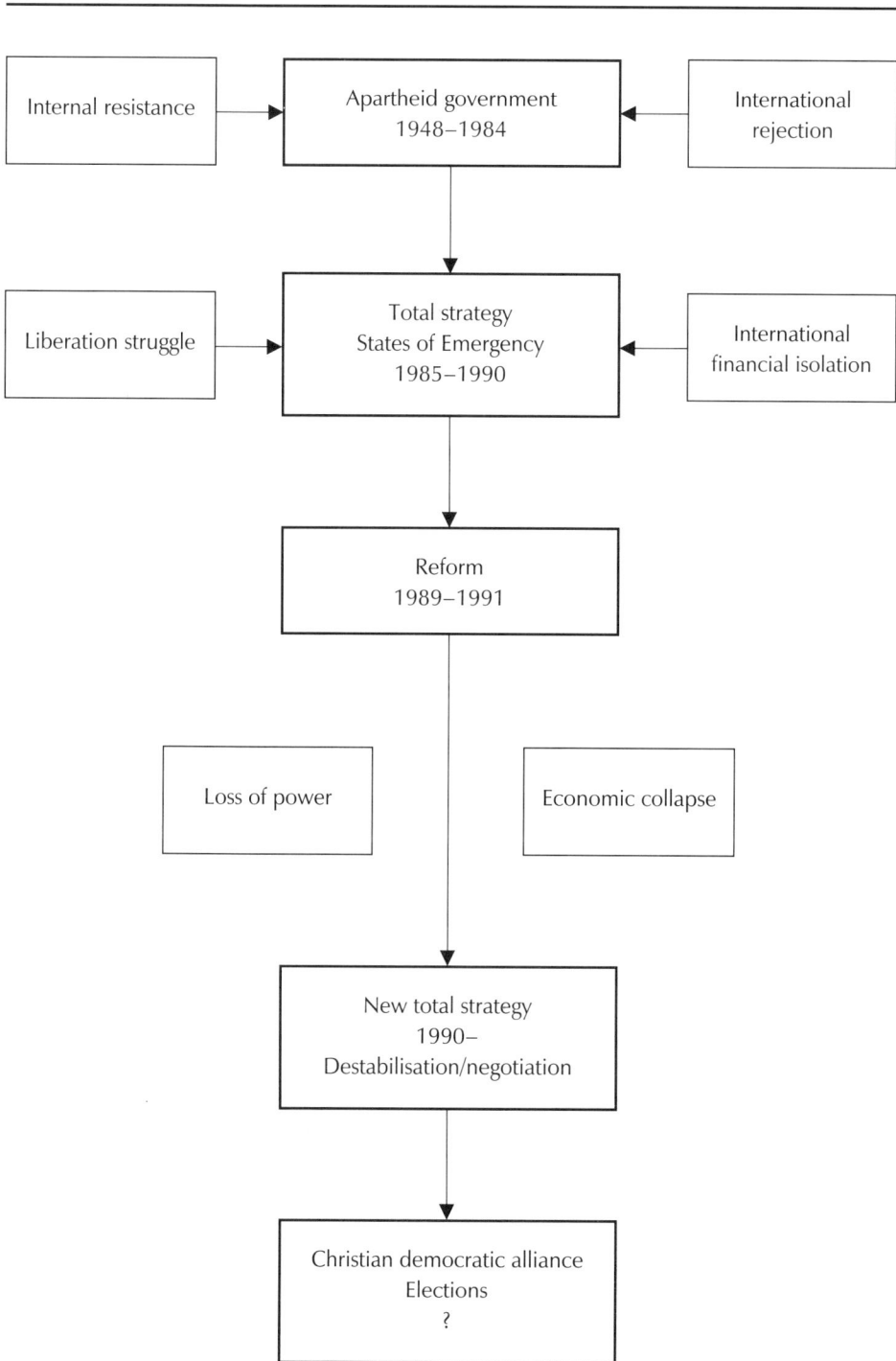

FIGURE 15
Evolution of Nationalist government strategy

In responding to the legitimate demands of the liberation movement, the government runs the risk of having to transfer power to the majority which, of course, is the essence of the creation of a democratic order in South Africa. As yet, there is no evidence whatsoever that there is a readiness on their part to do that, in fact, quite the contrary. Up to this point, there is overwhelming evidence to suggest that the government is addressing the threat of the loss of power by adopting a twin track strategy of negotiating and destabilising simultaneously.

The negotiating track includes, inter alia, a vigorous programme of attracting support for National Party policies from the white 'left', from 'moderate' and conservative elements within the black community (African, 'Coloured' and 'Indian') and forming alliances with any political, religious and business groupings which may be opposed to the ANC for their own particular reasons. Most of these constituencies have in one way or another been beneficiaries of the apartheid system and would have an interest in maintaining the status quo. Such a grouping is already being recognised by the label of the 'Christian Democratic Alliance' (CDA).

The destabilisation track involves a whole host of less legitimate activities focussed on township communities which has resulted in the loss of thousands of lives in the explosion of violence dating particularly from 6 August 1990 when the ANC announced its suspension of the armed struggle. The purpose of such destabilisation is to ensure the maximum disruption, disarray, disunion and fragmentation of the anti-apartheid camp.

The overall strategy of this twin track approach is designed to enhance the chances of the government winning an election (should an election be inevitable) and so averting the threat of the loss of power. Recent opinion polls show that the strategy has succeeded to some extent in that the level of support for the ANC has dropped to around 50% but the National Party is still unlikely to muster more than 20%, even in the event of an alliance with Inkatha who appear to be enjoying a support of no more than 4%. Furthermore, there is a high risk of the destabilisation tactic running out of control and having a negative effect on the efforts to re-establish the confidence of foreign investors and financiers.

In summary, a delicate and fragile balance exists between the inter-related threats to the apartheid government of economic collapse and loss of power. Withholding access to democracy could result in the former; granting access will lead to the latter.

Conclusion

It is clear that the Nationalist government is engaged in a war of survival, or to put it another way, a struggle to retain power. It is a war which dates back to 1948, when, upon its accession to power, it began to devise strategies to entrench that power for all time. Fig. 15 traces the evolution of the shift in strategy since that time in response to changing circumstances and pressures and helps to place today's strategy in context.

The strategy of grand apartheid occupied the years 1948 to 1984 with the development of the 'independent' and 'self-governing' homelands for the black rural population; the black local authorities for the black urban population; and the tricameral parliament, giving token representation to the 'Coloured' and Indian population but maintaining control in the hands of the whites. In spite of backing up these devices with repressive legislation and machinery, this strategy succeeded only in arousing the massive resistance of the disempowered majority and the rejection of the international community.

This reaction was so powerful that the Nationalist government was forced to shift into a different level of strategy, known as 'total strategy', tantamount to declaring war on the forces of resistance, and formalised in the declaration of a State of Emergency in 1985, continuing (with a minor interruption) until 1990. The simple objective of the strategy was to smash resistance and impose grand apartheid by maximum force.

Again the action produced an opposite reaction. Resistance stiffened and the liberation struggle intensified. The international financial system cut its links with South Africa. Total strategy turned into total disaster, and a new strategy became imperative in the interests of survival. The think-tank of the National Party, the secretive Broederbond organisation, is credited with analysing the probabilities of collapse and recommending the change in direction. So, the era of reform was born, becoming evident in 1989 with the unconditional release of Walter Sisulu and others and reaching a high point in February 1990 with the unbanning of organisations and the release of Nelson Mandela.

However, reform of itself, while designed to avert the threat of economic collapse, cannot ensure survival for the Nationalist government in terms of the retention of power and, in fact, as already mentioned, actually raises the spectre of the loss of power.

Thus, the strategy of reform must be supplemented by yet another level of strategy if the government is to walk the tight-rope between the twin threats of economic collapse and loss of power. That supplementary strategy we call the 'new total strategy'; total because it incorporates the use of all the forces at the government's command, including the state security forces, vigilantes and hit squads as described in this Special Report; total because it provides for simultaneous destabilising and undermining while engaging in negotiation. It is a strategy which has already been rehearsed in Namibia with some success and in violation of an agreement requiring the South African government to be an impartial administrator in the transition process. How then can they be trusted to administer South Africa's transition to democracy?

9 CHECKMATE FOR APARTHEID? July 1991–June 1992

In Chapter 8 we examined the emergence of a strategy of destabilisation alongside talks during the year from July 1990 to June 1991. It took the ANC up until April 1991 to fully recognise the tactic and to react to it by threatening to withdraw from all talks unless and until the government addressed the political violence. To emphasise the ultimatum, mass protest occurred throughout the country in May 1991.

The present chapter covers the second year of destabilisation (July 1991 to June 1992) which showed little abatement, if any, in the levels of violence but some shift in the patterns. Instead of the open massive forays from the hostels that characterised the first year, the violent events decreased in individual magnitude while increasing in frequency. For example, the number of incidents recorded went up by 63% for more or less the same number of deaths (over 3000 for each year) while the number of major massacres reduced from 34 to 15. This second year was also characterised by new and insidious forms of terrorising township communities, such as indiscriminate train attacks (accounting for 227 deaths) and attacks on busses and taxis (another 119 deaths). Assassination of political figures by unknown hit squads jumped from 28 to 96. But vigilantism remained the major source of political violence and even this was supplemented by alliances with notorious criminal gangs such as the Three Million Gang, the Black Cats and many others.

Mass protest, a national strike (November 1991) and international condemnation had the effect of forcing the Nationalist government into a national peace accord (September 1991) and the start of formal negotiations at CODESA I (December 1991) and CODESA II (May 1992). The second year of destabilisation, however, closed on a disastrous note, that of the appalling massacre in Boipatong (June 1992) which precipitated the withdrawal of the ANC from negotiations as an expression of their profound mistrust of the real intentions of the government. Nevertheless, it was a year in which apartheid power was beginning to run out of options and its continued survival was placed in question.

This chapter is based on the following appropriately titled special report: 'Checkmate for apartheid?' (August 1992)

Another feature of this particular document is its analysis of who the stakeholders are in apartheid power and what contribution they make to the 'third force' in their struggle to maintain and preserve that power.

CHECKMATE FOR APARTHEID?
A special report on two years of destabilisation July 1990–June 1992

HRC, August 1992

Part 1. The record of destabilisation
1.1 The toll of death and injury
1.2 The record of the security forces
1.3 The record of the vigilantes
1.4 The record of the hit squads
1.5 The record of the 'right wing'

Part 2. Destabilisation – the indictment
2.1 Centres of destabilisation
2.2 Acts of destabilisation

Part 3. Apartheid survival strategy
3.1 Structures and stakeholders of apartheid power
3.2 Threats to apartheid power
3.3 Evolution of apartheid survival
3.4 The chances of survival

Preface

South Africa has entered into the last stages of a struggle that may be likened to a hard-fought game of chess. On the one side it is a struggle for the survival of Apartheid Power, on the other a struggle by the majority population to emerge from the shadows and take its rightful place in the sun. At times, the movement of millions of people has been part of the play to arrange the pattern of the board to the liking of one of the players. At other times, pieces have disappeared from the board without trace or have been dealt with in many ways which are not to be found in any internationally accepted book of rules. While the game has essentially been fought on a black-and-white checkerboard pattern, growing numbers of white knights (and bishops) have joined the side of those struggling for liberation. Simultaneously some black pawns have allowed themselves to be co-opted onto the side of Apartheid Power in the hope that they might become kings, or at least continue to live in their castle. The game has gone badly for Apartheid Power, and in the last two years it has been fighting a bitter rearguard action in which thousands of black lives have been sacrificed. It is a play called Destabilisation. It was tried in Namibia and it failed. We believe it will fail here, and soon. Checkmate is nigh.

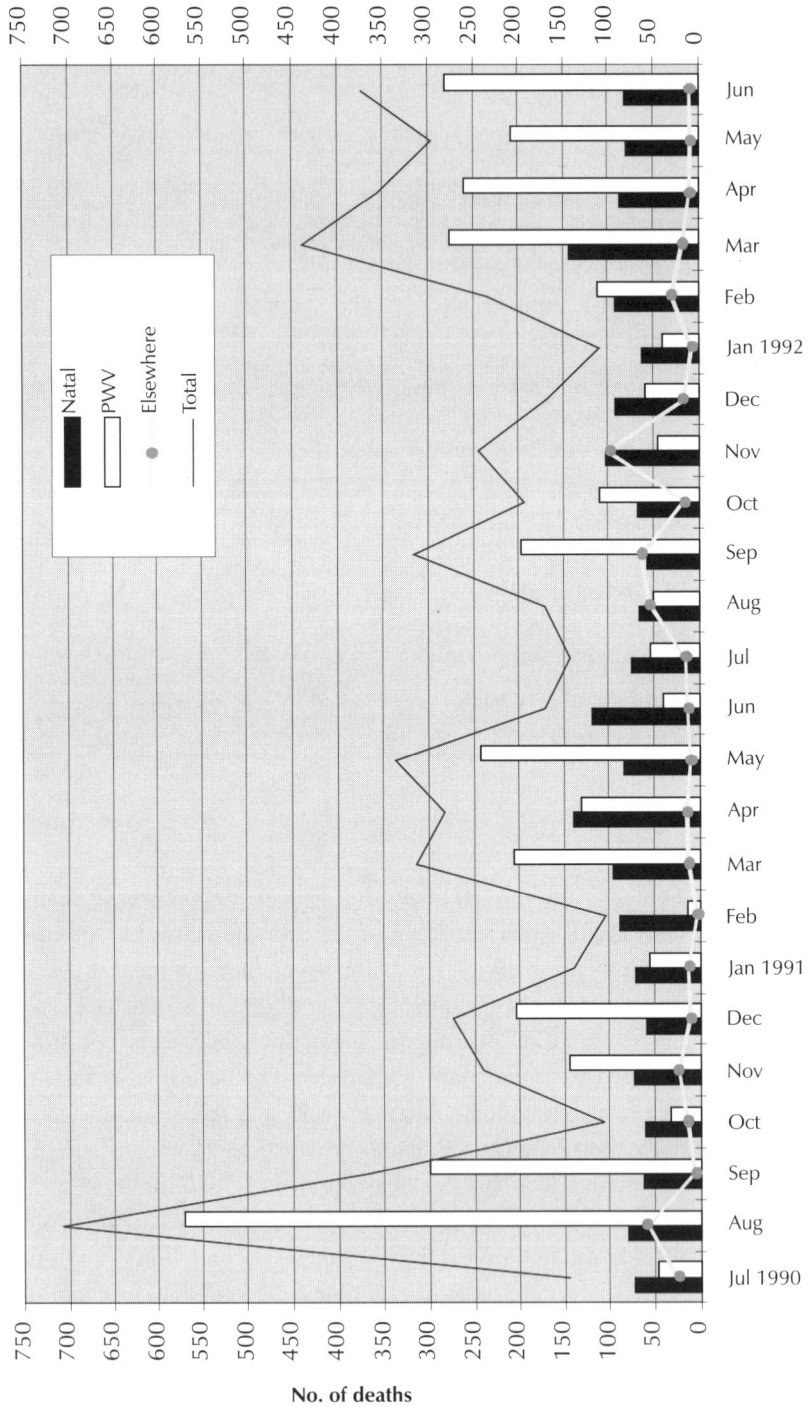

FIGURE 16
Politically related deaths

Part 1. The record of destabilisation

Introduction

The 2-year record of political violence contained in this report is drawn from 24 monthly issues of the HRC Area Repression Report, comprising the following:

- 2166 incidents from July 90 to June 91 (Year 1)
- 3534 incidents from July 91 to June 92 (Year 2)
- A total of 5700 incidents for the 2-year period.

1.1 The toll of death and injury

The death count

The month-by-month death count for the 2-year period is depicted in Fig. 16. Politically related deaths recorded by HRC amounted to a total of 6229 or an average of 260 per month or an average of 8.53 per day. Year 1 accounted for 3190 deaths while year 2 accounted for 3039 deaths, or a small reduction of 4.7%.

The early months of the period are highly significant. July 1990, although numerically a low month, signalled the start of the violence outside of Natal, particularly in the PWV region (Pretoria, Witwatersrand, Vaal) and coincided with the launch by Inkatha of a national political party, the Inkatha Freedom Party (IFP). August 1990 witnessed simultaneously the suspension of the armed struggle by the ANC in the Pretoria Minute of 6 August, and the full emergence of Inkatha onto the national stage from its previous base of Natal/KwaZulu. That month over 700 people died, 570 of them in the PWV alone; these are figures which have not been remotely approached since. However, in the last 4 months deaths have again reached horrifying levels, at an average of 366 per month, even more than the level of the 4-month period of August to November 1990.

The injury count

During the 2-year period, HRC recorded injuries inflicted on 11 888 persons. However, it is suspected that this is a very conservative figure, since many injuries would go unreported. Also it is impossible to assess how many of these injuries were so serious as to produce permanent disability.

Sources of the violence

The HRC discerns 4 sources of political violence which impacted on communities throughout the country during the 2-year period, namely:

1. Security force actions   352 deaths (5.7%)
2. Vigilante-related actions   5060 deaths (81.2%)
3. Hit squad attacks   126 deaths (2.0%)
4. Right wing attacks   44 deaths (0.7%)

In addition there were incidents responsible for 576 deaths (9.2%), around which there was insufficient information to determine a source; and a small number of definable actions not fitting into the above categories, responsible for 71 deaths (1.2%).

It is abundantly clear from the above statistics that vigilantism is by far the dominant factor in the carnage. It is no exaggeration to say that vigilantes have been the shock troops of community destabilisation.

Regional analysis of the violence

During the 2-year period the Natal region accounted for 32.2% of deaths, the PWV region for 58.9%, and the rest of the country combined for only 8.9%.

Natal region

The violence in Natal dates back to long before the present 2-year period. It has its origins in the rapid development of country-wide popular support for the Mass Democratic Movement (MDM) from 1984 onwards, a development which did not bypass Natal, and which was perceived by elements within Inkatha as a threat to Inkatha dominance in the region. That perceived threat intensified further when the ANC was unbanned in February 1990. Insofar as the current 2-year period is concerned, Fig. 16 shows that the month-by-month death count in Natal has been remarkably stable. In year 1, there were 1004 deaths and in year 2, there were 1004 deaths, producing a total for the period of 2008 deaths or an average of 84 per month.

PWV region

During the 2-year period, the PWV region recorded 3670 deaths or an average of 153 per month. By contrast with the pattern in Natal, the month-by-month death count in the PWV region shows very considerable fluctuation, from as low as 13 in February 1991, to as high as 570 in August 1990. Clearly it is the PWV region which is responsible for the on/off character of the overall monthly death count referred to previously.

Other regions

The fact that all other regions of South Africa outside of Natal and PWV account jointly for only 8,9% of all deaths, is an indication of the relative freedom of these areas from vigilantism and of the relative unity of the communities in these areas. There are, however, some exceptions:
- Vigilante groups sometimes with aligned criminal gangs were active in Eastern and Western Transvaal, often combining with police to oppose consumer boycotts, etc. or with mine security to attack mineworkers.
- Nearly half the deaths reported in the Western Cape were linked to the complex 'taxi-war'.
- The OFS region was plagued by the activities of a vigilante grouping known as the 'Three Million Gang'.

Major massacres

Amongst the 5700 incidents monitored by the HRC over the last 2 years, there were 49 incidents in which 10 or more people died and which the HRC has classified as major massacres. The first massacre occurred on 22 July 1990, at Sebokeng in the Vaal, around the launch of the Inkatha Freedom Party in the area and can be said to be the event which opened the floodgates of violence in the PWV region. The latest massacre on the list was the infamous Boipatong massacre of June 1992, which occurred but a few kilometres away from the first.

The 49 massacres accounted for 1250 lives, or 25 deaths per massacre on average. In 15 cases the death toll was higher than 25. Natal accounted for 11 massacres costing the lives of 167 persons while the PWV accounted for 38 massacres costing the lives of 1083 persons.

The victims of the violence

First and foremost amongst the victims of the violence that has swept the country have been the ordinary residents of black townships. White communities have physically been virtually untouched, and were it not for their newspapers, radio and TV screens they would hardly be aware that their black neighbours have been dying at the rate of over 250 per month for the last 2 years. Some of the violence has been targeted at specific groups or individuals active in the political arena but more and more of the violence seems to be totally random and indiscriminate with the only possible motive being to cause alarm, despondency and terror as a destabilising tactic. This is designed to discourage involvement in political activity. Some typical victims in both categories are analysed below.

Commuters

Commuters travelling on trains, buses and taxis have been coming under increasing attack and are daily being exposed to the danger of losing their lives while simply travelling to and from their places of work.

Train attacks in particular are taking a terrible toll of deaths and injuries during attacks in stations, on trains and being thrown from trains. The record of deaths and injuries in train attacks is as follows:

- Year 1   67 deaths and 284 injuries in 16 incidents.
- Year 2   227 deaths and 566 injuries in 230 incidents.
- Total   295 deaths and 850 injuries in 246 incidents.

In the second half of year 2, train attacks accounted for over 10% of all deaths, an indication of urban terrorism of a special kind. One particular train attack ranks as a major massacre. This was the incident starting at Jeppe Station in Johannesburg on 13 September 1990 which resulted in the slaughter of 21 passengers.

Bus and taxi attacks have appeared as a new form of terrorism supplementing the attacks on trains. In year 2, there were 27 attacks on buses, killing 53 and injuring 126; and 45 attacks on taxis, killing 66 and injuring 104.

In summary, 346 commuters died during year 2, representing 11.4% of all victims.

Women and children

Given the random and indiscriminate nature of many of the attacks on the community, it is not surprising that women and children should figure amongst the casualties. Whilst some of them may be ascribed to 'cross-fire' situations, there is no doubt that many have been deliberate and in cold blood. The records for year 2 show the following:

- Women   189 deaths and 227 injuries.
- Children   106 deaths and 87 injuries.
- Total   295 deaths during year 2 (close on 10% of all deaths).

In the Boipatong massacre, 25 out of 46 deaths were women and children.

Township communities

In reviewing the records of deaths and injuries within township communities, it is possible to determine from the reports the affiliation or location in the community of 50% of the victims. For the rest there is insufficient information to identify the victims. Within the identified victims, the records show the following for year 2:

- IFP/Inkatha members, supporters and occupants of Inkatha controlled hostels
  Deaths – 234
  Injuries – 306
- ANC members and identified supporters
  Deaths – 274
  Injuries – 310
- Township residents
  Deaths – 979
  Injuries – 1165

Thus, IFP victims account for 15.7% of the dead and 17.2% of the injured, while ANC and residents account for 84.3% of the dead and 82.8% of the injured.

Within the list of 49 major massacres over the 2 years, ANC and residents were the victims in 40 massacres, IFP supporters in 3 massacres, while in 6 massacres it was not possible to determine which party was the victim and which the attacker.

Security force members

In recent months, members of the security forces have increasingly fallen victim to political violence. During year 2, HRC recorded the following casualties incurred by the South African Police (SAP): 65 dead and 175 injured in 197 incidents. Figures recently released by the minister of law and order claim a higher figure of 97 deaths since January 1992. In addition, HRC recorded casualties incurred by the South African Defence Force (SADF) as follows: 3 dead and 104 injured in 8 incidents.

1.2 The record of the security forces

The security forces of the apartheid state include the South African Police (SAP), South African Defence Force (SADF), homelands police such as the KwaZulu Police (KZP), homelands armies, municipal and council police and other parastatal law enforcement entities.

Actions by the security forces which impact upon township communities are of 2 general kinds:

1. Actions which have the force of law under security and related legislation which apart

from providing powers of arrest also provide for the use of force that may lead to injury and even death.

2. Actions which fall outside of the law.

Incidents
Incidents involving overt actions by security forces were recorded by HRC as follows:
- Year 1 – 881
- Year 2 – 909
- Total – 1790 incidents

This represents 31.4% of all incidents recorded and is a high level of involvement.

Deaths and injuries
Deaths attributable to the security forces over the 2-year period, are as follows:
- Year 1 – 238
- Year 2 – 114
- Total – 352 deaths

The marked decrease in deaths in year 2 is indicative of the pressures put upon the security forces by public and even judicial criticism of their heavy handed approach to mass protest and demonstrations.

Injuries inflicted by the security forces show a similar pattern:
- Year 1 – 2248
- Year 2 – 1033
- Total – 3281 injuries

However, it should be noted that the level of injuries is extremely high, with the security forces accounting for 27.6% of all injuries, against 5.7% of all deaths.

The security forces have been directly responsible for, or directly involved in a number of massacres:
- SAP for the deaths of 12 in Daveyton on 24 March 1991
- SADF for the deaths of 11 in Sebokeng on 4 September 1990
- SADF for the deaths of 12 in Esikhaweni on 11 April 1992
- KZP for the deaths of 18 in Umlazi on 13 March 1992

Arrests
Arrests made by the security forces are a good barometer of the state's response to political resistance in the form of mass action of all kinds, such as protest marches, demonstrations, industrial action, boycotts, etc. Arrests are of course a precursor to the use of the courts to curb political activity, and are an expression of repressive legislation. The very extensive use made of the powers of arrest during the last 2 years can be seen by the following statistics:
- Year 1 – 8211
- Year 2 – 8725
- Total – 16 936 arrests

Unlike deaths and injuries, arrests by the security forces are on the increase, and are likely to accelerate further in the present climate of mass action. Over half the recorded arrests during year 2 were attributable to security force intervention in civic, labour, political and educational protest.

Unlawful actions

Apart from the 'legitimate' actions of the security forces as described above, the record abounds with allegations of unlawful actions perpetrated by the security forces during the 2-year period. Such unlawful actions run the full spectrum from acts of omission to acts of commission; from neglecting to act in performance of their proper and expected duties, to engaging in activities falling outside the law. Most of these alleged acts relate to security force involvement and complicity in vigilante attacks on township communities and are discussed in Part 2 of this report.

Foreign mercenaries

The 'dogs of war' which South Africa has inherited from the disintegration of colonial Southern Africa, including the Selous Scouts of Rhodesia, Koevoet of Namibia and elements of RENAMO and UNITA from Mozambique and Angola respectively, have in many cases found their way into the security forces to be formed into 'special' units such as the 32 Battalion. They have been used extensively in township patrolling, in spite of the fact that their training for lethal warfare makes them totally unsuited to a peace-keeping task. In this context their role is highly suspect.

1.3 The record of vigilantes

Vigilantism in the South African context arose directly out of the formation of homelands administrations and black local councils as essential components of the grand design of apartheid. Those willing to participate in these puppet structures found themselves isolated from the vast majority of the black communities in which they were located. In order to defend their vested interests against the hostile rejection of their undemocratic authority, they formed private 'armies' of vigilantes drawn from traditional and conservative elements, from the unemployed and even from criminal gangs. This development is known to have received tacit, and then active, encouragement of the apartheid state as an essential component of the total strategy of the Emergency years which served also to promote the image of 'black-on-black violence' at no political cost to the government.

Vigilante groups started making their appearance in several parts of the country in the mid-1980s, the most prominent and sustained of these groups being elements, primarily 'war-lords', from within Inkatha. Inkatha-supporting vigilantes bear the prime responsibility for the spread of vigilantism in Natal during the 1980s and in the Transvaal during the 1990s.

The initial targets of vigilantes have been community structures, organisations and individuals that were vocal or active in calling for the dismantling of homelands and black councils; but subsequently, during the general destabilisation period of the last 2 years, the targets have become much less selective and tactics have switched to indiscriminate terrorising of township communities.

Incidents

Incidents involving vigilante-related actions were recorded by HRC as follows:

- Year 1 – 884
- Year 2 – 1898
- Total – 2782 incidents

These figures indicate a strong upward trend in vigilante-related activity.

It must be noted that in reporting vigilante-related actions, the HRC includes not only attacks by vigilante groupings, but also retaliatory or pre-emptive measures taken by the affected community in a vigilante-initiated situation.

Deaths and injuries

Deaths attributable to vigilante-related actions were recorded as follows:

- Year 1 – 2640
- Year 2 – 2420
- Total – 5060 deaths

This represents 81.2% of deaths from all sources for the period and emphasises the pre-eminent role of vigilantism in the political death toll, and of vigilantes as the shock troops of destabilisation.

Injuries attributable to vigilante-related actions were recorded as follows:

- Year 1 – 4077
- Year 2 – 3186
- Total – 7263 injuries

The total represents 61.1% of injuries from all sources.

1.4 The record of hit squads

Evidence of the existence of professionally organised and trained hit squads stretches back to the 1970s, but it was only in the dying days of the 1980s that hard evidence came to light to confirm what had been suspected for a long time, namely, that these hit squads were the creation of the state, located within, trained by and financed by the state structures of the South African Defence Force, Police and National Intelligence Service. Before and during the States of Emergency, the state-based hit squads performed a designated role within the total strategy guided by the National Security Management System under the control of the State Security Council. Their activities encompassed South Africa, the Southern Africa region and the world beyond. Numerous hit squad entities have been identified and exposed thus far and doubtless there are others still to come. What is certain, however, is that the activities of organised hit squads continue to this day, in whatever modified or assumed form.

Hit squads are characterised by the clear possession of expertise in the use of weapons, explosives, chemicals, etc. and their ease of access to resources such as information, equipment, bases and funding. In contrast to the use by vigilante groups of widespread and indiscriminate terror to achieve their ends, hit squads are highly focussed in their objectives, which are to eliminate identified and designated political opponents, and to cripple or disrupt targeted organisations.

The record of the 2-year period July 1990 to June 1992 shows the manner in which these 2 specific objectives are currently being pursued by hit squads in their present role of contributing to the onslaught on township communities.

Incidents
Incidents involving hit squad actions were recorded by HRC as follows:
- Year 1 – 99
- Year 2 – 126
- Total – 225 incidents

Deaths and injuries
Deaths attributable to hit squad strikes were recorded as follows:
- Year 1 – 28
- Year 2 – 96
- Total – 124 deaths

Most of the deaths are, in effect, successful assassinations, whilst the rest of the deaths are family members, friends or associates caught in the firing line. It is clear that the trend is drastically upwards.

Victims
Over 100 of the victims listed of hit squads over the past 2 years are clearly identifiable as belonging to the anti-apartheid camp. Of these, 87 were officials, members or supporters of the ANC and its related organisations, 9 were members of civic associations, 4 were trade unionists, 5 were members of the PAC. Eleven victims belonged to the IFP.

In addition a disturbing new trend is the assassination of witnesses and of participants in peace accord structures. Within the list are to be found 6 witnesses (or their relatives) who were assassinated before they could give evidence; and at least two persons who were active in dispute resolution committees.

Finally, note should be taken of the practically non-existent record of success in solving these murders and bringing the perpetrators to book.

1.5 The record of the 'right wing'

The 'right wing' in the present South African context can be described as the residue of apartheid supporting whites left over after the National Party and government opted for a reformist strategy. It consists of the Conservative Party and a proliferation of extra-parliamentary groups bitterly opposed to the abandonment of legalised apartheid and comprises about one third of the white population or about 5% of the total population.

Within this residue there are militant elements, perhaps amounting to 1% or less of the total population, which are prepared to resort to violence to express their opposition. While some of this violence is directed at white groups supporting reform, the vast majority of actions are targeted on the black community and for that reason are included in this report.

In general there are 2 categories of right wing violence, the one involving semi-spontaneous and indiscriminate acts by individuals or small groups driven by emotional anger; the other organisationally based and involving planning and marshalling of resources.

Incidents

Incidents involving right wing actions were recorded by the HRC as follows:
• Year 1 – 93
• Year 2 – 114
• Total – 207 incidents

Such incidents include the bombing of buildings and attacks on people.

Deaths and injuries

Deaths attributable to right wing attacks were recorded as follows:
• Year 1 – 21
• Year 2 – 23
• Total – 44 deaths

Injuries were as follows:
• Year 1 – 246
• Year 2 – 101
• Total – 347 injuries

This represents a high injury rate relative to the number of deaths.

Prosecution of perpetrators

An extraordinary feature of right wing attacks has been the diligence with which the state has investigated them and the extremely high rate of success it has had in making arrests and obtaining convictions. What the reasons are for this outstanding display of political will is not clear but what is clear is that the capacity and ability exists for the solution of crimes of political violence.

Part 2. Destabilisation – the indictment

There are 2 centres of power in South Africa that both have a common interest, each for their own reason, in ensuring that the liberation struggle does not succeed in reaching its objectives. The one is the Nationalist government with its extensive security establishment, the other is the KwaZulu homeland. Both have over the years spawned mechanisms of destabilising the liberation struggle because it represents a threat to their ambitions, and this identity of interests has taken them along parallel, if separate, paths.

2.1 Centres of destabilisation

Nationalist government

The Nationalist government cannot be considered apart from its security establishment, since it has the full authority for its control through the relevant departments and ministers and for determining overall policy through the State Security Council and the former National Security Management System (now called the National Co-ordinating Mechanism); it must also accept ultimate responsibility for any actions undertaken by the security forces.

The government is also responsible for the security and related legislation which determines the parameters within which the security forces are able to operate at an overt level. Furthermore, it provides the funds for their operations and this would include the very considerable funds for secret operations not open to parliamentary or public scrutiny. Government cannot distance itself from involvement in destabilisation tactics carried out by their security forces.

It should also be pointed out that the government has a long history of practising destabilisation of its neighbours in the Southern African region by methods ranging from armed intervention through full-scale invasion, commando raids, abductions and assassinations, to the creation and support of surrogate forces, to the use of political and economic pressures designed to create dependency on South Africa. The heavy interference in the process towards Namibia's independence by promoting the Democratic Turnhalle Alliance and emasculating of SWAPO, was a precursor, a rehearsal, of what was to come when the Nationalist government was to turn its expertise in destabilisation inwards on its own population.

The Security establishment

While nominally under the control of the government and its cabinet, the security establishment is widely perceived as a force within a force, with waxing and waning fortunes. During the total strategy era spanning the States of Emergency, its star was in the ascendancy and the State Security Council was the body which effectively ran the country, completely overshadowing parliament and even the cabinet. After economic collapse began threatening about the time of military defeats in Angola in early 1988, the securocrats were obliged to agree to a shift in strategy and found themselves taking a back seat while the withdrawal from Angola and Namibia was being completed. The unbanning of their former enemies and the commencement of talks in early 1990 was a bitter pill to swallow but probably viewed by them as necessary measures to be followed in due course by others.

The considerable involvement by the security establishment in the destabilisation of the last 2 years raises the question as to whether it was doing the bidding of the Nationalist government along the lines of a carefully orchestrated plan, or whether it has been the prime-mover in the process and has been dragging a more or less passive government behind it, or even running away with the process. Regardless of the answer, final accountability rests with the government.

The security establishment has 3 component parts: South African Police (SAP), South African Defence Force (SADF) and National Intelligence Service (NIS).

South African Police (SAP)

Overt units of the SAP include the normal uniformed police attached to police stations around the country; the Internal Stability Units (ISU) formerly known as the 'Riot Police' and generally wearing camouflage uniform; and the Crime Intelligence Service (CIS) incorporating the security police.

Covert units uncovered so far include the 'counter-insurgency' section C1 based at security police headquarters in Pretoria and operating from bases such as 'Vlakplaas' and 'Daisy'. These were exposed by 'Askari' Almond Nofomela and commander Captain Dirk Coetzee in late 1989 as having a long involvement in political assassinations. More recently, a national network of covert structures was admitted to by the SAP after the discovery by the *Weekly Mail* in May 1992 of such a structure operating in the Vaal Triangle, involving the targeting of political activists.

South African Defence Force (SADF)

Overt units of the SADF, apart from the conventional forces, include special forces such as Reconnaissance Regiments 1,2,4, and 5, and Battalions 31 and 32 all of which perform roles beyond purely military matters. They also include Military Intelligence (MI) with a strong reputation for playing a political role.

Covert units of the SADF are also only acknowledged by the authorities as and when they are exposed. The existence of the complex network of the Civil Co-operation Bureau (CCB) was only revealed in late 1989 after being in existence for several years and its 'disbanding' in August 1990 was unconvincing. Numerous activities involving assassinations, abduction, arson, etc. by the CCB have been alleged or revealed prior to and during the Harms Commission of Inquiry. A more recent exposé has been that of the 'Hammer' units which have operated in the Eastern Cape and in the Witwatersrand. One such unit has been implicated in the assassinations of the Cradock Four in 1985. In addition, numerous front organisations posing as private companies have been exposed by the *Weekly Mail* as operating in conjunction with Military Intelligence.

National Intelligence Service (NIS)

The NIS is seen as the strategising wing of the security establishment but little is known of its operational role in the destabilisation of the liberation movement.

The KwaZulu homeland

Ever since its establishment in 1970, the KwaZulu homeland has exercised a destabilising influence on the course of the liberation struggle. Besides contributing to the division of the country along with the other homelands, an animosity towards the democratic movement (which gathered strength in 1984 around resistance to the tricameral parliament) was allowed and encouraged to develop within Natal. A territorial war for political influence ensued which continues to this day. It is a war which spilled over onto the national stage in July 1990, a few months after the unbanning of the liberation movements which raised longer-term threats to the continued existence of the KwaZulu power base.

Inkatha-supporting vigilantes

An extremely powerful culture of vigilantism, strongly opposed to progressive thought and activism particularly on the part of the youth, emerged as a reactionary force against the growth of the democratic movement in Natal during the 1980s. One of the earliest manifestations of this vigilantism was the 'lesson' inflicted on the students of the University of Zululand on 29 October 1983 when an impi of 500 Inkatha-supporting vigilantes descended on the University at Ngoye, killing 5 and injuring many more because of their intended boycott of an Inkatha rally. Similar vigilante groupings formed around influential warlords rooted in conservative traditionalism emerged in many parts of KwaZulu/Natal, and constituted the foot-soldiers of the war against the encroachment of the democratic movement that swept the rest of the country from 1984 onwards. They were to become the shock troops in the destabilisation of the liberation movements after their unbanning in February 1990 but now their field of operation extended beyond KwaZulu to encompass many parts of the country, in particular the Witwatersrand/Vaal area.

KwaZulu Police (KZP)

Although properly part of the security establishment, the KZP serves 2 masters. Since its establishment in 1980, it has continued to inherit more and more police stations and areas of jurisdiction from the SAP and its current commissioner is General Buchner, seconded from the SAP in November 1987. At the same time it has fallen under Inkatha control from which it is now virtually indistinguishable, especially in terms of allegiance. The KZP role in destabilisation is restricted to the KwaZulu area.

Hit squads

Strictly speaking it is unnecessary to distinguish hit squads as another centre of destabilisation as their existence has already been noted within the ranks of security force structures. This location has long been suspected and now been given ample confirmation by the revelations which began spilling out in November 1989. These revelations are now almost a daily occurrence. Nevertheless, it is important to recognise that more or less professional hit squads have emerged quite recently from backgrounds outside of the security forces but possibly with training and resources originating from within the security forces in some cases. These include vigilante-based hit squads, freelance hit squads and right wing hit squads.

Vigilante-based hit squads

A current trend in vigilante activity is generally away from large-scale swoops, towards small group, highly lethal, shock attacks in trains, taverns, night vigils, buses and homes. Such attacks indicate the existence of well trained, well-resourced squads which have had a remarkable record of making their getaway and concealing their identity.

Freelance hit squads

There are undoubtedly some criminal or mercenary hit squads in circulation whose services are for hire. What is less certain is who would avail themselves of, and pay for, such services.

Right wing hit squads

There is ample evidence that hit squads formed within the ranks of the right wing have been active. However, these have seldom shown a high level of professionalism and have in any event not in general been directed towards consciously destabilising the liberation struggle. One possible exception was the parcel bomb killing of computer consultant and ANC supporter Nicholas Cruse on 2 October 1990 by 3 members of Orde Boerevolk who, however, claimed that the SAP was implicated.

2.2 Acts of destabilisation

Role of the Nationalist government

The role of the Nationalist government in destabilisation has been one of failure, omission and neglect. First and foremost, it has failed to use its security forces to put a stop to the violence, something they have the duty and the capacity to do. In particular, it has neglected to secure hostels against their use as launchpads for violence, in spite of undertakings to do so and in spite of recommendations by the Goldstone Commission. Similarly, it has failed to secure trains against attacks and only after the deaths of nearly 300 victims and a train boycott, are the authorities beginning to take their first hesitant steps towards securing the rail transit system.

The government has vacillated on the issue of carrying dangerous weapons in public, including 'traditional' weapons. At first, in August 1990 the laws relating to traditional weapons were actually relaxed. Subsequently under pressure, the Dangerous Weapons Act was amended but is often not enforced. The present unclear position is that a ban on the carrying of all weapons is only in effect in unrest areas (of which there are none in Natal, where such a ban is most needed). All this despite the highly increased potential for violence which accompanies the carrying of traditional weapons in public and despite the recommendations of the Goldstone Commission 'that the carrying of any dangerous weapons in public should be outlawed – whether in respect of political meetings or at any other place.'

Another area of neglect is the failure to take meaningful steps towards transforming the security forces from an army of internal occupation with a war psychosis into structures which are accountable to the communities they are supposed to serve; or in the words of the Goldstone Commission 'transforming the police force into a body that has the confidence, respect and co-operation of the vast majority of the people of South Africa'.

The retention and continued use of repressive legislation such as the Internal Security Act and Public Safety Act is a serious omission; the declaration of unrest areas serves little purpose other than to antagonise township residents and add to their insecurity. One of the causes of violence ascribed by the Goldstone Commission is 'a history over some years of State complicity in undercover activities which include criminal conduct'. Failure to reveal and halt this activity is another serious omission.

The continued use of foreign mercenaries within the ranks of the security forces is another area of neglect. Such units (e.g. 32 Battalion, Koevoet, etc.) should have been disbanded long ago and their members returned to their country of origin or, at the very least, confined to barracks pending their demobilisation by an interim government.

Role of the security forces

The role of the security forces in destabilisation needs to be examined at 2 levels – the level of overt official operations and the level of covert extra-legal activities.

Overt official operations

The official role of the security forces and the reason for their existence is supposed to be the protection of the population and preserving the peace. The fact that over 6000 South African citizens have died in political violence over the last 2 years, with twice that number injured, is a measure of the extent to which the security forces have failed in their duty. This failure can be ascribed either to inability or to passive complicity or to active promotion of violence or to combinations of all three. In relation to the first possibility, the Waddington Report on police investigations into the Boipatong massacre of June 1992, found them to be 'woefully inadequate' and 'incompetent', and suggestive of 'an unaccountable police force.' Complicity aside, the nature of security force behaviour at an official level frequently confirms an active promotion of destabilisation and violence beyond the 'legal limits'.

The Security forces have in the last 2 years been responsible for 350 deaths, nearly 10 times that number of injuries and almost 17 000 arrests.

Security forces have frequently been engaged in operations, some of which fall under the category of massacres, in which 'excessive force' has been used and which have drawn the criticism and condemnation of various commissions of inquiry. Some of these are:

- Sebokeng, 26 March 1990. Police actions against demonstrations in the area resulted in 12 deaths and 281 injuries. A judicial commission of inquiry conducted by Judge Goldstone found the use of police violence as 'immoderate and disproportionate' and made reference to 'an attitude of unconcern for the lethal nature of their ammunition and for the consequences of its use. This is an attitude no police force should tolerate.' The prosecution of a number of policemen involved was recommended but well over 2 years later, the trial has not commenced.
- Sebokeng, 4 September 1990. SADF members opened fire without warning on a group of people, some seated, at Sebokeng hostel, killing 11 and injuring many others. Justice Stafford, who conducted a judicial inquest, criticised the SADF internal inquiry as a 'whitewash' and recommended prosecution of SADF members on 4 counts of murder and 10 of grievous bodily harm against people posing no physical threat. No trial has yet taken place.
- Daveyton, 24 March 1991. Police opened fire on a gathering of ANC supporters in an open field, killing 12 and injuring 37. Justice O'Donovan conducted a judicial inquest,

describing the incident as a 'slaughter', finding excessive use of force and recommending prosecutions for murder and culpable homicide. The attorney general declined to prosecute.

- Carletonville, 1990. The Welverdiend Unrest Unit of the SAP in the Khutsong district of the Western Transvaal was implicated during 1990 in the harassment, torture and killing of Khutsong township residents and activists. In July 1991 a police investigation was ordered into the 'ongoing allegations of irregularities'. Several policemen have been suspended, the unrest unit was disbanded in December 1991 and a number of trials are in progress.

- Phola Park, 8 April 1992. Members of 32 Battalion of the SADF attacked the Phola Park squatter camp and were accused of misconduct including assault and rape. A Goldstone commission of inquiry concluded that the members had acted in a manner entirely inconsistent with their peace- keeping function, had been guilty of unjustified violence and that the battalion should not be used for peace-keeping duties anywhere in South Africa. The response by General Meiring of the SADF was that 32 Battalion would be deployed as and where needed. During evidence, an officer of the Battalion said the existence of a 'war-type situation' justified the use of force.

The above are but a few examples of the 'war-psychosis' which seems to guide many security force units and personnel in their behaviour.

Covert operations

Covert operations of the security forces are now well known and no longer occasion much surprise when new facts come to light. The Goldstone Commission comments that in our recent history '[g]overnment has failed to take sufficiently firm steps to prevent criminal conduct by members of the security forces' but misses the point that such conduct is condoned within deliberately created covert structures. The practically non-existent record of solving the long catalogue of political assassinations is a product not so much of the lack of firm steps, as a desire and interest in avoiding disclosure. How much more there is to be disclosed is difficult to estimate but in the meantime the increasing frequency with which political assassinations occur is evidence of the continued existence of such covert operations and refutes claims that they have been disbanded. The following evidence, incidents and allegations are relevant:

- The assassination toll over the last 2 years has been 124 deaths, of which over 100 are clearly identifiable as assassinations of anti-apartheid activists or their families. This is 5 times the rate of assassinations during the years of total strategy.

- The Harms Commission of Inquiry into the activities of hit squads within the security forces confirmed the existence of such squads and that they had been engaged in illegal acts. Nearly 2 years after these findings no prosecutions have yet been brought by the state. The SAP Vlakplaas squad still exists, while the SADF CCB squad, though nominally disbanded, still has unfinished business.

- In a court before Judge Kriegler, General Lothar Neethling, an SAP forensic expert, was found to be lying to the court about supplying poison to the SAP hit squads for use against ANC activists.

- The Goldstone Commission is currently investigating disclosures by the *Weekly Mail* that the SADF has been funding and training hit squads for promoting destabilisation and violence in KwaZulu and in Wesselton in the Eastern Transvaal. This has involved the creation by Military Intelligence of a complex national network of front organisations with innocent sounding names, and most of which are still in existence. Training took place in a military base in Caprivi and at the Mkuze camp in a remote area of Zululand.

- Another Goldstone Commission inquiry pending, is one into the conduct of the SAP (CIS division) in the Southern Transvaal in instigating violence. This relates to a further *Weekly Mail* report that covert SAP units are operating in the Vaal from private property, using false company names, false telephone numbers and false registration plates.

- Yet another Goldstone Commission inquiry found prima facie evidence that 2 SAP members in Schweizer-Reneke had conspired to abduct and assassinate Jerry Maine, chairman of the Ipelegeng Civic Association in November 1991 and referred the matter to the attorney-general. Six months later Judge Goldstone had cause to complain about the tardiness of the police in investigating the case.

- Chief Mhlabunzima Maphumulo, member of CONTRALESA and ANC sympathiser, was assassinated in Pietermaritzburg on 25 February 1991, shortly after threats to his life. During the inquest, evidence was presented suggesting security police involvement in the attack, while the *Weekly Mail* claimed to have information linking Mkuze camp trainees to the assassination.

- The assassination of the Cradock Four (Matthew Goniwe, Fort Calata, Sparrow Mkhonto and Sicelo Mhlauli) near Port Elizabeth in June 1985 is having reverberations today. On 8 May 1992, the *New Nation* published information strongly implicating security forces in the murders. It had obtained a copy of a signal message sent from the Eastern Province JMC to the secretariat of the State Security Council proposing that Goniwe and others be 'permanently removed from society as a matter of urgency'. The message referred to a telephone conversation between Brigadier C.P. van der Westhuizen, then commanding officer of Eastern Province Command (now a lieutenant-general and chief of staff of Military Intelligence) and General van Rensburg, then serving on the State Security Council secretariat. Despite a public outcry, General van der Westhuizen has not been suspended pending a commission of inquiry. Furthermore, a Mr Andre de Villiers, said to be an informant about the participation of the covert SADF 'Hammer' unit in the killings of the Cradock 4, has himself been assassinated. The above samples of covert security force operations are probably but the tip of the iceberg.

Collusion with vigilantes

Over the past 2 years there have been extensive and persistent allegations by township communities of security force collusion with vigilantes during attacks upon them, primarily from hostels. Furthermore, there have been revelations emerging from press investigations, court actions and commission of inquiry which give support to these allegations. From HRC records kept during year 2 (July 1991 to June 1992) allegations of collusion were made on no fewer than 92 occasions. Similar allegations were made about 19 out of 49 major massacres. These various acts of collusion may be summarised as acts of omission and acts of commission as follows:

Acts of omission
- Absence from the scene of vigilante attacks or excessively late arrival.
- Not responding to forewarning of attacks or undertakings to protect communities.
- If present, standing idly by, even refusing or ignoring requests to intervene.
- Not countering, deflecting or dispersing attackers.
- Not disarming, arresting or detaining attackers.
- Not charging or prosecuting attackers and refusal to accept laying of charges by injured parties.
- Failure to solve murders, even when evidence is readily available.
- Failure to remove weapons from vigilante bases.

Acts of commission
- Indiscriminate attacks on township dwellers with teargas, guns, rubber bullets, etc. while defending themselves against vigilante attacks, resulting in deaths and injuries.
- Dispersing, arresting or detaining township dwellers and removing their means of defence.
- Vigilante groups escorted and even transported to and from the scene of the attack.
- Collaboration in the planning and executions of attacks and in the identification and targeting of specific individuals.
- Provision of weapons and other material to vigilante groups.
- Training and funding of vigilante groups.

Some examples of such collusion follow:
- The 'Inkathagate Scandal' in July 1991 uncovered State and Security Force support for Inkatha.

  The *Weekly Mail* disclosed that the security police had secretly been funding Inkatha activities, notably rallies in November 1989 and March 1990 (amounting to R250 000) and the Inkatha aligned United Workers Union of South Africa (R1,5 million). The government admitted to the allegations, claiming that the former was for 'anti-sanctions rallies' and the latter to 'counter intimidation, illegal activities and related violence on the labour front.'

  The *Weekly Mail* also alleged that Inkatha hit squad members underwent training at an SADF base in the Caprivi Strip in 1986 and that the SADF working through 'front organisations' funded further training at a camp in Mkuze established in 1989. De Klerk admitted SADF involvement in the 1986 training claiming that it was for VIP protection and security purposes. The Goldstone Commission is at present investigating the whereabouts and activities of the 200 persons allegedly trained at these 2 locations, and the operations of so-called 'front organisations'.

  On 29 November 1991 the *Weekly Mail* published evidence of security police funding of a further Inkatha rally at Mzumbe, Natal, in January 1991. The police admitted funding the rally, thereby undermining the claim made previously by President de Klerk that the secret funding of Inkatha had been stopped by March 1990.

- Trust Feeds Trial. In April 1992, Justice Andrew Wilson passed judgement in the now notorious 'Trust Feed' case. Five policemen, including Captain Brian Mitchell, were found guilty of murder. The case arose from the killing of 11 people at a funeral vigil in Trust Feeds, Natal, in December 1988. In the course of the trial it became clear that the context for these killings was an attempt by the SAP in alliance with Inkatha and the KwaZulu police to disrupt the community and oust the established residents' association, thereby enabling Inkatha to gain control over the area.

- Swanieville massacre. On 12 May 1991, a group of around 800 men, widely acknowledged to have been Inkatha supporters, attacked the squatter settlement of Swanieville on the West Rand. 29 people were killed and over 30 injured. According to eye-witnesses, survivors and newspaper reports (*Sowetan*, 20 May 1991), evidence of security force involvement included police and other unidentified white men allegedly participating in the attack; armoured vehicles escorting the attackers back to Kagiso One hostel afterwards; failure on the part of the police to halt or disarm the attackers. An internal police inquiry found there to be no evidence of police involvement in the attack.

- Boipatong massacre. On 17 June 1992 an attack was launched on the township of Boipatong in which 46 residents were killed. The *Weekly Mail* (26 June 1992) strongly suggested police involvement in the attack. For example, police failed to respond to warnings of an impending attack and the attack itself was carried out with 'military precision'. The Goldstone Commission discovered a covert Koevoet unit and arms at Greenside Colliery, a Gold Fields mine in Eastern Transvaal. The raid took place after the ANC obtained evidence of possible involvement by Koevoet members in the Boipatong killings. Furthermore, monitoring groups have collected statements testifying to police involvement in the attack. The Goldstone Commission is holding an ongoing inquiry into the incident.

- Ignoring advance warnings of impending attacks on a number of occasions, suggests complicity on the part of the security forces. A prime example of this was prior to the massacre at Sebokeng on 22 July 1990 in which 19 people died. Ample and specific warnings were relayed days before to the divisional commissioner of police, the national commissioner of police, as well as to the minister of law and order.

There can be no doubt that there is an overwhelming perception amongst township residents that the state and its security forces are in an unholy alliance with Inkatha-supporting vigilantes to destabilise township life and paralyse political organisation.

The role of Inkatha-supporting vigilantes

The statistical record
The records in Part 1 of this report show the predominant role of vigilante-related violence in the destabilisation of the last 2 years. This violence has accounted for 5060 deaths out of 6229, or 81,2% of the total deaths; it also accounted for 7263 injuries, or 61,1% of the total. Such a record justifies the description of vigilantes as the 'shock troops of destabilisation'.

Massacres
Within this appalling record of violence there are 49 massacres which have been analysed in Part 1 of this report. Regarding the character of the massacres, a number of points emerge very strongly from the record :
- The drive by Inkatha elements to establish political influence, membership and even territory, is the predominant theme.
- The tactics of extreme terror, used indiscriminately against township communities, to paralyse, immobilise and disorganise, is a complementary theme.
- The use of hostels as bases from which to plan and launch these activities.
- The persistent reports of security force complicity in these massacres, as well as involvement of unidentified whites.
- Retaliation which sometimes produces its own massacres.

Vigilantes as perpetrators of violence
Identifying perpetrators in violent incidents is obviously more difficult than identifying the victims. Nevertheless, reports sometimes indicate attacker identity by describing the emergence from or return to known hostels, wearing of identifying headbands, emergence from rallies, carrying of traditional weapons, chanting and singing, and many other indicators, especially the identification of the target victim.

In this way it is possible to assess the identity of the attackers in 20% of deaths and injuries that have occurred in year 2 (by comparison with 50% in the case of the victims). Within this identified 20% group, the records show that for year 2 Inkatha-supporting vigilantes were responsible for 584 deaths and 940 injuries while ANC and township residents were responsible for 40 deaths and 102 injuries. Thus, vigilantes were the perpetrators in 93,6% of the deaths and 90,2% of the injuries.

By way of confirmation, reference to the list of major massacres shows that of 39 massacres in which the identity of the attackers was assessed, vigilantes were responsible in 31 of these and jointly responsible with the opposing party in another 6 massacres.

The logistics of vigilante violence
The record of the last 2 years shows that one third of vigilante-related deaths has occurred in Natal and almost two thirds in the Witwatersrand/Vaal region. As shown in Fig. 16, the death toll in Natal is remarkably steady from month to month but fluctuates widely in the Witwatersrand/Vaal region suggesting an ability to raise or lower the scale of violence in response to political events or in order to manipulate them. High points have occurred in

August/September 1990 after the signing of the Pretoria Minute and the suspension by the ANC of the armed struggle; in December 1990 the month of the ANC Consultative Conference; in May 1991, a month of mass protest about political prisoners, township violence , educational crisis and anti-Republic Day observance; in September 1991 the month of the National Peace Accord signing; and in March 1992 the month of the referendum. Low points have occurred in October 1990 during F.W. de Klerk's visit to Europe; in January 1991 at the opening of parliament; in February 1991, after the signing of the ANC/IFP Peace Accord; and in June 1991 during the failed government-sponsored conference on violence.

Within the region of Natal there are several specific flashpoints which repeatedly flare up and die down again as the battle for territory rages on. In the Wits/Vaal region the pattern is somewhat different with the epicentre of violence moving from place to place, as if a mobile force were being continuously redeployed.

Hostels as vigilante bases

A number of hostels have acquired a reputation as launchpads for vigilante violence. A commonly repeated pattern has been for Inkatha-supporting vigilantes to 'capture' hostels by driving out non- supporters, instituting a militaristic regime, attacking the houses of township residents in the area surrounding the hostel, occupying those houses or keeping them empty to maintain a buffer-zone or no-man's-land around the hostel and then using these island bases as launch pads for destabilisation.

One of the most notorious hostels with a long record of terrorising its surrounding township community was the KwaMadala hostel in Boipatong, whose history culminated in the massacre which cost the lives of 46 residents. Other notorious hostels in the Wits/Vaal area are the Madala and Nobuhle hostels in Alexandra; Mzimhlope hostel in Meadowlands; Kwesini hostel in Katlehong; Sebokeng hostel; Denver, George Goch and Jeppe hostels in Johannesburg; Siphiwe hostel in Dobsonville; Nancefield hostel in Pimville; Kagiso No.1 hostel near Swanieville; Merafe hostel; Jabulani hostel; Tokoza, KwaThema and Vosloorus hostels on the East Rand.

All of these hostels and others have a history of involvement in violence affecting their surrounding areas. Together they constitute a fifth column permeating the entire fabric of township community life in the Wits/Vaal region. In the words of a Goldstone Commission report, 'Hostels are common to most of the worst areas of violence.'

Train massacres

The incidence of train attacks and massacres which have thus far cost nearly 300 lives is closely associated with hostels with a proximity to high risk stations and railway lines. There have been numerous instances of attackers being observed withdrawing into hostels and where attackers have been apprehended, invariably their addresses turned out to be in Inkatha-supporting hostels. Train violence is currently the subject of a Goldstone Commission of Inquiry. An interim report of the Commission states 'The violence on the trains cannot be separated from ongoing violence in the townships. The primary causes and participants appear to be the same ...Wherever a group of attackers was identified they turned out to be hostel dwellers.'

Vigilante linkages

An indication of the centrality, in operational terms, of vigilantes to the destabilisation of townships, is the multiplicity of relationships between them and other entities.

Government linkages are now well known in terms of the historical promotion of Inkatha and other groups as a counter-weight to the liberation movement, involving actual funding as well as other forms of support. Further evidence of government complicity is the almost total lack of success in prosecuting and convicting perpetrators of innumerable acts of vigilante violence. This is in stark contrast to the highly successful record of bringing right wing perpetrators to book, where a strong political will to do so is evident. Security force linkage is extensive and comprehensive in terms of funding, training, material and logistical support and even direct operational support (e.g. as in the Trusts Feeds massacre). Furthermore, there is overwhelming indication of extensive collusion between security forces and vigilantes, both through acts of omission and acts of commission.

Black councils, besides making use of their own vigilante groupings where they exist, have invited external vigilante groupings, such as Inkatha-supporting vigilantes into their areas as a counter to community-based Civic Associations, and in return for a base from which to extend their activities. A case in point is the township of Alexandra (next to Johannesburg) which from July 1990 to February 1991 was totally free of any of violence, which then erupted when such an alliance was struck.

Business interests have availed themselves of the services of vigilantes, both in support of mine security services against striking mineworkers in Transvaal and OFS, and against striking workers in a number of other industries. In addition they have turned a blind eye to the illegal occupation of hostels by vigilantes who have forcibly driven out the legal employee occupants.

Criminal gangs have linked in with vigilantes in their area of operation and preyed upon the political and civic life of the community.

The right wing, in spite of its racial dogma, has made overtures to the black right wing for some form of collaboration but so far nothing official has emerged.

Role of the KwaZulu police

The Goldstone Commission second interim report comments as follows:

> The widely held view by a large number of people in KwaZulu and neighbouring areas that the KwaZulu police are a private army of the Inkatha Freedom Party is a matter of great concern in relation to the curbing of violence in those areas. No less disturbing is the evidence that has been given concerning unlawful activities by senior members of the KwaZulu Police.

This statement echoes the findings of a comprehensive report on the KZP compiled jointly by Legal Resources Centre (LRC) and HRC (Natal) in December 1991 to the effect that accumulated evidence strongly indicates that KZP, or at least substantial elements thereof, have entered the arena of the conflict on the side of Inkatha. Based on a large number of case studies, the report lists the following as the most problematic allegations levelled at the conduct of the KZP:

- The perpetration of acts of harassment and intimidation, including shootings and assaults against persons perceived to be non-Inkatha;
- collusion with Inkatha vigilante elements and/or participation with such elements in carrying out acts of harassment and intimidation against persons perceived to be political opponents of Inkatha;
- disruption of political activity such as harassing persons at meetings and other events;
- failure to assist complainants and to investigate matters;
- failure to render or permit medical assistance to critically wounded persons.

The report compiled by the LRC and HRC lists over 120 incidents of unlawful attacks, shootings and/or assaults involving the KwaZulu police. The report also cites at least 54 cases where the KwaZulu Police acted in collusion with Inkatha resulting in the deaths of at least 68 people.

The following incident report implicating KZP in a massacre at Umlazi on 13 March 1992, is an extract from the HRC Area Repression Report:

> *Durban-Umlazi* (13 Mar 92)
> 18 people, including 15 women and 3 children under the age of 5 (one of whom was decapitated), were killed and 28 injured in an attack on the Uganda squatter settlement. Residents reported that the attack started at 5a.m., when between 100 and 200 KwaZulu police members led 300 Inkatha supporters from Unit 17 in the area and fired at houses, shooting mostly women and children who were fleeing. Another attack was then launched at about 9.30am when 2 KZP vehicles escorted a group of Inkatha men into the area. Residents have alleged that the SAP did not attempt to stop the attack. They also alleged that a SAP presence did not prevent the attackers as when the attackers became aware of a SAP presence, they relaunched an attack elsewhere in the area. Uganda is not part of KwaZulu.

Part 3. Apartheid survival strategy

3.1 Structures and stakeholders of apartheid power

From the moment the National Party came to power in 1948, it set about erecting an edifice of laws and structures designed to ensure the survival of that power for 'all time'. Building on the loose de facto system of racial discrimination that already existed at that point, they rapidly evolved the survival strategy that came to be known as 'grand apartheid'.

While most, but not all, of the laws have now gone, the structures are still with us and the stakeholders in those structures are faced with the decision of whether to cling to their vested interests or abandon them in anticipation of their imminent collapse. A brief examination of these structures of apartheid power is useful in assessing the balance of forces in South Africa today.

The structures are:

Tricameral parliament
Homelands
Black local authorities

The tricameral parliament

This structure in which central power is vested came into existence in 1984 and elicited widespread protest leading to a State of Emergency. It extended parliamentary representation previously reserved for the white population only, to the 'Coloured' and 'Indian' communities but incorporated mechanisms to ensure that ultimate control still vested in the white house. The population group classified as black was totally excluded and this is still the case 8 years later. Stakeholders with a vested interest in this structure of apartheid power are :

• White voters in general, but in particular the supporters of the National Party, Conservative Party and so-called right wing.
• The National Party government, the primary stakeholder.
• The security establishment within the government whose vested interests are perhaps the strongest of all.
• The civil service who may feel threatened by the disappearance of the tricameral parliament.
• The business community which faces perhaps the greatest dilemma of all, given the fact that they were the prime beneficiaries of apartheid in the past but now have the most to lose in the event of an economic collapse – a likely possibility if apartheid power is not abandoned.
• 'Coloured' members of the House of Representatives.
• 'Indian' members of the House of Delegates.

These last 2 stakeholders have limited support from their own communities and have been heavily criticised for allowing their presence in the tricameral parliament to confer legitimacy on this ultimate symbol of apartheid power.

Homelands

The homelands concept was an essential component of grand apartheid, intended to provide an outlet for the political aspirations of the black population group and, at the same time, to limit access of the black population to urban areas and to perpetuate the existence of docile labour reservoirs from which to feed mines, industry and agriculture. The homelands structures began to make their appearance in 1970, continuing into the 1980s, in a process that involved the dislocation or forced removal of some 3.5 million people and the loss of South African citizenship by some 8 million people. Present homeland structures are as follows:

'Self-governing' homelands
KwaZulu
Gazankulu
KwaNgwane

Lebowa
KwaNdebele
QwaQwa
'Independent' homelands (TBVC states)
Transkei
Bophuthatswana
Venda
Ciskei

Stakeholders with a vested interest in these 10 structures are members of the governments and administrations of the homelands, particularly those who agreed at their inception to participate in and collaborate with the homelands concept. Several of the original players have fallen away over time through coups and similar events. Several of the present players have already declared their hand as being committed to re-incorporation into a unified South Africa and therefore ready to give up their stake in apartheid power. Others, in particular Bophuthatswana, Ciskei, KwaZulu and QwaQwa, seem bent on clinging to their apartheid power and are searching for formulae, involving high levels of regionalism or federalism, that would perpetuate their power even in a new unitary constitution, if that became inevitable. Another stakeholder in homelands structures are those members of the business community who have investments within homelands, particularly in the so-called decentralised border industrial zones, and who have been the beneficiaries of an extraordinary range of incentive schemes. Finally, it must be mentioned that homeland governments in their attempts to impose their authority on, and to defend it against, their unwilling subjects, have spawned not only official police forces and armies but also private armies of vigilantes. KwaZulu is a prime example of a homeland dominated by a powerful police force (KZP) and by a highly developed vigilante element in the form of Inkatha warlords and their impis. It is also a special case in that its ambitions have extended beyond its borders.

Black local authorities

The segment of the population not catered for by the tricameral parliament and by the rural homelands, was the urban black population which could not be wished away. To address this gap, black councils were introduced more or less simultaneously with the tricameral parliament and this pointed and final exclusion from central power inevitably became the focus of the ire of the urban black population throughout the country.

Elections for black councils were almost totally boycotted; those who accepted office were widely regarded as sell-outs and collaborators; pressures mounted for the resignation of the black councillors and the dismantling of the councils; and the system has largely collapsed in most areas. Nevertheless there are a number of stakeholders in the form of black councillors surrounded by their municipal police force and sometimes by private armies of vigilantes. They clearly have an interest in trying to maintain their last vestiges of power inherited from apartheid by somehow carrying it over into new local government structures that will evolve under a new constitution.

3.2 Threats to apartheid power

Apartheid power today has not one, but two Achilles' heels. Firstly, the fact that over 75% of South Africa's population has no representation of any kind in the organs of central power; and in fact less than 15% have any meaningful representation. This is both a measure of the legitimacy of apartheid power and a measure of the resistance of the overall population to its continued tenure. Massive popular resistance then, is the first Achilles' heel. Secondly, international rejection of a system universally declared to be a crime against humanity has brought about an isolation from the world which has had severe consequences for the economy of South Africa and therefore on the capacity of apartheid power to continue. Since the declaration of a State of Emergency in July 1985 there has been a huge capital outflow from South Africa, totalling 36 billion rand up to the present time, in a country which requires capital in-flow in order to grow. We are currently in our third successive year of negative growth, with no prospects of stemming the capital bleeding, let alone reversing it, unless the world's financial system can be convinced that South Africa is politically stable and a secure area in which to place loans and investment. The foreign debt still stands at 18 billion dollars (US), having reduced by only 6 billion dollars since 1985, and pressures continue for the repayment of the debt. The pursuit of political stability has thus become an economic imperative and not to address it would mean certain collapse. Herein lies the second Achilles' heel of apartheid power.

In summary, the survival of apartheid power is under threat by 2 irreconcilable forces:
1. Denial of majority rule means continuing political conflict, leading to inevitable economic collapse.
2. Agreement to majority rule means political peace which will avert an economic crisis but involve the loss of apartheid power.

3.3 The evolution of apartheid survival strategy

Any government which has managed to hold onto power for 44 years in the face of total rejection by at least 85% of its population must have equipped itself with highly effective survival strategies. The figure below traces the evolution of apartheid survival strategy in meeting challenges to apartheid power as and when they arose.

The unfolding of the strategy of grand apartheid occupied the years of 1948 to 1984, culminating in the tricameral parliament. Of necessity, it was accompanied by the development of some of the most repressive laws the world has seen, backed up by powerful security forces. Nevertheless, resistance mounted over the years and, reinforced by international rejection, ultimately reached a dimension in late 1984 to early 1985 that forced the Nationalist government to shift into a different level of strategy that became known as 'total strategy'. This was in effect a full-scale war against its dissident population, intended to smash resistance and to impose its will by force. It was formalised in the declaration of a State of Emergency in July 1985, continuing (with a minor interruption) until 1990 and involved the full spectrum of repressive methods including mass detentions and arrests, media blackout, bannings, assassinations, abductions and vigilantism.

However, total strategy turned into a total disaster. Internally, resistance stiffened and the liberation struggle intensified. On the international front, the international financial community withdrew all support and massive capital flight soon placed the South African economy under severe strain.

Crisis point was reached as early as 1988 when the Nationalist government announced that it was disengaging its troops from Angola and was willing to implement UN resolution 435 setting out withdrawal from Namibia. These were the first signs that total strategy was giving way to the strategy of reform, now seen as essential to save apartheid power from collapse. The capital haemorrhage had to be stopped, and the only way was to establish political peace and stability. That meant talking to those whose demands had been ignored for 40 years and who were now in exile, in prison, banned, gagged or underground.

Thus the reform era started to emerge and to head in the direction of the negotiating table. Political organisations were unbanned, political leaders were released from prison and allowed to return from exile and talks were commenced. The first half of 1990 produced some startling advances towards the apparent removal of obstacles in the way of substantive negotiations for a new order.

It was only in the second half of 1990 that the sequel, or the alter ego, to the reform strategy began to appear, namely, the strategy of destabilisation as a companion to negotiation. This is a strategy which was rehearsed, to some effect, in Namibia in violation of an agreement requiring the South African government to be an impartial administration in the transition process. Within South Africa it was designed to have the same purpose, namely the emasculation of the liberation struggle in such a way as to destroy the capacity of liberation movements from translating their grassroots support into organised political support and ultimately into voter support at the ballot-box. It has involved the heavy hand

Derek Bauer, *Weekly Mail* calendar 1991

of the security forces, the naked terrorism of the vigilantes and the sinister stealth of hit squad assassins; and it has cost the lives of over 6000 people so far. It seems also to have run out of control and become counter-productive because the desired effect of reform strategy – to reverse the out-flow of foreign capital – is not likely to be achieved at the current high levels of violence which continue to frighten off foreign investors and financiers. The forces initially unleashed by the apartheid government in this strategy of destabilisation now seem to have taken on a momentum and agenda of their own. Strong and resolute action by their erstwhile master will be necessary to bring them to heel.

The latest, and probably last, chapter in apartheid survival strategy has been unfolding alongside of and within the climate of destabilisation. It is a strategy of negotiation aimed at securing a position of 'power sharing', a euphemism for the retention or prolongation of apartheid power. Instead of agreement to transferring power to majority rule (the essence of democracy), the government and its allies continue to propose formulae of 'power sharing', such as obligatory coalitions, rotating presidency, upper house with veto rights, autonomous regionalism and so on, which would ensure that apartheid continues to control from its grave. Up to this point in the negotiations that have taken place, there is no indication whatsoever that the Nationalist government is ready to abandon minority power in favour of unequivocal majority rule. It is still playing its game of survival strategy, of clinging to power.

3.4 The chances of survival

The further down the track apartheid power has gone, the narrower its options have become. It has been forced by internal resistance and international isolation out of the naked exercise of force and repression, and into the accountability of reform. It has been ensnared, reluctantly, into such structures as the Peace Accord and the Conference for a Democratic South Africa (CODESA) which commit it to yet more accountability and which limit its freedom of action. Its hopes of an early collapse of the liberation movement's negotiating strength in the face of severe destabilisation have not materialised and it is now trapped into processes of which it is no longer master. The violence is coming under the scrutiny not only of the Peace Accord mechanisms but also of the international community. Negotiation issues, as a result of the collapse of CODESA 2, have now become highly focussed and can no longer be obfuscated by 'power sharing' devices. With all irrelevancies swept aside, the issue of transfer of power to majority rule stands alone. The immediate task is to address the mechanisms for that transfer, and these are clear enough – the installation of a transitional government of national unity and elections for a constituent assembly which will prepare and adopt a new constitution and lay the basis for the election of a new government representative of the majority. It is very clear that the days of apartheid power are numbered, since any genuine election process conducted on the basis of universal suffrage will inevitably reduce the role of the National Party and its allies to that of an opposition party. Numbers are against the possibility of anything more. In a voter pool of 20 to 24 million, voter populations in old apartheid terms are approximately as follows:

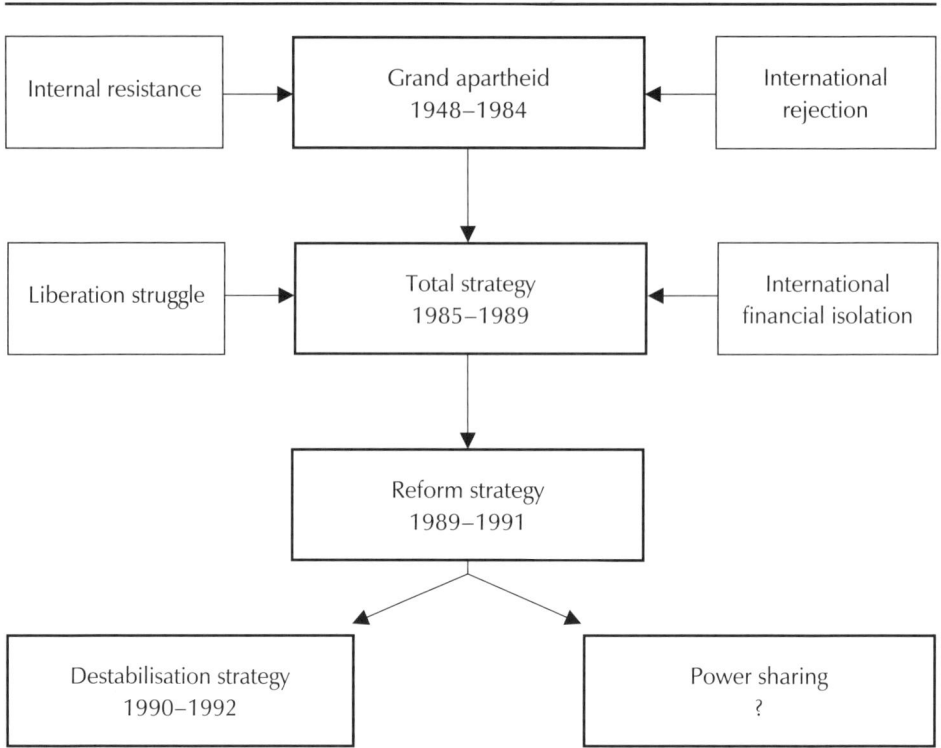

FIGURE 17
Evolution of apartheid survival strategy

- White   13%
- Coloured and Indian   10%
- African   77%

At an estimate most generous to the National Party and its allies, the highest percentages of votes that they could muster in a straight proportional representation contest with the liberation movements would be as follows:

- White   12% (92% of voters)
- Coloured and Indian   6% (60% of voters)
- African   12% (16% of voters)
- Total votes   30%

The only question marks around the balance of 70% are the unity of the liberation movements and their allies and their capacity to deliver their supporters to the polling booths. Nevertheless, the gap between the 2 blocs is so great that apartheid power would certainly be doomed in a free and fair election contest. To agree to such a contest, would mean the end of the struggle for the survival of apartheid power. That will only happen when the pain of holding on to power begins to exceed the pain of letting go. We are rapidly approaching that point.

10 LAST KICKS OF A DYING HORSE   July 1992–June 1993

The era of destabilisation entered its third year in July 1992 with the memory of the previous month's Boipatong massacre still fresh and negotiations having broken down. An atmosphere of profound mistrust of the apartheid government's real intentions now prevailed and serious doubts were being raised as to whether they had lost control of the elements used in the strategy of destabilisation.

Nevertheless, the year was marked by strenuous efforts by the liberation forces to pin the government down to a programme eliminating political violence and these efforts resulted in a Record of Understanding signed in September 1992 and ultimately in getting talks back on track in April 1993. The ultra right wing did their best to sabotage these efforts through the assassination of Chris Hani in April 1993 and to invade the venue of the now succeeding negotiations in June 1993. In spite of these setbacks, the third year of destabilisation closed on a high note with agreement to democratic elections now clearly in sight and the announcement of the date imminent.

The pattern of violence during the third year was largely an extension of the pattern during the second, namely, a war of attrition in which there were fewer major high-profile attacks (massacres declined to 12) but a high number of incidents (nearly 20% more) producing about the same number of deaths (3096) and exerting maximum disruption of township communities.

However, there was an important shift in the regional focus of the political violence, away from the PWV and into Natal from whence much of it had come originally. Natal accounted for 53% of all deaths, up from 33% for the previous year. PWV accounted for 35% of all deaths, down from 56% for the previous year. A shift of this magnitude suggests a deliberate decision to marshal forces on a provincial level.

The events and implications of this third year of destabilisation are described in the HRC publication entitled:

Three Years of Destabilisation *(August 1993).*

THREE YEARS OF DESTABILISATION
A record of political violence in South Africa, July 1990–June 1993

HRC, August 1993

1. The measure of the violence
2. Regional analysis of the violence
3. Components of the violence
4. Victims of the violence
5. Conclusions

Preface

The early months of 1990 held out great promise for the dismantling of apartheid; the Nationalist government, under intense pressure from the majority population of South Africa and from the economic crisis stemming from international isolation, seemed to respond to the demands for free political activity as a precursor to negotiating a political settlement. However, before long a two- pronged strategy began to make its appearance – that of destabilising the now-unbanned liberation movement while simultaneously negotiating with it. The destabilising prong, utilising an array of forces with an interest in defending their apartheid power, whether initiated or inherited, began to manifest itself in July 1990 with a massacre in Sebokeng in the PWV region, and by the following month was in full cry with the deaths of over 700 people in a single month.

Three years on, we are still in the grip of destabilisation. It may well be that the original authors of destabilisation, namely, the Nationalist government, are no longer as enthusiastic about the prospects of benefiting from the strategy (since it has now become counter-productive) but nevertheless they now seem unable to control their own creation. It also seems apparent that there are significant elements within the security apparatus who continue to pursue this strategy.

1. The measure of political violence

Incidents of political violence

The number of incidents of political violence recorded by HRC during the 3-year period is as follows:

Year 1	2166
Year 2	3534
Year 3	4178
Total	9878 incidents

The sharp increase in the number of incidents over the years is an indication more of the widespread nature of the violence over time rather than the intensity. As seen below, the greater number of incidents did not result in a greater number of deaths or injuries.

The death-count in political violence

The deaths in politically related circumstances recorded by HRC during the 3-year period are as follows:

Year 1	3190
Year 2	3039
Year 3	3096
Total	9325 deaths

This total represents an average of 259 deaths each month or 8.5 deaths each day.

The death toll for each of the 3 years has been remarkably constant with differences of less than 5%. However, this is simply coincidental, with extreme fluctuations taking place within the course of each year, as can be seen from the chronologies at the beginning of Part C.

Year 1	lowest month 105	highest 709 (6,8 times)
Year 2	lowest month 110	highest 437 (4,0 times)
Year 3	lowest month 175	highest 373 (2,1 times)

As time has gone by, the fluctuations have become less extreme, with the peaks reducing and the troughs rising, confirming the broadening of the violence as indicated by the increase in the number of incidents.

The major explosions and lulls which characterised year 1, came to be replaced by a different style of violence in year 3, which, while it produced much the same number of deaths, involved a much greater number of incidents, each of them claiming fewer victims on average.

This observation is confirmed by the decline in the number of major massacres, involving the deaths of 10 or more people which were recorded during the 3-year period as follows:

Year 1	34
Year 2	15
Year 3	12
Total	61 massacres

A notable feature of the month by month death toll over the 3-year period has been the surges which have taken place during months in which important political events have occurred. The correlation of the death toll with the political calendar is shown in the chronologies at the beginning of Part C.

The injury-count in political violence

Injuries were recorded as follows:

Year 1	6855
Year 2	5033
Year 3	5085
Total	16 973 injuries (an average of 471 per month or 15.5 per day)

Injuries are very approximately proportional to deaths at almost 2:1 but injuries are far more difficult to assess with any accuracy since so many go unreported. The true figure must certainly be in excess of 20 000 in total with no way of knowing how many are permanent injuries.

2. Regional analysis of the violence

The regional breakdown of the deaths for the whole 3-year period is as follows:

Natal region   3653 (39.2% of total)

PWV region   4756 (51.0% of total)

Elsewhere   916 (9.8% of total)

Natal region

Deaths recorded in the Natal region during the 3-year period were as follows:

Year 1   1004 (31% of total)

Year 2   1004 (33% of total)

Year 3   1645 (53% of total)

Total   3653 deaths (an average of 101 per month)

The Natal region is different from the rest of the country in that the current wave of political violence cannot be said to have started in July 1990 in this region. In fact, the political conflict in Natal dates back to at least 1980 when resistance emerged to incorporation of townships within the homeland of KwaZulu and educational and other conflicts arose. The emergence of the United Democratic Front (UDF) in 1984 as a strong unifying political force with popular support throughout the country, including Natal, intensified the conflict. This popularity was perceived by elements within the KwaZulu homeland as a threat to their thus-far unchallenged control. A struggle for political allegiance ensued and developed into a conflict in which both aggressor and victim were Zulu-speaking; clearly a political conflict and not an ethnic conflict as some have attempted to portray.

The 'Natal War' has since 1984 claimed the lives of around 7500 victims including 3653 during the 3-year period covered by this report. As can be seen from Fig. 18, the conflict in Natal has an unremitting character with deaths occurring month after month without a lull. In years 1 and 2, the average monthly death toll was constant at 84 with relatively little fluctuation from month to month. In year 3, a shift in gear took place with the average jumping to 137 (an increase of 64%) but still with little monthly fluctuation. The Natal region accounted for one third of the countrywide deaths in years 1 and 2 but jumped to over half in year 3. It can be concluded that an intensification of the 'Natal War' took place in year 3. Nineteen major massacres occurred in Natal during the 3 years for which months and places are indicated in Fig. 18.

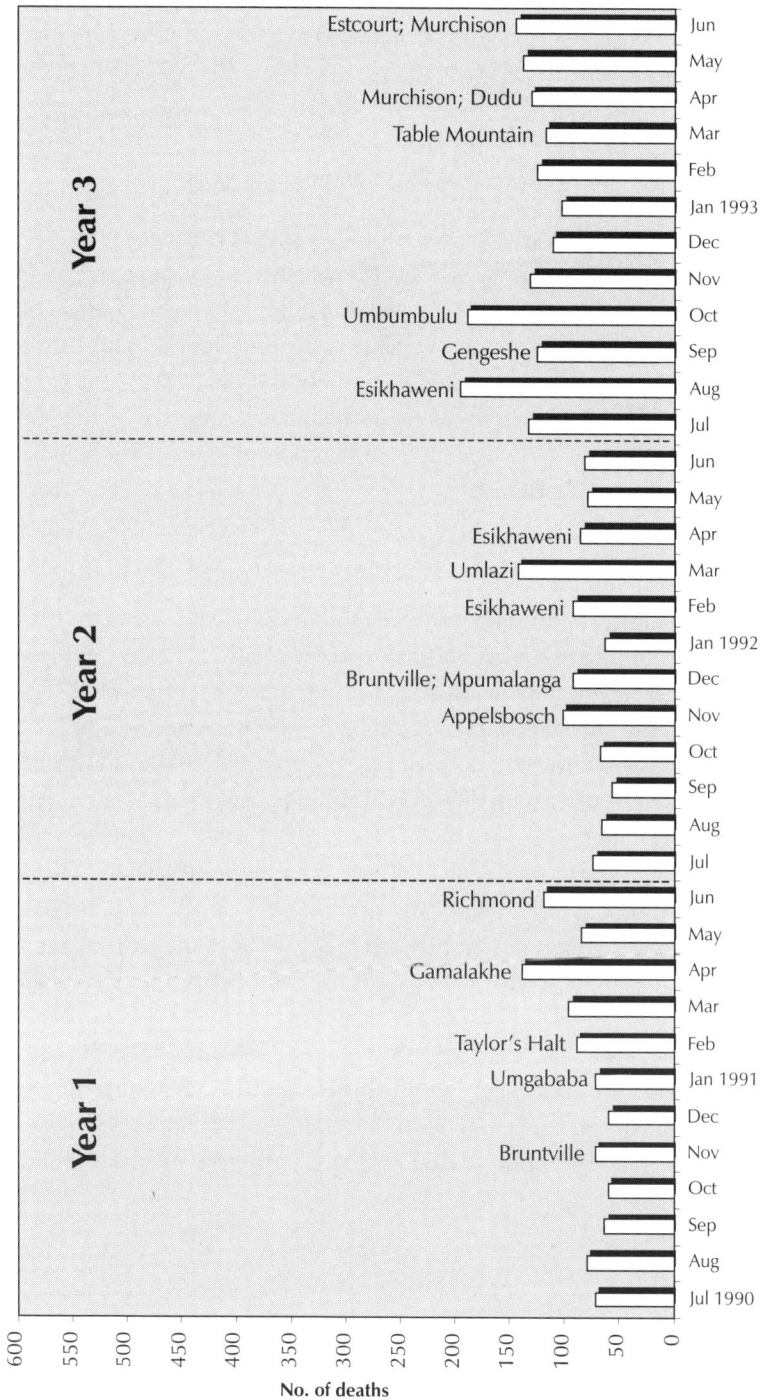

FIGURE 18
Politically related deaths in Natal (July 1990–June 1993)

PWV region

Deaths recorded in the PWV region during the 3-year period were as follows:

Year 1   1982 (62% of total)
Year 2   1688 (56% of total)
Year 3   1086 (35% of total)
Total   4756 deaths (an average of 132 per month)

Unlike the pattern in Natal, the character of the political violence in the PWV region is a highly volatile one with considerable fluctuations from month to month (see Fig. 19). After its ignition in July 1990, the PWV violence followed a roller-coaster course, evident to this day, and is clearly the underlying cause of the fluctuations in the national profile of political violence described in an earlier section. In fact the PWV region can be described as the barometer of political activity and is the region most affected by political events. The volatility of the PWV region is evident from the following death toll figures:

Year 1   lowest month 13   highest 570 (43.8 times)
Year 2   lowest month 40   highest 281 (7.0 times)
Year 3   lowest month 36   highest 182 (5.1 times)

Furthermore, a high proportion of major massacres has taken place in the PWV region (41 out of 61). The months and places of their occurrence are indicated on Fig. 19.

Noteworthy is the drop in the death toll during year 3 by 36% from the previous year. After accounting for around 60% of the total countrywide deaths in years 1 and 2, the PWV region accounted for only 35% of the country total in year 3. This drop occurred simultaneously with the escalation in Natal and raises questions about a switch in tactics and resources.

The East Rand is the most unstable sub-region within the PWV and towards the end of year 3 was contributing over 60% of PWV deaths. The Vaal also has a history of instability which is showing no signs of improvement. By contrast the situation in Soweto and Alexandra has improved greatly and towards the end of year 3 both were dipping below 10%.

Hostels have played a key role in the PWV political violence. An important factor in the abatement of violence particularly in the Soweto and Johannesburg sub-regions during year 3 has been the initiatives of hostel dwellers themselves to reach peace accords. Another has been the pressure placed on the government to make proper use of the security forces to secure the hostels.

Other regions

Deaths recorded in regions other than Natal and PWV during the 3-year period were as follows:

Year 1   204 (7% of total)
Year 2   347 (11% of total)
Year 3   365 (12% of total)
Total   916 deaths (an average of 25 per month)

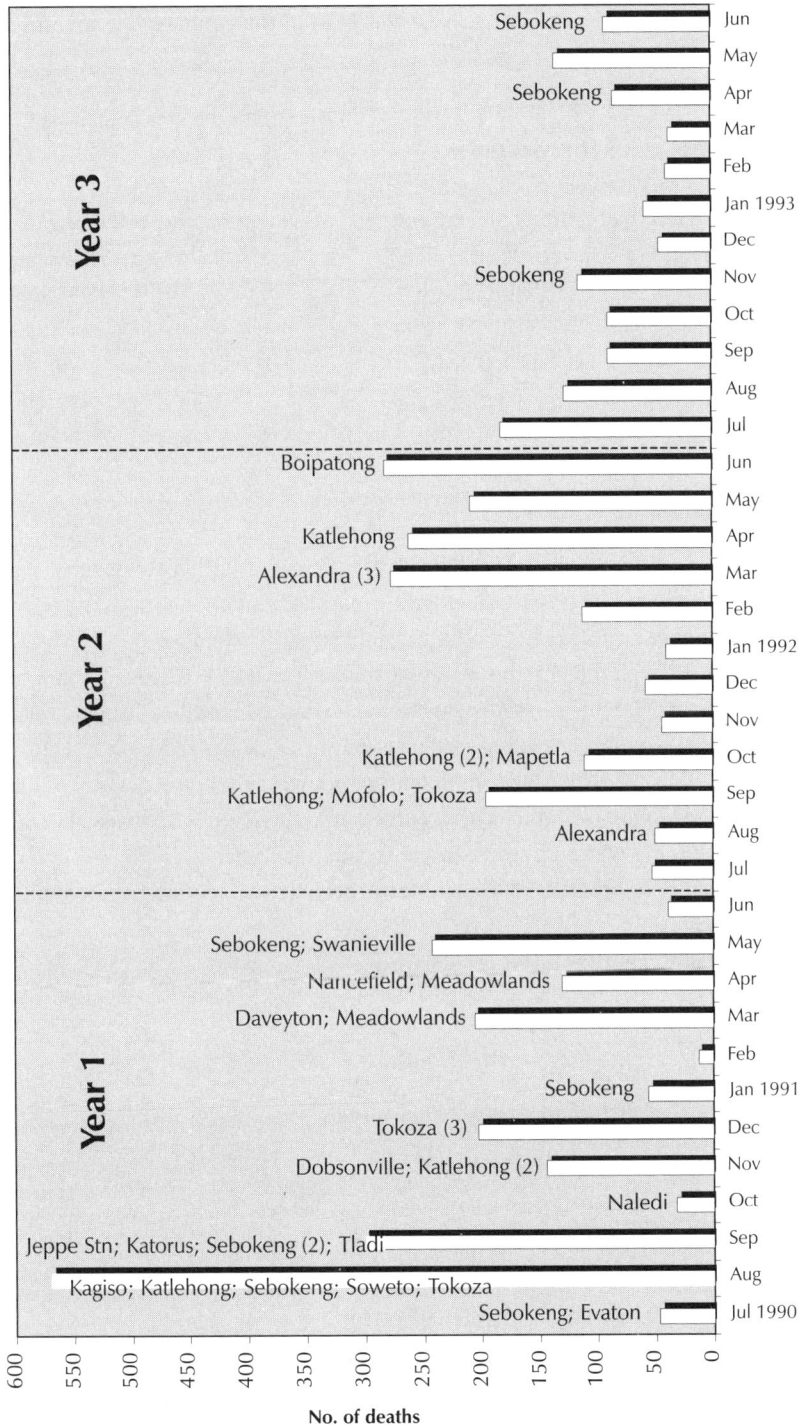

FIGURE 19
Politically related deaths in PWV (July 1990–June 1993)

These figures show a trend towards a broadening of the violence to regions outside of Natal and PWV as time goes on and reached 15% of the countrywide total in the second half of year 3.

3. Components of the violence

In terms of HRC categories of components of violence, the following deaths were recorded during the 3-year period:

General incidents	8580 (92.0%)
Security forces	518 (5.6%)
Hit squads	173 (1.8%)
Right wing	54 (0.6%)
Total	9325 deaths

General incidents

This category includes political violence which is based within township, rural and city communities, frequently hostel-related and frequently involving the activities of vigilante groupings against anti-apartheid political activists in particular, but also against whole communities at large. For the purposes of this report it also includes a range of actions emanating from elements normally associated with the liberation struggle but which can often only be seen as impeding progress towards democracy; such actions include sectional conflict, violence arising from industrial and educational conflict, attacks launched upon members of the security forces, attacks on white civilians, and the so-called taxi wars. While several of these actions can be understood as a backlash against destabilisation, they are frequently counter-productive in neutralising destabilisation.

Incidents recorded within this category were :

Year 1	1093
Year 2	2385
Year 3	3283
Total	6761 incidents (68.4% of total)

Deaths recorded within this category were:

Year 1	2903
Year 2	2806
Year 3	2871
Total	8580 deaths (92.0% of total)

Injuries in this category were:

Year 1	4315
Year 2	3864
Year 3	2806
Total	10 985 injuries (64.7% of the total).

It can be seen that while the number of deaths has not differed much from year to year, the number of incidents has climbed appreciably while the number of reported injuries has decreased.

Security forces

The security forces include the South African Police (SAP), the South African Defence Force (SADF), homelands police and armies, municipal and council police and other parastatal law enforcement entities. Actions involving the security forces during the 3-year period in a political context were as follows:

Incidents recorded:

Year 1	881
Year 2	909
Year 3	779
Total	2569 incidents (26.0% of total)

Deaths recorded:

Year 1	238
Year 2	114
Year 3	166
Total	518 deaths (5.6% of total)

Injuries recorded:

Year 1	2248
Year 2	1033
Year 3	2061
Total	5342 injuries (31.5% of total)

While the proportion of deaths inflicted by the security forces is relatively low (5.6%), the involvement in incidents of violence is high (26.0%) and the infliction of injuries is higher still (31.5%).

In addition the security forces effected the following number of arrests during political activity:

Arrests recorded:

Year 1	8211
Year 2	8725
Year 3	9137
Total	26 073 arrests (an average of 724 per month)

The security forces are also alleged to have been directly responsible for, or directly involved in a number of massacres:
- SAP for the deaths of 12 in Daveyton on 24 March 1991.
- SADF for the deaths of 11 in Sebokeng on 4 September 1990.
- SADF for the deaths of 12 in Esikhaweni on 16 February 1992.
- KZP for the deaths of 18 in Umlazi on 13 March 1992.
- Ciskei Defence Force for the deaths of 28 in Bisho on 7 September 1992.

The above record does not take into account the numerous allegations and reports of security force complicity in fuelling or condoning political violence.

Hit squads

The activities of professional hit squads located primarily within state structures has been recorded as follows:

Incidents recorded:

Year 1	99
Year 2	126
Year 3	34
Total	259 incidents

Assassinations recorded:

Year 1	28
Year 2	96
Year 3	49
Total	173 deaths

Injuries recorded:

Year 1	46
Year 2	35
Year 3	18
Total	99 injuries.

After a major increase in activity in year 2, there has been a dramatic fall-off in year 3, especially in the second half (January to June 1993) when only 2 incidents were reported, resulting in 2 deaths and 1 injury. There may, therefore, be some validity in the government's claim that all such operations have been terminated.

Right wing

Right wing violence is of 2 kinds, the one perpetrated indiscriminately against blacks in a more or less spontaneous manner by individuals or small groups of individuals; the other involving organisation and planning. Together they have produced the following:

Incidents recorded:

Year 1	93
Year 2	114
Year 3	82
Total	289 incidents

Deaths recorded:

Year 1	21
Year 2	23
Year 3	10
Total	54 deaths

Injuries recorded:

Year 1	246
Year 2	101
Year 3	200
Total	547 injuries

The ratio of injuries to deaths is much higher than for any other component of violence, indicating the level of assault and aggression employed. The killing of Chris Hani in April 1993 was an act with devastating consequences to the levels of violence throughout the country.

4. Victims of the violence

The overwhelming majority of the nearly 10 000 dead and 20 000 injured have been the ordinary residents of black townships throughout the country. Their lives during these 3 years of destablisation have been turned upside down and in so many cases, destroyed. Until year 3, the white community was virtually unscathed and largely unaware of the suffering being endured by their black neighbours. But as time went on, the violence began to permeate almost every corner of South African society in one way or another. Some specific groups or categories of victims are examined below:

Commuters

Many township communities, particularly in the PWV region, in addition to attacks upon their homes, have been exposed to serious dangers while travelling to and from their places of work by train, bus or taxi.

Train commuters:

Year 1	67 deaths	284 injuries	16 incidents
Year 2	227 deaths	566 injuries	230 incidents
Year 3	107 deaths	217 injuries	110 incidents
Total	401 deaths	1067 injuries	356 incidents.

Clearly this form of violence peaked in year 2 and showed signs of abating in year 3 in the face of a concerted clamour for countermeasures to be instituted. However, attacks on train commuters still continue.

Bus and taxi commuters:

Year 1	no figures available		
Year 2	119 deaths	230 injuries	72 incidents
Year 3	84 deaths	161 injuries	53 incidents
Total	203 deaths	391 injuries	125 incidents

These attacks serve to supplement train attacks in terrorising and destabilising communities.

Women and children

The ultimate in terror-tactics is to kill women and children and thereby strike at the very heart of the community. While some of these women and children will have been simply 'cross-fire' victims there have been numerous instances where their slaughter was deliberate. The record is as follows:

Women

Year 1	no figures available	
Year 2	189 deaths	227 injuries
Year 3	253 deaths	315 injuries

Children

Year 1	no figures available	
Year 2	106 deaths	87 injuries
Year 3	58 deaths	211 injuries

The combined totals for women and children represent 10% of all deaths. In the notorious Boipatong massacre, 25 out of 46 dead were women and children, a clear example of deliberate intent.

Security force members

Attacks on members of security forces and upon their vehicles and bases have increased in frequency and intensity, as the following figures show:

Year 1	no figures available		
Year 2	68 deaths	279 injuries	205 incidents
Year 3	200 deaths	264 injuries	569 incidents

Nearly 14% of all incidents of political violence in year 3 were attacks on the security forces.

White civilians

Attacks on white civilians in a politically related context only began to make their appearance in year 3, during which HRC recorded the following:

| 34 deaths | 43 injuries | 52 incidents |

This represents only around 1% of the casualties for the year but has raised concern in most quarters that efforts to carry the violence into the white community can only impact negatively towards an abatement of the violence.

5. Conclusions

Faced with the staggering record of political violence outlined in this report, the 2 questions most frequently asked are:
• What is the identity of the real perpetrators of this violence?
• What does it take to bring this violence to an end?

The perpetrators

In broad terms, all South Africans today sooner or later have to choose between belonging to the pro-democracy forces or the anti-democracy forces in the country. Those who have a vested interest in apartheid power and are reluctant to relinquish that power, place themselves squarely in the anti- democracy camp and collectively constitute the base of the so-called 'third force'. They are collectively responsible for the violence of destabilisation.

The past beneficiaries of apartheid power are not difficult to identify and this has been done in some detail in the previous chapter. In summary they were the stakeholders in the 3 primary structures in which apartheid power was vested:
1. Tricameral parliament
2. Homelands
3. Black local authorities (BLA)

The tricameral parliament stakeholders include:
*   The white electorate, white parliamentary parties, white government, the security establishment, the civil service and the business community;
*   members and supporters of the 'coloured' House of Representatives;
*   members and supporters of the 'Indian' House of Delegates.

The homelands stakeholders include the governments, administrations, security forces and supporters of 6 'self-governing' and 4 'independent' entities.

The black local authorities stakeholders are those who took office as black councillors, along with their hangers-on.

Some erstwhile stakeholders have fallen away, either through the collapse of their structures (as with most black councils) or their displacement from power (as with coups against homeland leaders). Other stakeholders have publicly committed themselves in advance to abrogating their power in favour of a unitary democratic constitution while elements within white, 'coloured' and 'Indian' structures and constituencies have openly committed themselves to a negotiated democracy and thereby renounced their claims to the privileges and benefits of apartheid power.

However, there remains a hard core of stakeholders who cling to their past power, have no intention of relinquishing it if they can possibly help it and actively oppose the arrival of a non-racial democracy. They are to be found within all of the structures and constituencies listed above, but particularly within the white right wing, the security establishment and a number of homelands. Together they constitute the anti-democracy camp in South Africa and together they are responsible for the activities of what is referred to as the 'third force'. Who else could possibly benefit from the apparently mindless and indiscriminate destabilisation of whole communities through such untargeted violence as the random slaughter of train commuters, taxi commuters, tavern patrons, beer hall patrons and funeral mourners?

Before leaving the issue of the identity of the perpetrators of the political violence, a word needs to be said about the criminal factor in the violence. There can be no doubt that some of the violence projected as politically inspired involves the hand of apolitical criminals but at 2 different levels. The one level is simply criminal activity for personal gain under the smokescreen of political violence; taking advantage of a turbulent situation and perhaps even promoting it; engaging in protection and extortion rackets; and even seeking cover within hostels and other community structures, often in 'alignment' with one or other political grouping. The other level is availability for hire, for involvement in planned assassination and massacres. Such hitmen are simply hired guns with special expertise paid by politically motivated sponsors.

Ending the violence

Three critical phases are crucial in bringing political violence to an end:
- the control of violence during the election campaign;
- the election itself;
- acceptance of the election results.

Violence during electioneering

South Africa is already effectively into a period of election campaigning which will culminate in election day on 27 April 1994. Crucial to the control or minimising of political violence during this period will be the proper and effective use of the total available security machinery of the country and the energetic promotion of peace initiatives and political tolerance through the already well-established Peace Accord structures and international observer teams. The security machinery needs to be under the multi-party control of the Transitional Executive Council (TEC) to ensure that its efforts are totally directed towards promoting and supporting free and peaceful political expression and participation. At the same time its considerable resources must be brought to bear instantly and resolutely when potentially violent situations arise, either from covert or overt sources. The resources exist but their improper use in the past has been part of the problem instead of the solution.

The various peace-promoting structures with their capacity to foster and encourage a peace culture and tolerance and to intervene in tense situations also have a vital role to play. They need to be fully supported and expanded, both politically and financially, in order to maximise their effectiveness.

At the rate of political killings of the last 3 years, 2600 people will die during the 10 month period from July 1993 to 27 April 1994, election day. Everything will depend upon the twin efforts of the peace-keeping and the peace-promoting structures, described above, as to whether that frightening figure can be substantially reduced or whether it will even be exceeded.

The election

The importance of the election itself in bringing an end to the violence, cannot be overestimated. Provided it is conducted in a free and fair manner, it will reveal the true support base for each and every participant and put an end to speculation about where the support lies. Political non-entities will be exposed and relegated to the rubbish heap of history; minor players will be cut down to size. Political posturing and grandstanding on the basis of imagined support will no longer have any meaning or impact and trying to win support by violence, threats, intimidation and dirty tricks will no longer have any relevance.

The Namibian experience is instructive. After a dirty election campaign into which the South African government had poured 100 million rand in an effort to affect the outcome by destabilising South West African People's Organisation (SWAPO) and promoting Democratic Turnhalle Alliance (DTA), the electorate's decision became known and a constitution was expeditiously adopted. Almost overnight political violence disappeared in spite of dire predictions to the contrary by those who warned that the ethnic diversity of Namibia would bedevil all efforts to bring about peace. But the end of the political struggle for power signalled by the election result brought with it the end to political violence. The purpose of such violence no longer applied.

In South Africa can we expect the same to happen? Certainly the violence related to the political jockeying for position must end once the election results are known. But will there then be dissidents who will not accept the results, will refuse to recognise them and have the power to act upon their refusal?

Acceptance of the results

If one examines the possible existence of groups powerful enough to fill the role of spoiler after an election and with enough muscle to mount a sustainable campaign of violence to thwart the result, then not one emerges at the level of UNITA in Angola, which is the example constantly referred to when pondering the acceptance of election results. The key questions in this issue are support base and sustainability; on both counts the 3 possible candidates fall short.

The first possible spoiler is the white political right wing including the members and supporters of the Conservative Party (CP) and extra-parliamentary groupings to the right of the CP. It could also include some disaffected members and supporters of the National Party. At the outside we are looking at 5% of the total population and probably less than 1% of total population if one is considering only those who are prepared to bear arms and engage in a violent confrontation. From where material support for this hard core would be forthcoming is difficult to imagine especially in a world where there will be strong international pressure for the acceptance of the outcome of democratic elections and for an end to apartheid.

The second possible spoiler is the white military right wing including elements in the security establishment which are unwilling to be part of the transformation of police, defence and intelligence into structures ready to serve a democratically elected government. It could also include members of the security portfolios within the Nationalist government. There is also an obvious overlap with the political right wing. However, material support and sustainability would be totally in the hands of the elected government and dependent upon a healthy economy. A military coup is totally out of the question having regard to the high proportion of blacks in both the police and defence forces. There must also be a significant number of whites in both forces who accept that their professional careers and aspirations will survive and even be advanced in a non-racial democracy.

The third possible spoiler is the black right wing in the form of governments and administrations of those homelands that struggle bitterly to cling to their inherited power. They can be expected to draw support from the white right wing, each for their own reasons, in spite of being the strangest of bedfellows. However, a big question mark hangs over the support they can expect from their own populations where the desire for democratic freedom is extremely compelling. Another compelling factor against sustainability of a go-it-alone attempt is the question of economic viability. During 1992, about 15% of the national budget (or nearly 14 billion rand) went as straight non-repayable grants to prop up the 10 homelands of which the greatest single beneficiary was KwaZulu at R3.148 billion (*Business Day*, 1 September 1992). In addition it was reported in *Business Day* on 15 September 1992, that loans in the region of 7 to 8 billion rand made by South African commercial banks and the Development Bank of Southern Africa to the 4 TBVC 'states', are guaranteed by the South African government. This generous support from parent to offspring will disappear on election day, if not before. Replacing it from other sources would be an impossible task, and collapse inevitable.

In summary, the HRC has strong hopes that a free and fair election will dramatically reduce political violence and that any attempts to reject the result will be non-sustainable. However, long-term stability and peace are going to depend on how a democratically elected government performs in delivering the fruits of democracy to all the people of South Africa. Therein lies our best guarantee that violence and destabilisation will never return to haunt us again.

11 COUNTDOWN TO THE ELECTIONS July 1993–April 1994

In July 1993, the date for South Africa's first non-racial democratic elections was announced: 27 April 1994. This announcement was the moment the whole nation had been waiting for and the next 10-month period of run-up to the elections was now being anticipated with a range of emotions from jubilation to apprehension. For those who were well aware of the ongoing strategy of destabilisation, a major concern was the anticipated impact on the loss of life during this period.

This chapter examines the actual course of destabilisation during the 10-month period and for that purpose draws upon HRC Monthly Reports from July 1993 to April 1994.

DESTABILISATION DURING THE ELECTION CAMPAIGN
HRC monthly reports, July 1993–April 1994

The announcement in July 1993 of the date of the election produced an instantaneous and electrifying reaction. (See Fig. 20). Deaths in political violence for that month shot up to 605 from the previous month's figure of 267 (very close to the monthly average of 259 over the past 3 years). The figure of 605 deaths in one month far outstrips any other month since August 1990 when 709 deaths were recorded and it seemed the country was being taken back in time to those apocalyptic days. This dramatic escalation of violence centred mostly around the PWV region where the death toll leapt to almost 4 times its previous levels, stayed there for a couple of months and then slowly settled back to more 'normal' levels as the elections came and went. The pattern for Natal, while also reflecting an immediate increase in the political temperature, was somewhat different – a less sharp increase occurred in July of about 50% on the previous year's average, but then kept rising in a sustained manner peaking in election month at around 2.5 times previous levels.

In total for the 10-month period, 4608 deaths were reported across the country or 2000 more than predicted from an extrapolation of the previous 3 years. In percentage terms, the political death rate for the period was 78% higher than during the previous 3 years and the incident rate was 102% higher.

To some extent the pattern of deaths in Natal does not come as a great surprise if one takes into account the history of a battle for political turf and the uncertainty generated by events leading up to the eleventh hour decision on 19 April of the IFP to participate in the elections. However, the pattern in the PWV is a totally different story and the sudden explosion in July, August and September 1993 cries out for an explanation. There is clearly a hidden hand in this pattern, with the express intention of subverting the election process by creating a situation in which free and fair elections would not be possible. The epicentre of this thrust was in the East Rand sub-region accounting for 90% of all deaths in the PWV. The record of this period abounds with high levels of vigilante activity in and around hostels in the East Rand and persistent reports of security force complicity; in other words, a re-run of the events of August 1990. The message emerging from this East Rand war was that elections at this level of violence would be impossible and that the process should therefore be aborted or, at least, postponed.

Vigilante activity was not the only element to experience a revival. Other stakeholders in the perpetuation of apartheid power were also galvanised into action as the day of reckoning became a reality that was drawing close. Most visible were the governments and administrations of the 'self-governing' homelands and the 'independent' homelands, now faced with the issue of how to realign themselves within an imminent democratic South Africa of a unitary nature. The greatest resistance to this prospect came from Bophuthatswana under the leadership of Lucas Mangope. He moved quickly to prohibit all activity related to election campaigning on the basis that Bophuthatswana was an independent country and its citizens could not participate in the elections of another country. All election meetings, voter education workshops and general campaigning were prohibited. When they did occur, police moved in to break up such gatherings, confiscated and destroyed election material, detained and arrested large numbers of people and pressed charges in court. Attempts by the ANC and church groups to 'enter' Bophuthatswana for the purpose of promoting free political activity were forcibly blocked, as was a proposed visit by Nelson Mandela. A ban was placed on any South African trade union from operating in Bophuthatswana. Human Rights Day (10 December) celebrations were banned and student unrest was severely dealt with and the university closed for a period.

From July 1993 to February 1994 the message was clear – the elections have nothing to do with Bophuthatswana and Bophuthatswana is not about to relinquish its sovereignty. However, this was not a message which was acceptable to the vast majority of the inhabitants of Bophuthatswana who were not to be denied their South African birthright nor their right to participate in their own liberation. During March, 1 month ahead of the election, a popular uprising in the face of extensive but crumbling security force action, succeeded in overthrowing the Mangope regime; this in spite of the intervention of white right wing 'commandos' whose only identity of interest was to thwart democratic elections. This mission impossible by Mangope and his right wing allies resulted in the loss of close on 50 lives with 150 injured.

Another apartheid power stakeholder that came to the fore during this period was the white right wing itself. During the year prior to the announcement of the election date, right wing activity had been relatively subdued, being responsible for 10 deaths in 82 incidents, although several incidents were of a serious nature. From January 1994 onwards it became very apparent that the AWB was adopting terror tactics with the express purpose of obstructing the election campaign. The tactics involved the use of commercial explosives to bomb targets such as ANC offices, polling stations, taxi ranks

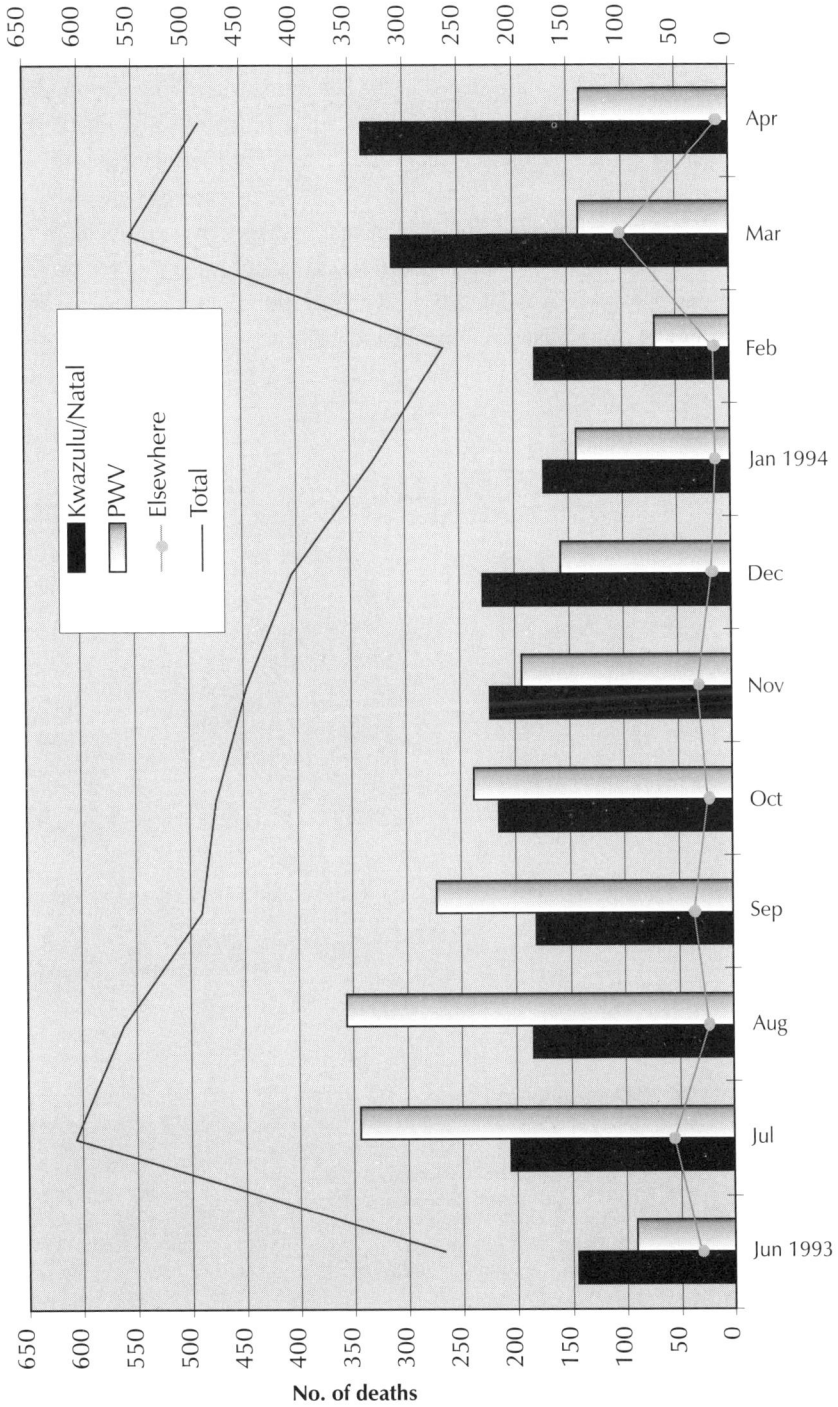

FIGURE 20
Deaths in political violence (June 1993–April 1994)

and civilian high traffic areas. During the 4 months of January to April 1994, the HRC recorded 80 such bomb attacks of which close on half occurred in the last couple of weeks prior to the election date. Several of these were massive bombs and the murderous intent is evident from the fact that 2 bombs placed in the last week caused the random deaths of 19 people in high movement public areas. For the total 10-month period, the right wing caused the deaths of 48 people and the injury of 279 more in 172 incidents which included 85 bombings.

By the time election day arrived, the human cost of taking the process from the start of negotiations in mid 1990 to the actual elections to install a democratic government, a period of just under 4 years, was 14 000 dead and 22 000 injured. These are the terms in which the strategy of destabilisation must be judged.

PART D
IN THE AFTERMATH OF DEMOCRATIC ELECTIONS MAY 1994–DECEMBER 1996

Introduction

The South African elections of April 1994 have been widely hailed as a 'political miracle' and the subsequent installation of South Africa's first democratically elected government referred to as the result of a 'negotiated revolution'.

As predicted, there ensued a dramatic cooling of the political temperature manifested in a rapid and marked decline in the political death-toll in the months that followed. Also, as expected, no major force with any significant muscle emerged to challenge the validity of the election results or to pose a threat to their acceptance. On the contrary, a realignment of the political landscape, imagined or actual, has taken place with the departure or evaporation of some previous aspirant stakeholders in political power; and with the re-positioning of others anxious to retain whatever power possible from their apartheid inheritance.

Part D of this book examines the residual destabilisation activity continuing beyond the transfer of power to a democratically elected majority government in an attempt to assess from where such activity emanates and whether it poses any threat to our fledgling democracy.

Calendar of major events after elections

Date		Event
1994	May	Inauguration of Nelson Mandela as president. Opening of first democratic parliament of South Africa.
	October	Constitutional court established.
1995	June	Truth and Reconciliation Commission approved by parliament.
	July	Local government elections announced for 1 November.
	October	Local government elections postponed for KwaZulu/Natal.
	November	Local government elections (except KwaZulu/Natal and parts of Western Cape).
	December	Truth Commission starts work Shobashobane massacre.
1996	May	Local government elections in Western Cape (29th).
	June	Local government elections in KwaZulu/Natal (26th).
	December	Final constitution approved by the constitutional court and signed by president Mandela.

12 POST-ELECTION POLITICAL VIOLENCE

As South Africa went to the polls on 27 April 1994, many voters must have wondered what the future would hold. After 4 years of unremitting destabilisation in which 14 000 lives had been lost, would the elections simply open the door to further violence and instability along the pattern of the rejected election outcome in Angola or would they result in instant success in eliminating or at least markedly reducing political violence as happened after the elections of Namibia? The coming days, weeks and months would be critical in revealing which direction South Africa was to take.

What actually unfolded after the elections is described in some detail below, relying upon careful monitoring of some 4600 incidents by HRC during a subsequent period of 32 months.

POST-ELECTION STATISTICS
HRC monthly reports, May 1994–December 1996

The abrupt and dramatic decline in political violence after the democratic elections of 27 April 1994 is starkly illustrated in Fig. 21, which traces the deaths in political violence throughout the country recorded by HRC from January 1994 to December 1996. During the month of the elections, HRC recorded 487 such deaths. During the next month the figure plummeted to 195, a drop of 60%, followed by a further drop of 10% the following month. Since then, with minor fluctuations, the trend has been ever downwards. By way of comparison, the average monthly death tolls from political violence recorded by HRC in successive periods are shown below

Average monthly political death tolls

- Run-up to the elections (July 1993 to April 1994)   461

- Post election months (May 1994 to December 1994)   133

- Year of 1995 (January to December)   100

- Year of 1996 (January to December)   83

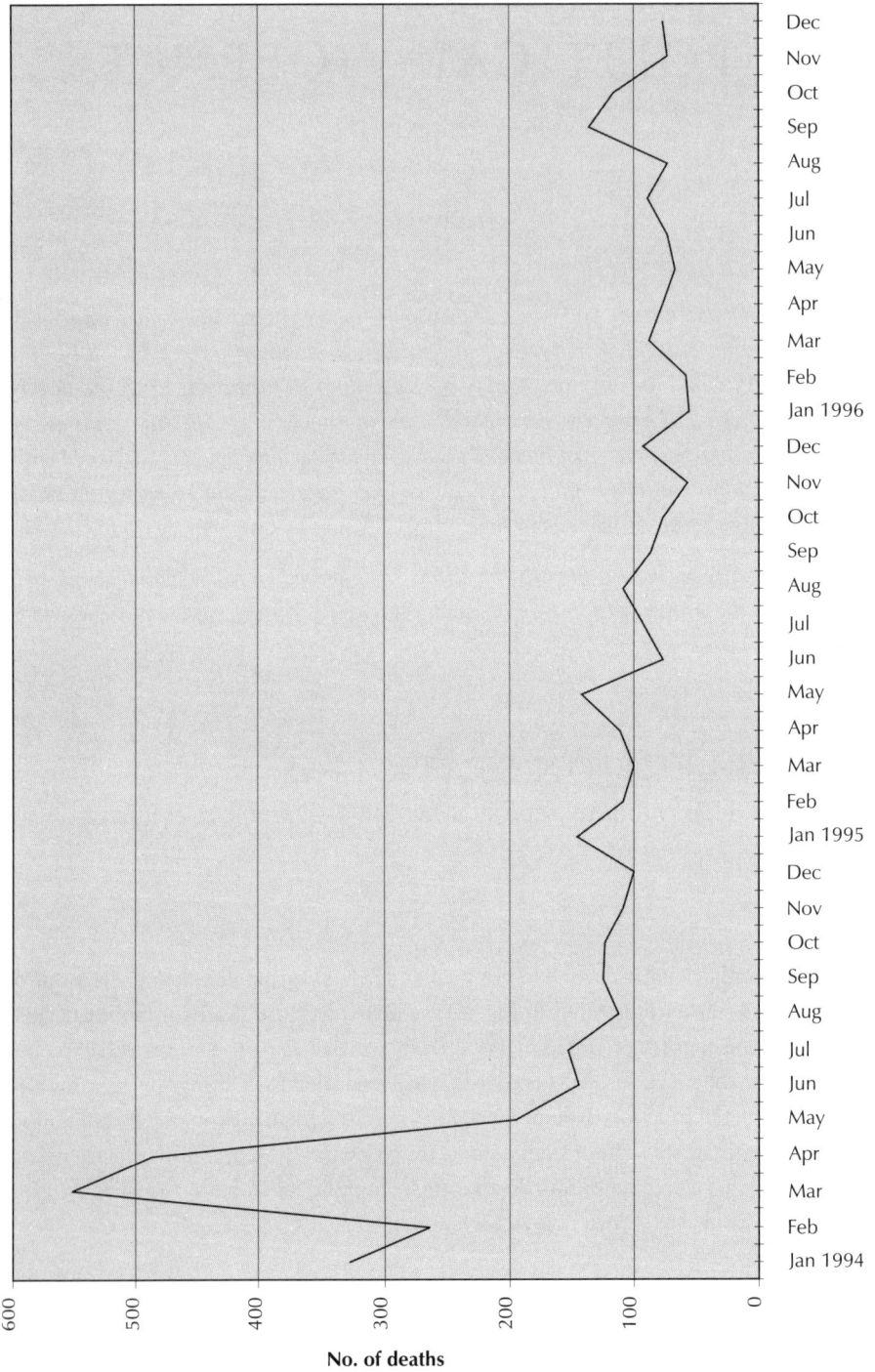

FIGURE 21
Deaths in political violence (January 1994–December 1996)

Unpacking the statistics

Even the above statistics do not reveal the full extent of the de-escalation in political violence subsequent to the elections. To obtain a clearer picture we need to examine various components contributing to these statistics and in particular to focus attention on 3 forms of violence which, while they had strong political origins, can now, in present circumstances, best be described as socio-economic violence with, at most, political overtones. These are: taxi violence, stock-theft violence and mine violence.

Taxi violence

This is certainly a form of violence which harks back to the era of destabilisation. It first emerged as a variant of indiscriminate terror attacks on commuters (train, bus and taxi) but there is no doubt that its character has changed to a war for turf in an emergent form of survival for tens of thousands engaged in the informal sector. Deaths in this form of violence are occurring in virtually all of the provinces of South Africa. Numbers of deaths recorded by HRC in the periods referred to above, are as follows:

	Total	Monthly average
• July 1993 to April 1994	76	7.6
• May 1994 to December 1994	164	20.5
• January 1995 to December 1995	200	16.7
• January 1996 to December 1996	312	26.0

Stock-theft violence

A not yet fully explained phenomenon, first noted in September 1993, has arisen in the Tsolo and Qumbu districts of Transkei in the Eastern Cape and, for want of a better description, is being referred to as stock-theft violence. The death toll in this conflict is quite considerable and because of its undeniable political overtones cannot be ignored in general reporting of political violence. However, because of its isolated and particular nature, it makes sense to separate out such statistics when assessing, as we are doing in this chapter, the national levels of ongoing political destabilisation. For the record, the number of deaths in stock-theft violence are as follows:

	Total	Monthly average
• July 1993 to April 1994	17	1.7
• May 1994 to December 1994	46	5.8
• January 1995 to December 1995	77	6.4
• January 1996 to December 1996	128	10.7

Mine violence

Clashes amongst workers on mines have taken place during 1995 and 1996 which are difficult to categorise as political, ethnic, socio-economic or as a combination of these.

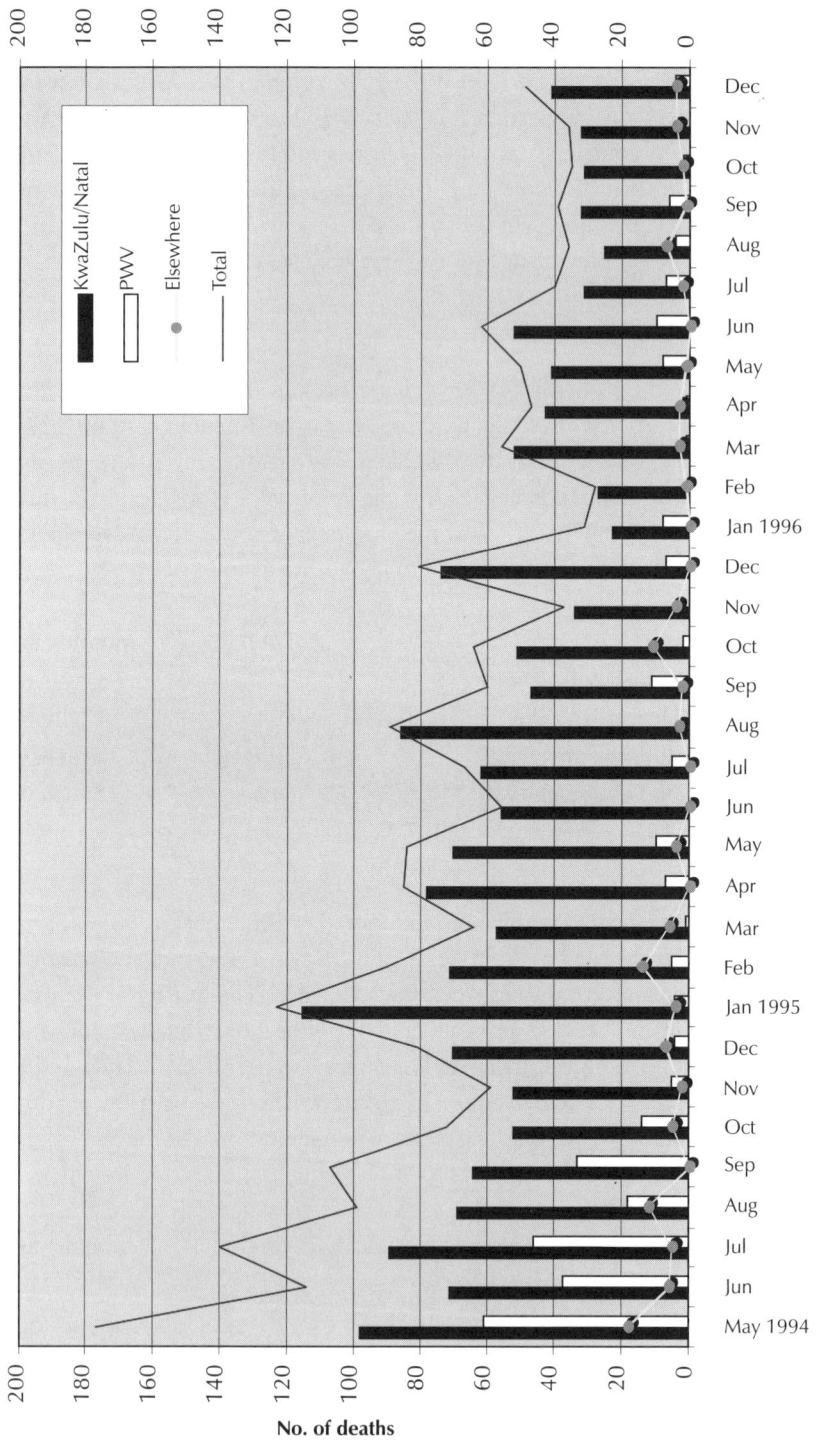

FIGURE 22
Adjusted death toll (May 1994–December 1996)

There is no doubt where the origins and responsibility for such conflict lie, but it makes no sense to distort violence levels in the statistics of a particular province in which the mines happen to be located. The total numbers are in any event, relatively small. In 1995 there were 15 deaths attributable to mine violence while in 1996 the number rose to 31.

Adjusted post-election statistics

By separating out the deaths caused by taxi, stock-theft and mine violence we are left with a more meaningful and undistorted picture of post-election political violence. Below is an adjusted version of the previous figures taking this separation into account.

Adjusted monthly death toll
- Run-up to the elections (July 1993 to April 1994)   452
- Post-election months (May 1994 to December 1994)   106
- Year of 1995 (January to December)   75
- Year of 1996 (January to December)   42

On this basis, political tension and destabilisation was running during 1996 at a level less than 10% of that during the run-up period to the elections. Just where the residual tension continues and at what intensity is shown in Fig. 22.

KwaZulu/Natal clearly emerges as the main contributor. In the 8 post-election months of 1994, KZN accounted for 67% of the political deaths, rising to 89% in 1995 and reaching 84% in 1996. Gauteng, after accounting for 26% of political deaths during the cooling-off post-election period of 1994, was almost eclipsed as a contributor in 1995 (5.7%) and 1996 (10.0%). Other areas combined came close to being free of political deaths contributing only 7.8% in post-election 1994, 5.2% in 1995 and 5.5% in 1996. In summary it can be said that, except for KwaZulu/Natal, South Africa is now substantially free of the kind of political violence which results in deaths on an ongoing basis.

13 APARTHEID STAKEHOLDERS – WHERE ARE THEY NOW?

South Africa can heave a collective sigh of relief that its democratic elections produced an outcome which closely parallelled the Namibian experience and not that of Angola. Transfer of political power to a democratically elected government was essentially accomplished and accepted. However, it would be naive to think that the acceptance of the outcome was unqualified in all quarters and that the orchestrated destabilisation of the past came to an abrupt end on the day the election results were announced. It must be expected that the forces which had been at work to defend and retain apartheid power would want to salvage what benefits they could from their erstwhile privileged position.

In Chapters 9 and 10 detailed analyses were made of the beneficiaries of apartheid power and it now seems appropriate to consider each of these stakeholders in turn, in order to assess their potential for further destabilisation into the future.

Apartheid casualties

The tricameral parliament (TCP)

The tricameral parliament with its dominant white house, token houses for 'coloured' and 'Indian' populations and total exclusion of African blacks, has disappeared to be superceded by a democratically elected non-racial parliament. Three tiers of representative government have been established under a constitution, initially in a negotiated interim form and now in a democratically adopted final form, which is the highest law in the land and to which all governmental structures and indeed all citizens are accountable.

However, traces of the past are still present, at least until the next elections in April 1999. At the national tier of government the transitional phase commits us to an obligatory government of national unity which allows the National Party to play a role of power sharing for a 5-year period (even though, for tactical reasons, they have decided to withdraw from playing this role). The NP during final Constitutional negotiations made strenuous efforts to have the compulsory power sharing arrangement extended beyond April 1999 but they were denied this extra lease of life.

Within the second tier of government, the provincial tier, there exists a relatively high degree of federalism that serves to perpetuate the survival, at least for the present, of 2 of the old stakeholders in apartheid power. In the Western Cape the National Party holds a dominant position, while in KwaZulu/Natal the old KwaZulu homeland lives on in the somewhat modified form of the KZN provincial government. Especially in the case of the latter it is clear from post-election statistics that a significant measure of instability still exists and the potential for destabilisation continues.

At the third tier, the level of local government, the distortions of apartheid still persist. We are squarely in a transitional phase which incorporates by agreement the presence of racially skewed representation in local councils in the interests of continuity and to allow for a period of development of skills and experience within previously disadvantaged communities. This temporary arrangement must be brought to an end by 1999 but some resistance and potential for destabilisation must be anticipated, particularly in historically conservative white towns and also in rural areas dominated by traditional leaders, both past beneficiaries of apartheid power.

Homeland structures

Homeland structures have also been relegated to the scrapheap of history. One after the other, the 4 'independent' and the 6 'self-governing' homelands melted away, capitulated or were deposed in the headlong and irrepressible run-up to South Africa's first democratic elections. But although the structures have disappeared their legacy lingers on in the form of a multiplicity of effects with which we will have to grapple for some time to come. Homelands' administrations, armies, police forces and assets have had to be integrated into the New South Africa, with the new provincial administrations bearing the brunt of this rationalisation. The homeland system opened up huge opportunities for corruption, self-advancement and enrichment and irresponsible management of resources. As a result, the new South Africa has inherited debt, missing assets, 'ghost' pensioners, 'ghost' workers and self-promoted officials, to mention but a few forms of mismanagement, fraud and corruption. Many of the old beneficiaries of homelands are still there, clinging onto their benefits and making a negative contribution to the growth of a healthy democracy.

Apartheid survivors

The National Party (NP)

Nominally the NP has survived the transfer of power to a majority government, in itself a remarkable feat under the circumstances. Given their past record they can count themselves extremely fortunate not to have been summarily banished to the political wilderness. They can attribute their good fortune either to the generosity of spirit shown by the majority or to the good sense of the majority in pursuing a path of compromise in order to limit the possibility of violent conflict or perhaps a mixture of both. In any event, the architects of formal apartheid were permitted to participate in democratic elections and to test their support at the polls. They emerged with 20.4% of the national votes cast, and with a majority in the Western Cape Province of 53%. Both results were attributable to their support within the white electorate and those within the Afrikaans speaking 'coloured' community whom the NP contrived to attract on the basis of the 'devil you know.' In terms of the interim constitution, this support entitled the NP to take its place in the government of national unity and to play a controlling role in the Western Cape provincial legislature.

Surprising as this outcome may have been to some, the NP has lost its political power and with it the access to the trappings of power such as the security forces and public administration. Furthermore, local government elections in November 1995 and May 1996 indicate declining support for the NP, while almost daily revelations about atrocities of the apartheid past continue to batter their already badly dented image. The struggle to throw off the baggage of the past and to create a new identity appears to be an impossible task. All the indications are that the National Party is a spent force and is unlikely to survive in its present form. As a spent force, its potential for further destabilisation is limited.

The white right wing

The white right wing has also survived the transition to a non-racial democracy but in a radically altered form. Never a monolith, it can be said to have split broadly into 2 blocs, a process which preceded the elections.

The first bloc emerged as a political party, the Freedom Front (FF), which opted to pursue its political objectives by peaceful and constitutional means. It participated in the elections, emerging with 424 555 votes, or 2.17% of the votes cast; in 4 provinces, (PWV, Eastern Transvaal, OFS and Northern Cape) it was able to muster around 6% of the votes. Amongst its objectives are the establishment of a volkstaat (an Afrikaner homeland) on the basis of 'substantial proven support'. To this end it negotiated the inclusion of a provision in the interim constitution (and extended into the final constitution) for the establishment of a volkstaat council. In addition, the final constitution provides for the establishment of a commission for the promotion and protection of the rights of cultural, religious and linguistic communities. Armed with these concessions, the Freedom Front has been able to convince nearly half-a-million supporters that they are not about to lose their cultural identity and that their future lies in peaceful and constitutional processes. Their problem now lies in how to demonstrate 'substantial support' within geographical pockets and how to string these pockets together to form an entity which is politically and economically viable.

The second bloc consists of those right wing organisations which chose to pursue extra-parliamentary and often violent means of reaching their objectives. This non-homogeneous bloc includes the old Conservative Party of the tricameral parliament and the *Afrikaner Weerstandsbeweging* (AWB) amongst many others. As we have seen in Chapter 11, their rejection of democratic elections was expressed in the form of a paroxysm of violence which reached a peak in the week preceding election day, costing 19 lives in that week alone. However, it is significant that no bombings or other organised attacks by the white right wing were recorded in the 31 months following the elections from May 1994 to November 1996; the only incidents and casualties recorded in that time arising from the actions of individuals, such as farmers shooting child trespassers or alleged chicken thieves, or racial clashes at schools and tertiary education institutions. Then, on Christmas Eve 1996, the long period of freedom from right wing bomb attacks was shattered by 2 explosions in Worcester, Western Cape which claimed 4 lives and injured 60 others. A group by the name of *Boere Aanvals Troepe* claimed responsibility.

But it seems true to say that the AWB which was from February 1990 to April 1994 involved in well over 100 organised violent acts including about 100 bomb attacks, has since the elections refrained from any further similar violence. It is of interest to note that the AWB in a submission to the Parliamentary Portfolio Committee on Justice when debating the bill to establish a Truth and Reconciliation Commission in January 1995, stated the following:

> As far as the AWB ... is concerned, we would very much like to become part of an all inclusive political settlement in South Africa. We would like to be able to call a full meeting of our general staff and senior officers to discuss burning issues such as participation or otherwise in the upcoming local elections; an official meeting with the present government leadership; and general discussions with the government on how possible solutions may be found.

The problem of the AWB at the time of making the submission (and the reason for making it) was that many of their general staff and senior officers were either in detention or awaiting trial (for the violent acts of early 1994) under severe bail conditions, and more to the point, ineligible for amnesty because of the cut-off date in the Constitution for acts committed after 5 December 1993. The AWB went on to plead 'for the sake of peace' that the cut-off date be extended so as to qualify their members for amnesty for acts committed up to election day. In their submission they stated: 'We would submit that this cut off date is the last stumbling block lying in the way of a final and peaceful resolution of our country's problems.'

The AWB had to wait nearly 2 years for their plea to be agreed to but in the meantime they adhered to what seems to have been a self-imposed moratorium on violent acts. It now remains to be seen if they will adhere to the spirit of their submission and engage in becoming 'part of an all inclusive political settlement in South Africa'.

In summary, the white right wing with its deep divisions, limited support and minimal resources, cannot be considered as a meaningful survivor from the apartheid era which would be capable of derailing democracy in South Africa. At worst, any continuing destabilising role will be limited to sporadic and declining racial acts and incidents of sabotage.

The security establishment

Few will deny the seminal role that the security establishment played as the instrument of repression and destabilisation in the past but given that a democracy, too, requires security institutions for its continued well-being, the transformation of these institutions from instruments of repression to friendly protectors of citizens rights, is critical. The new constitution spells out the responsibilities, objectives and norms of behaviour to which our defence, police and intelligence services must aspire and thereby establishes the mould of the end-products of transformation which began some time ago and is ongoing. The task of successful transformation is formidable when one considers the starting ingredients of apartheid security forces, homelands police and armies, and the armed wings of the liberation movements.

Within this context it is not surprising that elements from the old apartheid security apparatus are resisting and impeding transformation. Old attitudes and old networks still persist, both within state structures and within the privatised security industry which has sprung up to capitalise and thrive upon the new criminal instability which has taken hold. This industry has become the home for former members of security force special units, mercenaries and 'dogs of war'. In some cases their tentacles even extend into the international arena (as with the externally based activities of Executive Outcomes) and with a capacity to engage in illegal arms trade and the peddling of state secrets to which they have been privy in the past.

A particularly worrying aspect is the extent to which these elements, located both within state and privatised institutions, have a vested interest in instability and simultaneously are strategically positioned to foster that instability, particularly criminal instability for personal gain. Their emphasis has shifted from being engaged in obstructing the advent of democracy to promoting (criminal) self-interest. This is manifesting itself in police and other complicity in crime syndicates, gun-running, drug trafficking, taxi wars, protection rackets, vehicle hijackings and scams, stock theft, theft of state assets, and so on ad infinitum. Taken together these activities amount to economic sabotage on a massive scale, every bit as crippling to an emerging democracy as the political destabilisation of the past.

The public service

The new constitution defines the basic values and principles of democratic administration to which the public service must aspire. Not surprisingly there is a huge gap between this ideal and the practices of the past apartheid structures. Here too, then, a radical transformation has been necessary but on a scale which comes into some perspective when it is realised that over a million public servants were involved and that the existence of 10 homelands administrations complicated the task enormously.

Responses by the old inherited public servants to the transformation challenges have been varied. There have been those who have genuinely and enthusiastically welcomed the arrival of a new atmosphere of openness, transparency and accountability in administration after long years of suffocation. Then there are those with a resistance to change, for ideological or attitudinal reasons, which results in an uncooperative passivity. Finally there are those who are actively engaged in what can only be described as economic sabotage by profiting personally from the opportunities that have been exposed during this period of transition for corruption, taking of bribes, theft of state assets, drawing of salaries by ghost workers, sale of forged documents and scams of every conceivable kind. This amounts to destabilisation of an extremely debilitating nature.

The business community

The history of the business community as a role player in the development of apartheid in South Africa goes back much further in time than that of the National Party. For economic reasons the early business community was an enthusiastic promoter and supporter of a system which ensured an unlimited supply of cheap compliant labour for its mines, industry and agriculture. The advent of National Party power in 1948 with a penchant for tightening apartheid controls within an ideological framework, served only to enhance the benefits which the business community could derive from the economic practices of apartheid. Amongst the additional benefits were an extraordinary range of government incentives for establishing and running so-called border industries located close to homeland labour reservoirs; government support for 'strategic' industries (often of doubtful viability) through high levels of protection against imports and competition; and the award of valuable government contracts to those who gave their support to the system of apartheid.

However, the wheel of fortune was to turn and from being a prime beneficiary of, and stakeholder in, apartheid power, the business community watched in dismay as apartheid began turning into an albatross around its neck. The revulsion of the international community against apartheid practices resulted in the South African economy being threatened with collapse, with the business community as the biggest potential losers.

Against this background, the business community must count itself fortunate not only to have survived the demise of the apartheid system but to have survived with its assets intact. Survival also implies transformation from apartheid economic practices to democratic economic practices which will address the needs of 100% of the population and not only 15% as in the past. The extent to which such transformation is taking place has so far been slow to emerge and we have yet to see much enthusiasm on the part of the business community for substantive fixed productive investment which will create jobs and ensure growth. Moreover, resistant elements within business are frustrating the development of a democratic culture through engaging in white-collar crime of all kinds, money laundering and the illegal transfer of assets abroad. It is in the business community's own best interests to take steps to counter the impression that it has not yet unequivocally shifted its allegiance from apartheid to democracy.

Transformation of the 'third force'

If one accepts the concept of a 'third force' as an amalgam of stakeholders in apartheid power which actively opposed the arrival of non-racial democracy in South Africa, whether they acted individually or at times in concert with one another, then it is a valid question to inquire how the surviving stakeholders fit together today and what transformation the third force has itself undergone.

Firstly, the membership of the team has changed, as we have seen, with some dropping out, some relegated to a minor role and others going their own way. Secondly, the objectives have altered quite radically in that, having lost the battle to prevent the advent of a democratic order, the emphasis has now shifted to the individual pursuit of personal interests. There is little scope for teamwork when it comes to salvaging remnants of benefits and privileges from the wreck of apartheid and so the days of the third force are numbered. In its dying form it has assumed the ugly characteristic of an economic saboteur, which opportunistically and criminally exploits the instability inherent in a transforming society.

A summary of residual destabilisation potential

In summarising the remaining potential for destabilisation in South Africa we focus on the post-election period of May 1994 up till December 1996, under the 3 headings of:

1. Political violence
2. Socio-economic violence
3. Economic sabotage

POLITICAL VIOLENCE

- Warlordism in KwaZulu/Natal claimed 1800 lives post-election (430 in 1996).
- White right wing claimed 22 lives post-election (5 during 1996).
- Old security force elements. Covert activities.

SOCIO-ECONOMIC VIOLENCE

- Taxi industry wars claimed 676 lives post-election (312 in 1996).
- Stock theft wars claimed 251 lives post-election (128 in 1996).
- Mine clashes claimed 46 lives post-election (31 in 1996).
- Crime syndicates.

ECONOMIC SABOTAGE

- Old homeland elements.
- Old and existing security force elements.
- Old and existing public service elements.
- Business community elements.

EPILOGUE

In the opening chapter of this book the reader was introduced to the many faces of apartheid repression which were clearly recognisable at the time of its writing in 1989. Yet more faces were soon to emerge from the shadows, but few could have anticipated the extreme ugliness of the final mask of destabilisation that was to bring down the curtain on this cruel saga.

By the time the liberation struggle had run its full course and a democratically elected government was installed, the human cost, in the simple terms of loss of life, reached the appalling total of around 21 000 dead. What was of particular significance was the fact that of this total, 14 000 lives were lost in the 4 years immediately preceding the elections, i.e. during the destabilisation era. In other words, twice as many people died during the 4 years of destabilisation as died during the preceding 40 years. This pattern is echoed in the numbers of major massacres recorded by the HRC – 91 during the 4 years of destabilisation as compared with 46 during the 40 years of total strategy. Likewise, assassinations by hit squads escalated 6 times in annual rate during the first 3 years of destabilisation as compared with the rate during 1980 to 1989. This highly skewed pattern of destructive repression speaks volumes about the callous duplicity of destabilisation strategy. It must surely rank as the mother of all covert operations.

Ultimately, this is a book that runs the risk of falling into the wrong hands. As a chronicle of every imaginable form of repression and control devised by the apartheid regime, it may well serve as a manual, a field guide, for any aspirant dictator or repressive regime for the purpose of establishing and exercising control over a resistant population. Numerous examples could be quoted of contemporary regimes taking a leaf out of the apartheid book in order to tighten up or refine their own repressive arrangements.

How then, to prevent further leaves being taken from this book? Fortunately history has already begun to provide answers, both at the global level and at the level of South Africa as the prime victim of apartheid repression.

In the global village of today, the observance or violation of human rights is no longer regarded as a domestic matter. The international community gave a clear and unequivocal demonstration of this principle when it declared apartheid to be a crime against humanity, not only that part of humanity that was the direct recipient of the evils of apartheid, but all humanity. This declaration was an important enunciation of the universality and indivisibility of human rights in today's world. The price to be paid for practising repression increases daily and in the case of the apartheid regime proved to be fatal.

In the new South Africa where there is a natural concern that the repression of the past may never again be visited upon us, a shield has been erected to guard against such a possibility. That shield is the Bill of Rights guaranteed by a constitution which is itself underpinned by a system of checks and balances and agreed to by the overwhelming majority of our population. It is true to say that our Bill of Rights can stand proud with any similar document anywhere in the world today. The strongest guarantee that repression in any form not be allowed to creep back into our lives, is to ensure that the government of the day observes the classic four layers of its obligations towards our Bill of Rights, namely, to respect, to protect, to promote and to fulfill these rights, and in so doing, deliver the fruits of democracy to all the people of South Africa.

Political deaths in police custody (non-security) 1984–1989

This is a list of deaths in politically related circumstances while the victim was in the custody of the police, not prison authorities. They are deaths which occurred on arrest, during transport to a police station, during interrogation or while being held awaiting trial in a police lock-up. In general security branch police were not directly involved, but in 5 instances this was the case and the victims' names will also be found under deaths in security detention listed in Table 7.

Date	Name (Age)	Affiliation	Place	Description
1984				
15 July	Ngalo, Johannes (26)		Parys	Found dead in cell due to serious internal injuries.
29 September	Moleleke, Jacob (16)		Sebokeng	Shot in head by policeman during altercation between police and other arrested youths in police van.
5/7 November	Masunyane, Anthony		Katlehong	Police informed victim's family of death in custody after stayaway.
11/19 November	Maseko, Samson (19)		Katlehong	Found at mortuary with terrible marks & bruises after reported arrest.
22 November	Ngwenya, Abel (31)		Daveyton	Police reported epileptic fit as cause of death while pathologist indicated violence involved in death and family denied any history of epilepsy.
late 84/early 85	Korotsoane, Tatlheho (28)		Vereeniging	Reported to have been in security detention, but police denied this.
1985				
29 March	Mvulane, Bheki (18)		Katlehong	Brain injuries from alleged police violence while awaiting trial.
5 May	Mutsi, Sipho (20)	COSAS	Odendaalsrus	Died during interrogation; post-mortem revealed head injuries and severe sjambok weals.
6 May	Raditsela, Andries (29)	COSATU, CWIU	Tsakane	Died of head injuries after being violently confronted by police while producing documents to counter car theft accusations.
3 July	Muggels, Mzwandile (20)	Karoo Youth Congress	Steytlerville	Died from gunshot wounds during arrest at memorial service.
5 July	Spogter, Johannes (13)	Nephew of Muggels	Steytlerville	Found dead (attributed to head injuries) during routine cell visit.
16 August	Mokoena, Sonnyboy (24)		Pilgrim's Rest	Allegedly found hanged in cell.
16 August	George, Thembalake (15)	KWT Youth League	Kingwilliam's Town	Mother found victim unresponsive at hospital with badly swollen face after arrested at a student gathering.
18/19 August	Ndzandze, Loyiso (20)	KWT Youth League	Kingwilliam's Town	Circumstances same as George above, except died a few days later.
21 September	Mbotya, Mbuyiselo (35)	KWT Youth League/UDF	Kingwilliam's Town	Died from head injuries.
24 September	Ndondo, Batandwa (22)	SRC – University of Transkei	Cala, Transkei	Allegedly shot several times by police on the outskirts of Cala.
18 October	Ramalepe, Ngwako	President SRC – Modjadji Teacher Training College	Kgapane, Lebowa	Assaulted by police at station and later dumped along a road.
17 November	Mogale, Meshack (16)	Student	Mamelodi East	Sister, arrested with him at a night vigil for unrest victim, alleged he was kicked and sjambokked by police.
1986				
1 April	Phoshoko, Joel (28)	CCAWUSA	Pretoria	Allegedly assaulted by police during interrogation

5 April	Kutumela, Lucky (25)	Journalist/ AZAPO/ MWASA	Mahwelereng, Lebowa	Found dead in police cell with more than 40 sjambok weals.
11 April	Nchabeleng, Peter (59)	President of Northern Transvaal UDF	Schoonoord, Lebowa	Allegedly tortured by police.
12 April	Ngomane, Eric (22)	Student	KaNgwane	Police claim he was shot dead while trying to escape.
19 April	Mashego, Johannes (26)		Parys	Police state he collapsed during interrogation; relatives reported extensive bruising and swollen face upon identifying the victim's body.
26 July	Stuurman, Mlungise (18)		Cradock	Interrogated and then killed by 2 'unrest unit' members who were later sentenced to death for his murder.
11 December	Mapumolo, Matthews	ANC	Swaziland	Accosted and shot at home by a group of armed men; abducted to South Africa while wounded, then died.
13 December	Mogotsi, Joseph	Teacher	Pretoria	Assaulted after police forced car off the road.
15 December	Olifant, Benji (25)		Klerksdorp	Allegedly shot while attempting to escape
1987				
16 February	Unknown youth (17)	Soweto		Allegedly jumped from Casspir in an attempt to escape from custody.
9 July	Cele, Edwin (22)	Lamontville Youth Congress	Durban	Shot by police while allegedly trying to pull the pin from a hand grenade.
9 July	Kriel, Ashley (20)	Bonteheuwel student activist	Athlone	Police reported victim killed during arrest scuffle while post-mortem indicated victim shot in the back at 'point-blank' range.
24 July	Mntonga, Eric	IDASA/SAAWU	Mdantsane	Killed by 6 Ciskei security officers at police cells.
23 August	Nyoka, Caiphus	Student leader	Daveyton	Shot dead by police, execution-style, while raiding his father's home.
4 November	Marume, Ndiko		Sasolburg	Died inside a police van while being transported to Sasolburg police station.
1988				
20 March	Kobe, Andile (22)	George Youth/Civic Associations	Sandkraal	Beaten for at least 30 minutes by police in front of eyewitnesses.
1 December	Khoza, Amos (18)		Johannesburg	Fell seven stories from a flat where he was allegedly escorting police to identify the place where he had made contact with an ANC member.
1989				
23 January	Dakuse, Patrick (36)		Khayelitsha	Shot dead by police after allegedly tried to prime a hand grenade from an arms cache that he had taken the police to see.
21 April	Mbetheni, Dinana (21)		Alice	Found in cell hanging from an electric wire tied to a bar.
22 December	Ruiters, Kevin (22)		Bellville South	Mother found that his face had been 'badly bashed'

Note:

Of the 38 victims listed above, the ages of 31 at the time of death are recorded:

- 13 were under 21 (or 42% of those of recorded age)
- 14 were 21-30 (or 45% of those of recorded age)

List of political assassinations 1974–1989

Date	Place	Name	Affiliation	Description
1974				
February	Botswana	Abraham Onkgopotse Tiro	SASO	Parcel bomb.
–	Zambia	John Dube	ANC	Parcel bomb.
1978				
8 January	Durban	Dr. Rick Turner	Banned political scientist at University of Natal	Shot dead at home.
–	Swaziland	John Majola	ANC	Killed after being abducted.
–	Swaziland	Khela (codename)	ANC	Abducted and killed.
1980				
4 June	Manzini, Swaziland	Patrick Makau, and his child (9)	ANC/MK	Bomb attack on 2 houses.
1981				
1 August	Harare, Zimbabwe	Joe Gqabi	ANC National executive committee member and chief representative in Zimbabwe	Car bomb (several attempts on his life before).
October	Vlakplaas	Peter Dlamini Vuyani Mavuso	ANC ANC/MK	Dlamini handed himself over to C-10, Mavuso was captured in the Matola raid, both were shot dead and burnt.
October	Komatipoort	Sizwe Kondile	ANC	Detained in PE, brought to Komatipoort, killed and burnt
19 Nov.	Umlazi, Durban	Griffiths Mxenge	Civil rights attorney, former ANC member	Found stabbed after being abducted.
–	Gaberone, Botswana	Unnamed man	ANC & unionist (SACTU)	Car bomb.
1982				
4 June	Mbabane, Swaziland	Petrus Nzima Jabu Nzima	Both ANC	Car bomb.
June	Maseru, Lesotho	Z.P. Mbali	ANC	Found decapitated after disappearance on 27 June 1982.
August	Lesotho	Unnamed person		car bomb meant for Chris Hani (MK)
17 August	Maputo, Mozambique	Ruth First	ANC, academic, wife of Joe Slovo (SACP)	Parcel bomb.
1983				
–	Driefontein	Saul Mkize	Community leader	Shot dead while addressing a crowd on forced removal.
22 Nov.	Manzini, Swaziland	Keith McFadden, Zwelakhe Nyanda	Both ANC	Shot dead by 2 gunmen.
1984				
28 June	Lubango, Angola	Jeanette Curtis Schoon, and daughter Katryn (6)	ANC and unionist (SACTU)	Parcel bomb.
13 Sept.	Soweto	Bongani Khumalo	Student activist (COSAS)	Shot dead by police.
1985				
–	Vryburg	Gasuebe Hubhuli	Activist	Shot dead.
14 May	Gaborone, Botswana	Vernon Nkadimeng	Son of SACTU General Secretary	Car bomb.
June	East Rand	Alex Pilane	Student activist (COSAS)	Abducted and beaten to death.

June	near Port Elizabeth	Matthew Goniwe, Sparrow Mkhonto, Ford Calata, Sicelo Mhlawuli	UDF and Cradora UDF and Cradora UDF UDF	Disappeared on 27 June 1985. Later found killed.
1 August	Umlazi, Durban	Victoria Mxenge	UDF, lawyer	Shot and hacked to death.
25 August	Natal north coast	Toto Dweba	UDF and Natal Freedom Charter Committee	Found mutilated.
August	East Rand	Brian Mbulelo Mazibuko	Activist, former prisoner	Stabbed.
September	Durban	Thabo Mokoena	UDF and unionist	Abducted and killed.
19 Sept.	Pimville	Godfrey Thuso Phuso	High School pupil	Shot dead by passing motorist.
–	Thabong, OFS	Sello Mofokeng (15), Teboho Bokopane (17), Oupanyana Mabenyana (17)	All youths	Killed by vigilantes.
24 Sept.	Cala, Transkei	Batandwa Ndondo (22)	ANC and student leader	Found shot dead the day he was picked up by security police.
16 Nov.	Gaborone, Botswana	4 South African exiles killed		Car bomb.
December	Tumahole, Parys, OFS	Lefu Rasego	Student activist (COSAS)	Found hacked and burnt to death after being abducted.
December	–	Ian Zamisa	Unionist (SAAWU)	Abducted and shot dead.
–	Zwelitsha, Ciskei	Zalisile Matyholo	Student activist (former SASO)	Found dead.
1986				
12 March	Atteridgeville/ Saulsville	Esther Masuku	Mother of youth activist and SACC member Oupa M.	Handgrenade thrown in house (Oupa was injured).
April	Atteridgeville, Pretoria	Frank Martin		Petrol bomb attack on home.
April	Bongweni, Eastern Cape	Lindile April	Organiser of local consumer boycott	Found dead.
14 April	Koster, Western Transvaal	William Oliphant	Unionist (SAAWU)	Found dead on a farm after being abducted 2 weeks earlier.
19 May	Kagiso, West Rand	5 family members	Entire family of Morgan Montoedi (Krugersdorp resident's organisation)	Petrol bomb attack on home.
28 May	Oukasie, near Brits	Joyce Modimoeng	Wife of unionist David (MAWU)	Bomb thrown in house (husband was injured).
May	Soweto	Diliza Matshoba	UDF and SACC	Doubtful car crash.
2 June	near Mbabane, Swaziland	Pansu Smith, Sipho Dlamini, Busi Majola	All ANC	Found shot dead.
June	Bronkhorstspruit	Stanley Nhlapo		Abducted, his body was found later.
19 June	–	Joseph Mothopeng	Allegedly ANC	Abducted, escaped, shot dead the same day.
20 June	Chesterville	Muntu Khanyile, Joseph Mthembu, Sandile Khawula, Russel Mngomezulu	All Chesterville Youth Organisation	Shot dead.
–	–	Sidney Mbisi	Former bodyguard of Oliver Tambo (ANC)	Abducted from Swaziland in July 1986, detained, shot dead after his release.
–	near Port Elizabeth	Sonwabo Ngxale	AZAPO	Abducted, later found stabbed and shot dead.
August	Port Elizabeth	Fuzile Lupulwana	AZAPO	Abducted, stabbed and burnt to death.
19 Sept.	Atteridgeville, Pretoria	Walter Ledwaba (16)	Youth	Bomb attack on home.

October	Mbabane, Swaziland	3 people	ANC (2)	Shot dead in home.
October	New Brighton, PE	Mzimkhulu Sogawayi	Former prisoner, possibly PAC	Shot dead after having received death threats.
1 December	Mamelodi	Dr. Fabian Ribeiro Florence Ribeiro	Former detainee, activist His wife, sister of PAC leader	Shot dead (there was an earlier attack on their home in March 1986
–	–	Jomo Mkize	Detainee support group worker	Beaten, stabbed and hacked to death in view of locals.
1987				
January	Mbabane, Swaziland	4 people	Allegedly ANC	Killed.
5 April	Mozambique	Gibson Ncube	ANC	Poisoning.
10 May	Soweto	Yvonne Ntsele	Senaoane Secondary School pupil	Shot dead.
14 May	Harare, Zimbabwe	Tsitsi Chiliza	Wife of ANC Chief Representative R. Mzimba	Booby-trapped TV.
24 May	outside Mbabane, Swaziland	Theopholis Dlodlo, Tutu Nkwanyane, Mildred Msomi	ANC members	Shot dead in car.
5 June	Soweto	Nkosinathi S. Shabangu	SOSCO and Senaoane Secondary School pupil	Shot dead.
24 July	Ciskei	Mxolile Eric Mntonga	IDASA Border Region director & civic activist	Found stabbed in his car – the trial revealed that he was killed in police cells.
29 July	Mbabane, Swaziland	Cassius Make, Paul Dikeledi, Eliza Tsinini	ANC (NEC)/MK ANC	Shot dead after their car was stopped near Matsapa Airport.
6 August	Swaziland	1 South African, 1 Mozambican		Shot dead.
23 August	Daveyton	Caiphus Nyoka	Student leader	Shot dead while police raiding his home.
2 Sept.	Dube Village (Soweto)	Samuel Siliso Ndlovu	Student activist (SOSCO)	Died from bullet wounds.
14 Nov.	Western Cape	Mr. Mtosana	Executive member of Western Cape Civic Association	Found shot dead.
15 Nov.	Sebokeng	Petrus Mnisi	UWCC and Vaal Youth Congress	Stabbed (second attack).
17 Nov.	Tsakane	Amos Tshabalala	Civic activist & CCAWUSA	Stabbed.
1988				
8 January	Francistown, Botswana	Jacob Molokwane	ANC	Shot dead in his car.
11 January	Bulawayo, Zimbabwe	1 person killed		Car bomb in front of house of alleged ANC members.
13 January	Swaziland	Sipho Ngema	ANC	Shot dead in restaurant.
25 January	Soweto	Sicelo Godfrey Dhlomo	DPSC	Abducted and found shot dead.
29 January	Heldemoed, OFS	Linda Brakvis	UDF	Found stabbed 3 days after release from detention.
10 February	Clermont, Durban	Pearl Tshabalala	UDF	Shot dead.
27 February	Germiston	Amos Boshomane	Unionist (SEAWU)	Shot dead (he survived an earlier attack on 25 November 1987).
6 March	–	Nomsa Nduna	Mother of unionist	Shot dead.
March	Clermont, Durban	Emmanuel Q. Khuzwayo	School principal	Found dead.
19 March	Paris, France	Dulcie September	ANC Chief Representative in France	Shot dead after receiving death threats.

22 March	Maseru, Lesotho	Mazizi Maqekeza	ANC	Shot dead whilst in hospital.
8 June	near Piet Retief	Makhosi Nyoka, Lindiwe Mthembu, Surendra Naidu, Nontsikelelo Cothoza	All ANC	Shot dead in an ambush as alleged 'infiltrators', none was armed.
12 June	near Piet Retief	Jabulani Sibisi, Joseph Mthembu, Sifiso Nxumalo, Nkosinthi Thenjekwayo	All ANC	Shot dead in an ambush as alleged 'infiltrators'.
1 July	–	Michael Banda	Unionist (POTWA)	Killed, police claim he died in a limpet mine blast.
July	Western Cape	Mthuthuzali Payi	Cape Youth Congress and unionist (FAWU)	Disappeared during stayaway in June 1988, later found mutilated.
–	Pimville, Soweto	Sipho Henry Tshabalala	Secondary School pupil	Shot dead.
September	Tumahole, OFS	Lefu Nakedi	Chairman of Tumahole Youth Congress	Shot dead.
November	Zambia	Z. Mkhonza	ANC	Car bomb.
November	–	Mzuzwana Ndyogolo	unionist (General Secretary of NEHAWU)	Died in 'mysterious circumstances'.
November	Naboomspruit	2 shop stewards	Unionists (CAWU)	Shot dead.
23 Dec.	near Zeerust	Gladstone Sewela	former Mandela United Football Club	Found hanging from a tree the day of his release from Bophuthatswana security police custody.
1989				
February	Adelaide	Sawutini Booi	President of Adelaide Youth Congress	Petrol bomb attack on home.
12 February	Swaziland	Derrick Mashobane, Thabo Mohale, Porta Shabangu	Student activists, all SANSCO	Found shot dead in a forest.
27 February	Clermont	Sithembiso Dlamini, Siphephelo Dlamini	Both Clermont Youth League	Killed in Sithengele High School.
14 April	near Durban	Chris Ntuli	Former detainee, Kwa-Mashu/Ntuzuma youth activist	Stabbed after returning from reporting to Inanda police station in compliance with his restriction orders.
April	near Lusaka, Zambia	Seddhan Naidoo, Mtunzi Thole	Both ANC	Killed in attack on ANC farm.
1 May	Johannesburg	David Webster	Wits University lecturer, DPSC member	Shot dead outside home.
21 May	Imbali, Pietermaritzburg	Jabu Ndlovu, Jabulani Ndlovu, and their daughter	Both trade unionists (NUMSA)	Shot and burnt in attack on their home, Jabu later died in hospital.
May	near Cape Town	Zolani Dala	Khayelitsha civic activist	Shot dead.
July	Sekhukhuneland	David Gayisa	Student activist (Pathudi College of Education)	Found stabbed, police informed parents a few weeks later.
19 July	East Rand	Bofana Sigasa	Unionist	Found floating in a dam bound hand and foot.
July	Potchefstroom	Bashi Gugushe	Former prisoner, student activist (AZASM)	Stabbed.
July	Kempton Park	Stanford Mazikwana	Unionist (SACWU)	Died as a result of injuries sustained in an attack by 4 whites.
July	Uitenhage	Andile Sapotela	Brother of NUMSA member Joe S.	Firebomb attack on home of brother Joe.
11 August	KwaMashu	Eric Gumede	Youth League activist	Shot dead 1 week after release from detention.
August	Cookhouse	Samson Godola	Youth activist	Shot dead.

12 Sept.	Windhoek, Namibia	Anton Lubowski	SWAPO, advocate	Shot dead with an AK47 at his Windhoek home.
4 November	Phola Park	Themba Myapi	Church fieldworker	Mutilated body found.
28 Dec.	Witbank	Eric Liberty	Civic leader	Stabbed after numerous death threats.

Summary

| Period | Place | | |
	Internal	External	Total
1974–79	1	4	5
1980–84	6	12	18
1985–89	89	38	127
Total	96	54	150

Sources of information

Community Resource and Information Centre (CRIC)

DPSC files and reports

HRC files and reports

IDAF: 'Focus'

Indicator SA

Jacques Pauw: 'In the Heart of the Whore'

Press reports

SAIRR: Race Relations Survey

APPENDIX 2B
List of political assassinations 1990–1994

Date	Place	Name	Affiliation	Description
1990				
7 April	Alexandra	Aldo Mogano	Executive member of Alexandra Youth Congress	Shot dead outside his home.
23 April	Gaberone, Botswana	Sam Chand, his wife and 3 children	PAC	Shot dead.
23 May	Soweto-Naledi	Simon Maswanganye	Executive member of Soweto Civic Association	Allegedly shot dead by group of men in a white minibus.
26 May	Langa, Western Cape	Sidwell Nonno (32)	SARHWU shop steward	Mutilated body found.
1 June	Vosloorus	Lindiwe Maziya (wife), Zwelakhe and Elizabeth (mother)	Vosloorus Crisis Committee (all relatives of chairperson – Ali M.)	Killed by unknown gunmen.
1 June	Vosloorus	Bella Motsupi (grandmother of Vosloorus activist, Thuli Motsupi)	Relative of activist.	Killed.
7 June	Oukasie, Western Transvaal	Abel Molokwane (31)	Executive member of Brits Action Committee	Shot dead by unknown gunmen.
13 June	Umtata	Sipho Pungulwa	ANC dissident	Killed.
4 July	Soweto	Sam Mabe	PAC; deputy editor of *Sowetan*	Shot dead in car by 2 gunmen.
2 August	Johannesburg	Clement Msomi	NUMSA organiser	Shot dead by 2 men in a passing car.
30 September	Ndwedwe, Natal	Iris Magwasa	ANC organiser	Shot dead at home
2 October	Durban	Nic Cruse	Worked for PC Plus, which had been started by people within the Mass Democratic Movement	Killed when he opened a parcel containing a computer, which exploded.
2 October	Durban	3 guards of ANC lawyer	ANC lawyer	Shot dead by 8 men.
4 October	Umtata	Selby Ngendane	PAC	Gunned down outside home.
12 October	Mdantsane, Ciskei	Jeff Wabena	ANC, unionist	Shot dead at ANC branch meeting
18 October	Khayelitsha, Western Cape	Nomsa Mapongawana (34)	Wife of chair of the UDF affiliated Western Cape Civic Association, Michael Mapongawana	Died from a bullet wound in the chest.
27 October	Durban	Revd. Wallace Ngcibi	Methodist Church	Shot dead by gunman.
5 November	Ntuzuma, Natal	Thami Zondi Mr Nene	ANC Civic worker	Killed.
19 November	Soweto	Fawcett Mathebe	ANC Youth League	Knifed and killed, car stolen.
13 December	Soweto	Lele Mabele	PAC, unionist	Shot outside home.
1991				
24 January	Heidelburg, PWV	Revd. Modisele	ANC, NECC	Killed; burnt body found with bible on it.
8 February	Durban	Mthunzi Njakazi	ANC	Shot dead on street.
16 February	Soweto	Bheki Mlangeni	ANC, human rights lawyer	Killed by walkman bomb meant for Dirk Coetzee.
25 February	Pietermaritzburg	Chief Mhlabunzima Maphumulo	CONTRALESA, ANC	Shot dead getting into car.
24 March	Table Mountain, Natal	Dinzy Maphumulo	Step-father of Chief Maphumulo	Shot dead at home.

14 April	Alexandra, PWV	Zweli Tshabalala	Azanian Youth Organisation	Shot dead at home.
24 April	Mooi River	Derrick and Mavis Majola	ANC	Shot dead by 4 armed men bursting into home
01 May	Thokoza	Jackie Matjili	MK	Shot dead.
17 May	Soweto	Tumi Padi	MK	Shot dead.
17 May	Soweto	Nokuzolo Ncalo	MK	Shot dead.
7 June	Soweto	Phanuel Molaudzi, Rose Kota, Darkmore Tshabalala	ANC, SACP	Gunned down in a train.
19 June	Cape Town	Mziwonke 'Pro' Jack	ANC	Gunned down near home.
1 July	Mmakaunyane	Joseph Mathe	?	Body discovered by Bophuthatswana police in the boot of a burnt car.
2 July	Braklaagte, Bophuthatswana	William Rantoa, Kgosimang Mafora	Pro-Bophuthatswana faction in Braklaagte	Killed when gunmen opened fire on them at a bus stop.
3 July	Mphopomeni, Natal	3 occupants at ANC home	At home of chair of local ANC branch	Killed.
3 July	Boipatong	Constance Sotsu (49), Margaret Sotsu (33), Samanta Sotsu (4)	Relatives of COSATU official and ANC education officer, Revd. Ernest Sotsu	Family members shot dead; house petrol bombed.
8 July	Cape Town	Michael Mapongwana and driver of taxi	Chair of Western Cape Civic Association	Killed in taxi.
12 July	Katlehong	Aubrey Sibiloane	MK	Shot dead entering the yard of his home.
20 July	KwaThema, PWV	Pepsi Mahlangu	Returned exile	Shot and killed by an unknown gunman.
21 July	Pietermaritzburg	Muntu Gasa (26)	Former Imbali Special Constable and Inkatha member, turned ANC member	Shot in the head 3 times by gunman.
4 August	Umbumbulu, Natal	Boy Chonco	Working for Flora Mkhize, widow of Sipho Mkhize, who had allegedly been killed by a KwaZulu police member	Shot dead while driving his car.
14 August	Natal midlands	Chauffeur of Chief Mhlabunzima Maphumulo	Witness at inquest into Chief's death	Killed.
14 August	Khayelitsha, Western Cape	Florence Tshuku, her children – Lundi, Mncedisi, Abigail, Edward Gebe	ANC	Killed when home was attacked and burnt.
9 September	Athlone, Western Cape	Igsaan Sharief Adriaanse (34) Dorothy Spencer (26)	Witnesses for the state's case against a CCB operative	Shot dead in the back of the head at close range.
19 September	Mbayi, Natal	Joseph Twala (35)	ANC official	Shot dead at home of girlfriend.
19 September	Soweto	John Papo Monyakalle	ANC Youth League leader	Found dead in the toilet of his home.
22 September	Folweni, Natal	Nhlanhla Makhanya (14), Revd. Mntambo, his son and an employee, Mr. Mtshali, Mr. Ngwenya and Siyabonga Goodwill Mohlomi	ANC supporters	Shot in the back of their heads at close range.
29 September	Thokoza, PWV	Sam Ntuli (31)	General Secretary of CAST, chair of Thokoza Civic Association and ANC member	Shot dead when gunmen forced his car off the road.
5 November	Thokoza, PWV	Phumzile Mbatha	ANC activist and COSATU worker	Killed while returning from anti-VAT protest rally.

6 November	Alexandra, PWV	Jama Makhosi, Fihlokwakhe Nxumalo	ANC, SACP and Alexandra Civic Organisation activist, Relative of chair of local IFP branch	Shot dead outside the local ANC offices.
19 November	Greytown, Natal	Sifiso Khumalo (13), Msani Chamane (13), Sibongiseni Makhathini (12)	ANC youth	Killed in their homes.
24 November	Wattville, PWV	Dr. Lindiwe Mbambo	Wife of an ANC official and member of Wattville Concerned Residents Committee	Shot dead by gunman at home.
15 December	Murchison, Natal	2 active COSATU affiliated trade union members	Trade union members	Killed by a group of men.
17 December	Table Mountain, Natal	Thomas Mshoki Gcabashe	Local IFP official	Killed; shot 45 times in the neck and shoulder.
18 December	Khayelitsha, Western Cape	Jongikaya Witbooi, Lumkile Maxiti, Agnes Maseti	At home of civic leader	Shot dead.
22 December	Mpumalanga, Natal	James Khanyile	Community leader	Shot dead while sitting outside his home.
1992				
10 January	Daveyton, PWV	Almond Tshabalala (36)	Daveyton Interim Committee	Shot dead by an unknown gunman.
22 January	Empusheni, Natal	7 members of Nkwazi family	ANC	Killed at their home; shot at close range.
27 January	Mdantsane, Ciskei	Sipho John Thembani (69)	ANC and member of Mdantsane Residents Association	Killed; shot in the head.
5 February	Folweni, Natal	6 people	ANC members	Gunned down by a group of men.
5 February	Pietermaritzburg	Precious Chiliza (6), Nkanyiso Sithole (9), Noluthando Mkhizi (11)	In car of Abdul Awetha, senior Inkatha official and deputy-mayor of Imbali	Killed when 16 gunmen opened fire on the car they were in.
7 February	Umlazi, Natal	Winnington Sabelo	IFP Central Committee member and KwaZulu MP	Gunned down at his shop.
9 February	Pietermaritzburg	S'kumbumso Ngwenya	ANC official	Shot dead after leaving a restaurant in the centre of town
27 February	Nyanga, Western Cape	Nyanga Lucas Mbembe (60)	ANC official and chair of Western Cape Hostel Dwellers Association	Gunned down after coming from a civic unity meeting
27 February	Thokoza, PWV	Mr. Madondo	Thokoza Civic Association	Killed in his house by a group of unknown men.
29 February	Estcourt, Natal	Mr. Zulu	ANC official	Shot and killed while driving his car.
9 March	Sharpeville, PWV	'Doctor' Mkopidi Motsisi	Witness to killing of an ANC activist	Shot dead.
21 March	Umlazi, Natal	Sifiso Mabaso	ANC member	Shot dead.
22 March	Sebokeng, PWV	Saul Tsotetsi, Alfred Yika, Elias Motloung	SACP and ANC official, SACC employee	Killed when a hand grenade exploded.
12 April	Wesselton, Eastern Transvaal	Chris Ngwenya and his wife	IFP Youth Brigade official and leader of the vigilante gang, 'Black Cats'	Shot dead by unknown men.
12 April	Wesselton, Eastern Transvaal	Christina Khabe	IFP member and mother of witness at Goldstone Commission	Attacked and killed at her home.
17 April	Esikhaweni, Natal	ANC member	ANC	Shot dead while driving.
29 April	Sebokeng, PWV	Alinah Smith (52)	Mother of ANC Youth League official	Killed when a hand grenade exploded in house.

15 May	Alexandra, PWV	Simon Nxumalo	Chairperson of IFP Alexandra Branch	Shot and killed by unknown gunmen.
17 May	Soweto	Ernest Mabaso	Chairperson of ANC Zola Branch and member of Soweto Civic Association	Shot dead as he was leaving his home.
29 May	Pretoria	Jan Choba (35)	PAC member (senior)	Shot dead 7 times in the chest and head
3 June	Piet Retief, Eastern Transvaal	Goodwill Sthuli Shlaza (22)	Chairperson of the Piet Retief ANC Youth League and of the ANC Youth League zonal structure	Shot dead at his home.
3 June	Butterworth, Transkei	Fanie Jannes Jiba (36)	Chairperson of SACP and MK member	Shot dead at a taxi rank.
11 June	Umtata	Julayi Hlekiso	Chairperson of the Transport and General Workers Union	Shot at point blank range outside his office.
14 June	Empangeni, Natal	ANC member	ANC member	Shot dead.
14 June	Empangeni, Natal	Ewert Mzimela, Stanley Mabaso	ANC activists	Bodies found by children playing on a local beach.
15 June	Tembisa, PWV	Revd. Tseleng Namane (47)	PAC member	Died in hospital three days after he was shot at his home.
19 June	Malukazi, Natal	Sbu Pitiyase Mnguni	ANC member	Shot dead by group of gunmen.
19 June	Umlazi, Natal	Vusimuzi Mabaso, Thabani Memela, Mazwi Mkize	ANC supporters	Shot dead.
20 June	Umlazi, Natal	Pitso Moekoena	ANC member	Shot dead.
22 June	Umlazi, Natal	Lizzy Makhathini (62), Nhlanhla Mbatha (36)	Makhathini member of the ANC Women's League	Killed at Ms Makhathini's home.
26 June	Wembezi, Natal	Isaac Mswane (49)	IFP organiser	Shot dead while driving to his home.
9 July	Umtata	Chief Julius Matatu	Former Transkei government minister and prominent traditional leader	Shot and killed at his home in Mqanduli.
15 July	Umbumbulu, Natal	Dominic Mahlangu	IFP's Etholeni leader	Shot dead when unidentified attackers in a car pulled up outside his home.
16 July	Alberton, East Rand	Bernard Mafiyeka	NUMSA shop steward	Gunned down by one of a group of 4 men who approached him as he walked to work.
18 July	Umlazi, Natal	Dome Wellington Ngobese	Chair of the IFP branch at Glebelands Hostel	Gunned down in his hostel room.
8 August	Rosslyn, PWV	NUMSA chair	Chair of NUMSA's Rosslyn local	Kidnapped and murdered by unidentified men.
18 August	Addo, Eastern Cape	Andre Maasdorp de Villiers (42)	Disclosed information to the ANC and Natal-based weekly paper on activities of the SADF's 'Hammer' unit	Gunned down as he parked his vehicle on his farm.
23 August	Richmond, Natal	Fana Nzimande, his wife and 4 children (aged between 4 and 15)	IFP supporting headman	Shot dead in their home by a group of 5 unidentified gunmen.
26 August	Tentergate	Thembinkosi Dywshu	ANC	Shot 5 times; body found by the Ciskei police.
26 August	Esikhaweni, Natal	8 people, including Sam Nywayo	Nywayo – chair of the ANC Empangeni branch, others – ANC, present at homes of attacked ANC members	2 hour attack on homes of ANC activists.

27 August	Tentergate	Welile Oliphant	ANC	Shot dead at his home.
28 August	Richmond, Natal	Washington Duke Sosibo	Traditional headman and local IFP organiser	Shot dead as he left a local supermarket.
31 August	Ezingolweni, Natal	ANC member	ANC	Killed when he was attacked at the home of a friend.
15 October	Alice, Eastern Cape	Elby Ngece	ANC	Killed at home.
15 October	Alice, Eastern Cape	Ben Badi, Nowinile Badi and granddaughter Vuyokazi Badi (11)	ANC	Killed at home.
26 October	King Wiliam's Town	Jackson Lufele	ANC Quinzini Village branch executive member	Shot and killed by gunmen introducing themselves as members of the African Democratic Movement.
27 October	Richmond, Natal	Reggie Hadebe	ANC Natal Midlands deputy chair	Gunned down in an ambush on a vehicle transporting senior ANC officials.
27 October	Thokoza, PWV	Vusi Tshabala	Thokoza township civic leader	Shot by gunmen in the head and back while walking.
2 November	Piet Retief, Eastern Transvaal	Tulani Eric Nkosi and friend Elias Kunene	ANC	Gunned down.
12 November	Madadeni, Natal	Professor Hlalanathi Sibankulu	ANC regional executive committee member, Newcastle branch chair	Found dead in his car.
5 December	Imbali, Natal	Nhlalayenza Ngcobo	Chair of the Inkatha Youth Brigade at Imbali	Shot dead during an attack on his home.
1993				
24 January	Esikhaweni, Natal	Matilda Ndlela	ANC	Killed by alleged hit squads.
February	Mdantsane	Mlungiseleli Venkile, Zwelinjani Tshandu	ANC	Shot dead in a pre-dawn attack on their home.
February	Tigane	Andries Khoza, Koos Seokolo	IFP Youth Brigade leaders	Killed.
March	north coast, Natal	Mbonlongeni Zulu	Inkatha leader	Killed; home torched.
March	Alexandra, PWV	Mxibilo Phoswa	Wife of Alex Inkatha general secretary, Peterson Phoswa	Killed when gunmen burst into home.
March	Vaal, PWV	James Mthombeni, Sizwe Mkhwanazi	Mthombeni – trained member of Umkhonto we Sizwe, Mkhwanazi – Vaal Civic Association (sub-branch chair)	Shot dead by a contingent of SAP and Internal Stability Unit.
23 March	Umlazi, Natal	Emphraim Ndebele (44), Robert Sekobi (44)	Ndebele – Inkatha supporting councillor, local Dispute Resolution member	Killed days before peace meeting.
10 April	Boksburg, PWV	Chris Hani	Executive member of ANC and SACP	Shot and killed outside his home.
April	Natal	Caiphus Dlamini	IFP Northern Natal regional chair	Killed.
April	Protea	Sam Tambane	General secretary of ANC Soweto branch	Shot and killed by police during a march outside the Protea Police Station.
May	Thokoza, PWV	Dennis Makhanya	Thokoza ANC and Civic branch treasurer	Abducted on 25 May on his way to work; body subsequently found at Germiston mortuary on 27 May.
May	–	Solly Smith	ANC's former chief representative in London	Killed.

June	Ipelegeng, Western Transvaal	Paul Dintoe	Chair of the IFP Youth Brigade Ipelegeng branch	Killed after being abducted from his home.
6 June	Empangeni, Natal	Mkhombiseni Buthelezi	IFP branch chair at Ekusayeniward, kwaNtewa	Shot and killed.
June/July	Piet Retief, Eastern Transvaal	Mphikeledi Malinga, Star Magudulela	SANCO officials	Shot dead by a man who claimed to be a member of Umkhonto we Sizwe.
June/July	Tembisa, East Rand	Zephania Ndoda 'Mosebetsi Mathebula', Boy Petsie	MK	Shot and killed on their way to work.
June/July	Empangeni, Natal	Khulekani Mhlongo	SRC member and secretary-general ANC Northern Natal region	Shot dead at the campus.
June/July	PWV	Ishmael Moloane	Former Umkhonto we Sizwe logistics officer	Died when police exchanged fire with ANC leader Walter Sisulu's bodyguards.
June/July	OFS	Tejibe Ndlovu	Secretary of Free State ANC Women's League	Killed in front of her house.
July	Wembezi	Bonginkosi Sithole	Senior IFP official	Shot and killed outside his home.
July	Katlehong, PWV	Absolom Anderson, Boy Shozi	Senior IFP official, deputy chair of the Katlehong Local Peace Committee	Burnt body found in Katlehong; had been shot and stabbed before being set alight by a group of youths.
September	Kwa-Tema-Springs	Samuel Motha	IFP chair of Kwa-Tema branch	Shot in the head on his way to work.
September	Meadowlands, Soweto	Prince Mafoko	Official of the ANC Youth League	Shot and killed by police.
September	Komba	Mbulelo Archie Mbelekane	ANC local executive member	Stabbed and stoned to death after answering a knock on the door.
19 October	Vulindela, Natal	Michion Mkhize	IFP student leader at the University of Zululand	Stabbed to death.
November	Pongola, Natal	Zolana Michael Mcetywa	Chair of the Pongola region of the ANC	Shot and killed in front of a furniture store.
November	KaNgwane	Abraham Vilakazi, Wilson Maseko, Mischalk Motha, Mandla Mabaso	ANC Deepdale branch executive members	Killed when their car was ambushed.
6 November	Transvaal	Felix Mvelase	Son of IFP Transvaal chair Vitus Mvelase	Killed by gunmen.
20 November	Johannesburg	John Lawrence	Winnie Mandela's bodyguard	Died after a shoot-out in the centre of Johannesburg.
December	Bekkersdal	Robert Hlomuka	IFP Bekkersdal secretary	Stabbed to death.
December	Yeoville, Johannesburg	Patrick Shuma	Bodyguard of ANC NEC member Jacob Zuma	Shot and killed while waiting at a bus stop.
December	Tzaneen, Eastern Transvaal	Johannes Pilusa	Chairman of an area ANC branch	Shot dead at his home by 2 gunmen.
27 December	Vosloorus	Samuel Magaula Mabuja	East Rand MK commander	Shot and killed by the police.
31 December	Western Cape	Frederick and Clifford Nissen	Brothers of the ANC assistant secretary of the Western Cape, the Revd. Chris Nissen	Shot dead.

Statistical summary of political assassinations 1990–1994

ANALYSIS BY PERIOD:

1990	29 victims
1991	62 victims
1992	86 victims
1993	43 victims
1994	Nil recorded
Total	220 victims

Notes:

- Some victims were not the intended target but died through association with the target or were caught in the line of attack.
- The above figures are somewhat higher than will be found in the texts of Chapters 8 to 10; additional reports have come to light since the texts were written.

ANALYSIS BY REGION:

KwaZulu/Natal	101 victims
PWV (Gauteng)	58 victims
Transvaal rural	19 victims
Western Cape	18 victims
Eastern Cape	17 victims (includes Transkei, Ciskei)
External	5 victims

VICTIM ANALYSIS:

ANC/UDF affiliation	152 victims
IFP	36 victims
PAC/AZAPO	10 victims
Trade Unionists	7 victims

Political abductions and disappearances

The list of names in this Appendix is drawn from files maintained by DPSC and HRC of reports received from numerous sources at the time the events occurred or subsequently came to light. In the case of known abductions, some of the victims have reappeared to resume their lives, some have been found dead or their fate accounted for, while the fate of others has yet to be explained. In the category of disappearances in general, stretching back to 1977, some of the disappeared may have in the meantime resurfaced without our knowledge, some have been accounted for in the recent probing that has taken place (and this number will undoubtedly grow), but many mysteries remain which may never be resolved.

Date	Name (Age)	Affiliation	Place	Details
1970s	Nduli, Joseph Ndhlovu, Cleopas Ramotse, B.S.	Exile Exile Exile	Botswana/ Swaziland	Abducted from Botswana/Swaziland.
1977				
February	2 un-named detainees		Johannesburg	Allegedly escaped from John Vorster Square police station.
March	Molekeng, Malebelle Joseph			Wife claimed had been redetained by police; originally detained and tried under the Terrorism Act earlier in the year.
1981				
30 January	3 persons		Mozambique	Abducted during Matola raid.
1982				
14 April	Mthimkulu, Siphiwe Madaka, Topsie	COSAS Activist	Port Elizabeth	The 2 disappeared during the institution of lawsuit proceedings against the minister of law and order for allegedly poisoning Mthimkulu while in detention.
1984				
2 May	4 ANC members	ANC	Swaziland	Abducted in Swaziland.
1985				
January	Nqwelo, Monde		Ciskei	Escaped from detention.
May	Mokobo, Billyboy (17)	COSAS	Thabong	Disappeared after having been interrogated by police 3 times.
8 May	Godolozi, Qaqawuli Hashe, Sipho Galela, Champion	Activists	Port Elizabeth	An airport worker who was later fired stated that 7 men (1 in police uniform) escorted the 3, allegedly at the airport to meet a British Consul Official, to a waiting car.
10 May	Maluleke, Jabulani	COSAS Soweto branch secretary		Allegedly arrested by railway police while returning with COSAS publications; rumoured to have gone into exile.
July	De Jonge, Klaas		Pretoria	Escaped from detention.
11 August	Hassan, Solomon	Youth Forum – Durban	Durban	Last seen leaving parent's house to get a lift to the funeral of lawyer Victoria Mxenge.
September	Mokoena, Sonny-boy		Pilgrim's Rest	Mother informed that son had escaped from custody; later found hanging from bars of his cell.
21 December	Mahlalela, Vincent		Pietersburg	Allegedly escaped from jail.
1986				
20 March	Thlapi, Nicholas 'Boikie'		Stilfontein	Allegedly taken into police custody after he stopped at a roadblock while leaving Ikageng to attend a death vigil in Klerksdorp.
14 May	Mahlangu, Petrus Vusi		Vlaklaagte Number 2	Disappeared after being shot in the foot at a taxi rank while on his way to a meeting at Chief Mabogo's kraal at Weltevreden.

12 June	Manyeki, Thomas		Tweefontein	Seen on morning of 12 June running from Imboko vigilantes and later seen being taken into an ambulance; KwaNdebele prisoner claimed to have spoken to him in a neighbouring cell.
July	Msibi, Sidney		Manzini, Swaziland	Abducted from Manzini; returned November.
August	Seme, L.	ANC	Swaziland	Kidnapped from a Swaziland police cell.
12 December	1 ANC member 4 others	ANC/?	Swaziland	Abducted in cross-border raid in Swaziland and later handed over again.
15 December	Ebrahim, E.	ANC	Swaziland	Abducted from Swaziland and later tried in South Africa.
1987				
6 February	Shabangu, George		KwaNdebele	Police allege that he escaped from custody while pointing out an arms cache in the veld.
11 February	Mahlangu, Jim Msebenzi	Headman of Tweefontein	Tweefontein	Last seen in a white E20 combi at 152 Tweefontein.
May	Mfeti, Phindile	SASO	Durban	Went missing on a shopping trip; search of hospitals, mortuaries and local police stations proved fruitless.
25 May	Nyanda, S.	ANC	Swaziland	Abducted in Mbabane.
15 July	Makope, Andrew Harold		Mamelodi	Taken into a light blue combi a short distance from his home by armed men claiming first to be policemen and then ANC cadres.
26 July	Sefolo, Harold Sello			Business partner of Makope; disappeared after allegedly receiving a call from Makope and going to meet him.
3 November	Mofokeng, David			Police claimed he escaped from custody after being arrested in connection with a robbery in August – a month in which he was in detention.
25 December	Leoate, Phineas 'Mokotjo' Phakone, Edgar Sandile Mabaso, Thulani Makhuba, Ntanda		Protea	4 alleged to have been part of group of 6 people who escaped from police station.
1987/1988	Thibedi, Jerry	former Northern Transvaal COSATU chairman	Mabopane	Reported missing after a petrol bomb attack on his home.
1988				
22 March	Ngona, Mbulelo		Lesotho	Disappeared after shootout with the Lesotho police in February – allegedly seen detained by Lesotho police on 22 March; investigations concluded that he was 'probably dead'.
31 March	Seema, Mthabatha	PAC		Last seen first in the company of a policeman at the Seshego magistrate's court where he had gone to attend a criminal hearing and later at the Pietersburg prison unable to walk on his own.
April	Sengulane, Denis	Anglican bishop of Lebombo		Last heard of when telephoned bishop of Johannesburg, Duncan Buchanan, from Jan Smuts Airport; source claimed that bishop living in Maputo.
May	Mbatha, Nhlanhla	Azanian National Youth Unity	Dube	Allegedly apprehended by a number of white men at a taxi rank.
17 May	Rathogwa, Elvis	Chair of FAWU shop stewards' council	Wynberg	Farmfare management claimed that they had accompanied him to the Kew police station; police denied that he was in detention.
June	Payi, Mthuthuzeli			Disappeared during a 3-day stayaway; body found badly mutilated in August.
June	Mtshali, Herbert Nkosi (14)	ANC		Captured ANC guerrilla; police claimed he was released.
12 June	Bopape, Stanza	UDF		Allegedly escaped from a police van while being transported to Vereeniging.
August	Kgatle, Clifford Anthony	Student		Last seen by a worker on the Turfloop campus.

5 August	Tshabalala, Daniel		Soweto	Allegedly taken from his home by 4 men (2 black men in police uniform and 2 white men in private clothes).
4 September	Mashiqana, Siyolo	COSATU	Johannesburg	Went missing on his way to a COSATU meeting.
20 October	Lange, Charlotte			Picked up from house by 8 whites and 1 black in a combi.
23 December	Mapisa, Ryan Byisile		Duncan Village	Dragged into a car at his home by 5 men who identified themselves as policemen while another 2 men in a car with GCJ registration followed.
1989				
March	Molapo, Sekhonyana		Lesotho	Abducted from Lesotho; released 9 days later after interrogation and attempts to recruit him as an agent.
1990				
13 March	Moema, Frank	Reverend/ community leader	Bulfontein	Allegedly abducted from home by men dressed in camouflage gear.
22 June	Gwala, George		Durban	Missing since dropped off at a taxi rank by police after taken from place of employment by them in order to help trace his son, who had jumped bail.
1991				
27 March	Mufamadi, Lawrence	NUM/ANC	Johannesburg	Went missing after attending a conference.

Summary

Known or reported abductions	30
Reported or alleged escapes from detention	13
Other disappearances	25
Total	68

List of major massacres 1948–1989

The list is arranged chronologically. Major massacres are defined here as incidents in which 10 or more people lost their lives, but also including some events of particular historical significance in which fewer than 10 people lost their lives.

Date	Place	Deaths	Alleged attackers	Victims	Remarks
1950					
27 March	Witzieshoek, OFS	14	SAP	Peasants	Protest against policy of stock-culling.
1 May	Alexandra, other areas on the Reef	18	SAP	Residents	Police attacked general strike held in favour of full franchise and against discriminatory laws.
1952					
18 October	Port Elizabeth	11	SAP	Protestors	Events arising from defiance campaign.
October	East London	10	SAP	Protestors	Events arising from defiance campaign.
1958					
May	Sekhukhuniland	16	Security forces	Peasants	Revolt against imposition of bantu authorities.
1959					
10 December	Old Location, Windhoek	25+	SAP, SADF	Residents	Resistance to forced removal.
1960					
24 January	Cato Manor, Durban	9	Rioters	SAP	Hundreds of rioters ambushed a police raiding party.
21 March	Sharpeville	69	SAP	Protestors	Police opened fire on demonstrators.
6 June	Ngquza Hill, Pondoland	11	SAP	Pondo tribesmen	Revolt against imposition of bantu authorities; meeting of unarmed tribesmen attacked by heavily armed policemen.
1976					
16–21 June	Soweto	128 (Official fig.)	SAP	Pupils/ residents	Uprising as a result of a march initiated by pupils against the use of Afrikaans as a medium of instruction.
1978					
4 May	Kassinga, Angola	600+	SADF	Namibian refugees	Air and ground strike on SWAPO refugee camp.
1980					
17 June	Elsies River, Cape Town	25	SAP	Pupils	School boycotts and general rioting.
1981					
30 January	Matola, Mozambique	12	SADF	ANC	Cross-border raids by commando group of army.
1982					
9 December	Maseru, Lesotho	42	SADF	Residents/ ANC	Cross-border raid on Maseru.
1983					
20 May	Pretoria	19	ANC	SADF/SAP personnel	Car bomb attack, SAAF headquarters.
23 May	Maputo, Mozambique	6	SAAF	Residents/ ANC	Impala jet strike on 6 alleged ANC bases.
1984					
3/4 September	Vaal Triangle	26	SAP	Protestors	Residents protesting over rent increases clashed with police.
1985					
18–19 February	Crossroads, Cape Town	18	SAP	Residents	Police dispersed 400 shack dwellers protesting against forced removal to the newly-built township of Khayelitsha.

21 March	Langa, Uitenhage	20	SAP	Residents	Police opened fire on funeral procession.
14 June	Botswana	13	SADF	Residents/ ANC	Commando raid on 10 alleged ANC homes and offices.
26 June	KwaThema	10	Police spy	Township youths	Activists use booby-trap grenades.
5–14 August	Durban townships	70	SAP/ vigilante/ residents	SAP/ residents	Police, amabutho and activist clash.
11 August	Duncan Village, East London	23	SAP	Residents	Police action during protest.
28–31 August	Cape Town	31	SAP	Residents	Rioting after Mandela march.
18 November	Queenstown, Eastern Cape	14	SAP	Residents	Police used violence to break up a township meeting.
21 November	Mamelodi, Pretoria	12	SAP	Residents	Police opened fire on crowd gathered to protest the army's presence in the township, high rents, and restrictions on the holding of funerals.
20 December	Lesotho	9	SADF, Lesotho Liberation Army	South Africans (6), Lesotho nationals (3)	Renegade Lesotho Liberation Army claimed responsibility for the attack, while the Lesotho government blamed South Africa.
30 December	Guguletu, Cape Town	11	Vigilantes	Residents	Police allegedly refused to intervene in clashes between 'Fathers' and 'Comrades' following the killing of a community councillor.
1986					
1 January	Moutse, KwaNdebele	12	Kwa-Ndebele vigilantes	Residents	KwaNdebele vigilante attack on Moutse villagers triggered by government's promise that Moutse would be transferred to the homeland on New Year's Day
2 January	Moutse, KwaNdebele	8	SAP/SADF/ residents	SAP/ residents	Keerom and Klopper villages under police and SADF siege following protest meetings in response to Moutse's incorporation into the KwaNdebele homeland.
15–21 February	Alexandra '6-day war'	27	SAP/SADF/ residents	Residents	Police and youths clashed after the funeral of a schoolboy who was killed by a shopping complex security guard.
3 March	Guguletu	7	SAP	ANC	Police ambush on alleged ANC guerrillas.
8 March	Motetema, Lebowa	6+	SAP	Funeral goers	Violence erupted when police tried to stop mourners from Pretoria, Witbank and other areas from attending the funeral of an unrest victim.
26 March	Winterveld, Bophuthatswana	11	Bophutha-tswana police	Protestors	Bophuthatswana police opened fire on a 5000–10 000 strong crowd gathered at a meeting called by youths to discuss detentions and police brutality.
26 March	KwaZakele, Port Elizabeth	13	SAP	Rioters	Police fired shots to disperse a large crowd that stormed a bottle store.
23 April	Alexandra	9	SAP/ residents	Residents	Police and residents clash after rent stayaway called by the Alexandra boycott committee.
13–14 May	Vlaklaagte, KwaNdebele	12	Villagers/ SAP/ Mbokotho	Residents	Funeral of Mbokotho victim sparked widespread violent demonstrations against 'independence'; one such gathering of 25 000 was violently dispersed by police.
17–26 May	Cape Town squatter camps	44	SAP/ vigilantes	Residents	Police/'witdoeke' and 'comrade' clashes.
20–25 May	KwaMashu	11	Youth/ amabutho	Youth/ amabutho	Youth and amabutho clashes.
9–11 June	Cape Town squatter camps	21	SAP/ vigilantes	Residents	Police/'witdoeke' and 'comrade' clashes.
6 July	Katlehong/ Vosloorus, East Rand	9	Unknown	East Rand develop-ment board officials/ assailants	Development board members shot while patrolling township in two attacks.
26–27 August	White City, Soweto	24	SAP	Demonstra-tors	Police and residents clash over rent boycott.

1987					
21 January	KwaMakutha, Durban	12	Vigilantes	Residents/ guests at Ntuli family home	Family of UDF supporter gunned down.
25 September	KwaShange, Pietermaritzburg	13	SAP	Inkatha Youth Brigade	Group of men attending a meeting in a house attacked by group including 3 off-duty police officers.
1988					
3 December	Trust Feed, New Hanover, Natal	11	SAP/ IFP	Residents	Attack on all night funeral vigil aimed at remedying lack of support for Inkatha chairman Jerome Gabela.
1989					
6 September	Cape Town	29	SAP	Protestors	Attack on election protestors.

Statistical summary of major massacres 1948–1989

ANALYSIS BY PERIOD:

1948 to 1959	6
1960 to 1969	3
1970 to 1979	2
1980 to 1984	6
1985 to 1989	29
Total	46 massacres

ANALYSIS BY REGION:

Northern Transvaal	6
PWV	11
OFS	1
Western Cape	8
Eastern Cape	7
Natal	6
External	7
Total	46

ANALYSIS BY CHARACTER:

Suppression of peasant revolts	3
Suppression of civil protest	21
Vigilante attacks on residents	9
Reported collusion between vigilantes and security forces	8
Cross-border massacres	6

List of major massacres 1990–1996

The list is arranged chronologically within regions and subregions. A major massacre is defined as an incident in which 10 or more people lost their lives. It should be noted that while most incidents occurred over a period of a few hours, some of them took days or even weeks to unfold.

Date	Place	Deaths	Alleged attackers	Victims	Alleged collusion	Remarks
1990	**PWV/Vaal**					
22 July	Sebokeng/Evaton	19	IFP	Residents	SAP/IFP	IFP launch in Sebokeng Stadium.
23–25 July	Sebokeng/Evaton	30	IFP/ residents	IFP/ residents	SAP/IFP	Retaliatory actions.
1–11 August	Sebokeng	13	IFP/ residents	IFP/ residents	SAP/IFP	Continuing actions.
4 September	Sebokeng	19	IFP vigilantes	Hostel residents	Whites/ IFP	Attack aimed at hostel takeover.
4 September	Sebokeng	11	SADF	Hostel residents	–	SADF opened fire on negotiators.
1991						
12 January	Sebokeng	45	Unknown	ANC mourners	–	Attack on funeral vigil for ANC member.
23 May	Sebokeng	13	Unknown	Residents	Whites (?)	Attack on beerhall.
1992						
17 June	Boipatong	46	IFP	Residents	SAP/ whites/ IFP	Night attack on residents.
18 November	Sebokeng	10	MK member	Party-goers	–	An alleged member of MK pulled a grenade at a party.
1993						
18 April	Sebokeng	19	Unknown	Residents	–	Gunmen driving through the area fired randomly at residents for 4 hours.
26 June	Sebokeng	12	Unknown	Residents	–	Gunmen in a vehicle fired randomly at residents.
12 July	Sebokeng	14	Zulu-speakers	Residents	Whites	Driving gunmen fired randomly.
1990	**PWV – Soweto**					
5–23 August	Soweto	122	IFP	Residents	SAP/IFP	Sustained widespread attacks.
8–9 September	Tladi	26	Vigilantes	Residents	Whites	Night attack on residents.
28 October	Naledi	16	IFP	Residents	–	Thought to be revenge attack for death of IFP member.
26 November	Dobsonville	13	Vigilantes	Hostel residents	–	Attack on hostel housing civic association members.
1991						
3 March	Meadowlands	24	IFP	Xhosa speakers	–	IFP takeover of Mzimhlope hostel.
14 April	Nancefield	11	IFP/ANC	IFP/ANC	SAP/IFP	Clash between Nancefield hostel and Power Park squatter camp.
28 April	Meadowlands	10	IFP mourners	Residents	SAP/IFP	Attack after service for assassinated IFP leader.
8 September	Mofolo	13	IFP	Residents	–	Circumstances unclear.
13 October	Mapetla	10	Unknown	Residents	–	Gun attack on tavern.

1990	PWV – West Rand					
5–23 August	Kagiso	30	IFP	ANC supporters	SAP/IFP	Attacks aimed at takeover of Kagiso hostel
1991						
12 May	Swanieville	27	IFP	Residents	SAP/ whites/ IFP	Sustained attack on squatter camp.
1990	**PWV – East Rand**					
12–15 August	Tokoza	150	IFP/ hostel dwellers	Residents	SAP/IFP	Forced expulsion of non-IFP from hostels and attacks on Phola Park squatter camp
14 August	Katlehong	24	IFP	Residents	SAP/IFP	Pre-dawn attacks on Crossroads squatter camp.
1–2 September	Tokoza, Tembisa, Vosloorus	44	IFP	Residents	–	Attacks on townships from hostels.
15–19 November	Katlehong	34	IFP	Residents	Whites/ IFP	IFP takeover of Zonkezizwe squatter camp.
26 November	Katlehong	11	Vigilantes	Residents	Whites/ vigilantes	Night attack on Mandela View squatter camp.
2 December	Tokoza	30	IFP	Residents	–	Night attack on township.
3–8 December	Tokoza	33	IFP/ residents	IFP/ residents	–	Ongoing actions and reactions.
11 December	Tokoza	52	IFP/ residents	IFP/ residents	SAP	Large scale attacks and counter-attacks
1991						
24 March	Daveyton	12	SAP	ANC supporters	–	Police dispersed 'illegal' gathering.
8 September	Tokoza	23	Unknown	IFP supporters	–	3 gunmen fired on an IFP march.
10 September	Katlehong	10	IFP	Commuters	–	Train attack.
7 October	Katlehong	20	Unknown	Mourners	SAP	Gunmen opened fire on mourners at Sam Ntuli's funeral.
10 October	Katlehong	10	Unknown	Commuters	–	Bus occupants shot, stabbed and fire-bombed
1992						
3 April	Katlehong	23	Unknown	IFP residents	–	Night attack on Crossroads camp (IFP)
1993						
5 July	Katlehong, Tokoza	22	IFP	Residents	–	Ongoing township violence.
6 July	Katlehong	16	Unknown	Residents	–	ANC–IFP related violence.
7 July	Katlehong	11	Unknown	Residents	–	Due to ongoing violence in Tokoza and Katlehong.
21 July	Daveyton	10	IFP/ hostel dwellers	Residents	Whites	Residents suffered from stab and gunshot wounds.
25 July	Katlehong, Tokoza	20	Unknown	Unknown	–	Police reported bodies found in area.
30 July	Tembisa	30	Toaster gang/ hostel dwellers	Residents	SAP	Attack on ANC dominated Umthambeka.
1 August	Katlehong, Tokoza	14	Hostel dwellers/ residents	Residents	–	Result of clashes between Tokoza hostel dwellers and Phola Park residents.
2 August	Katlehong, Tokoza, Phola Park	27	Unknown	Residents	–	Police reported bodies found.
3 August	Katlehong	16	Unknown	Residents	–	Police reported bodies found.
5 August	Katlehong, Tembisa	12	Unknown	Residents	–	Police reported bodies found.
7 August	Katlehong, Tokoza	10	Unknown	Residents	–	Police reported bodies found.
9 August	Katlehong, Tokoza, Vosloorus	10	Unknown	Residents	–	Police reported bodies found.

22 August	Germiston	14	Hostel residents/ unknown	Residents	–	Men with AK47's opened fire on a group of people at a hostel housing Scaw Metals employees.
8 September	Wadeville	24	Unknown	Commuters	–	10 gunmen attacked a taxi rank.
21 September	Kliprivier	20	Unknown	Commuters	–	Gunmen travelling in 2 minibuses opened fire on vehicles and pedestrians.
6 December	Katlehong	12	SDU	ANC Youth League	–	Result of bloody feud between ANC Youth League and SDU
1994						
25 April	Germiston	10	BBB (Blanke Bevrydings -beweging)	Commuters	–	100 kg bomb exploded at taxi rank.
13 May	Tokoza	12	Unknown	Youths	–	Linked to conflict between SDU factions in Katlehong.
6 July	Germiston	11	Unknown	Commuters	–	Possible IFP-ANC related attack on minibus taxis and private vehicles.
1991	**PWV – Alexandra**					
8–10 March	Alexandra	45	IFP	Residents	–	Large scale attacks and counter-attacks
17 March	Alexandra	10	IFP/ residents	IFP/ residents	–	Clash arising from IFP rally.
27 March	Alexandra	15	Unknown	Mourners	SAP	Gun attack on a funeral vigil.
11 August	Alexandra	19	IFP	Residents	Whites	Attacks from Madala hostel.
1990	**PWV – Johannesburg**					
13 September	Jeppe Station	21	IFP	Commuters	–	Attack on train passengers.
14 September	Denver Station	26	Unknown	Commuters	–	Attack on commuters.
1994						
28 March	City centre	54 (incl. 8 outside Shell House)	IFP/Zulus/ marchers/ ANC members in Shell House	Crowd/ gatherers/ workers/ commuters/ marchers	Sharp-shooters in building	Day of violence centered around IFP supporters' march to the ANC headquarters in Shell House
1990	**Natal – Midlands**					
8 November	Bruntville	16	IFP	Residents	SAP/IFP	Attack by hostel dwellers and bussed-in IFP.
1991						
10 February	Taylor's Halt	18	Unknown	IFP supporters	–	Ambush attack on buses.
21–23 June	Richmond	16	IFP	ANC supporters	SAP/IFP	Attack days before planned peace talks.
3 December	Bruntville	18	IFP	ANC supporters	SAP/IFP	Retaliation for protest against cultural weapons.
19 December	Mpumalanga	11	Unknown	Residents	–	Attack by gunmen.
1992						
26 September	Gengeshe	11	Unknown	Residents	–	About 30 unknown attackers opened fire on residents.
1993						
5 March	Table Mountain	11	Unknown	ANC/ residents	–	A vehicle transporting workers from an ANC stronghold was ambushed.
4 June	Estcourt	11	IFP	ANC	–	Gunmen using the same weapons attacked 3 homes in the area.
20 October	Loskop	24	IFP	IFP	–	Due to intra-Inkatha conflict.
1994						
6 February	Masunkazane, Richmond	12	Unknown	ANC	–	Pre-dawn attack by a group of 20 men.

Date	Location		Attacking party	Target	Other	Description
18 February	Mahlele, Creighton	15	IFP	ANC	–	Attack on youth volunteers for ANC voter education workshop.
1996						
21 March	Junction Location, Donnybrook	11	IFP	ANC/ residents	SAP	Attack thought to have been aimed at ANC displacees from previous month's ANC–IFP fighting in ANC-supporting St. Charles.
1991	**Natal – North Coast**					
21 November	Applebosch	10	IFP	ANC supporters	–	Attack on launch of ANC branch.
1992						
16 February	Esikhaweni	12	IFP/SADF	ANC supporters	SAP/ SADF/IFP	Attack on houses and hostels.
11 April	Esikhaweni	11	IFP	Residents	–	Attack after return from funeral.
2 August	Esikhaweni	11	Unknown	Residents	–	Killers in balaclavas and armed with pump action shotguns similar to KZP issue indiscriminately fired at residents.
1993						
9 July	Ezakheni	10	IFP	ANC	SAP	Dawn attack by large group.
7 November	Nqutu	11	IFP	ANC Youth League	–	Attack on home of ANC supporting Chief Molefe.
25 December	KwaMsane	10	Unknown	Residents	–	Related to faction fighting between residents of KwaMthole and Madwaleni.
1994						
26 December	KwaMbonambi	10	IFP	ANC	–	Retaliation attack on the kraal of an ANC supporter.
1995						
9 May	Sundumbili	11	IFP	ANC	KZP/ foreigners (Mozam- bicans) with para- military training	Group shooting spree in Okhovothi and Mombeni.
1991	**Natal – South Coast**					
4 January	Umgababa	27	IFP	ANC supporters	–	Large scale attack on Emagcino area.
14 April	Gamalakhe	10	IFP	ANC supporters	–	Attack on gathering.
1992						
26 October	Umbumbulu	20	Unknown	IFP	–	Gunmen opened fire on occupants of the house of an IFP member who were attending a party/ religious ceremony.
1993						
5 April	Murchison	10	Unknown	ANC refugees	–	ANC refugees were shot and grenaded in an attack on a house.
9 April	Dudu	10	Unknown	Residents	–	Unknown gunmen attacked the area.
20 June	Murchison	13	Unknown	ANC	–	Balaclava clad gunmen attacked the area.
1994						
27 October	Gcilima	14	IFP	ANC/ residents	–	Group of over 100 heavily armed men attacked residents, vehicles and houses.
1995						
16 December	Nsimbini	10	Unknown	IFP	–	2 attacks on homes of IFP supporting Lushaba and Cele families.

25 December	Shobashobane	19	IFP	ANC/ residents	–	Attackers trying to wipe out ANC 'eyesore' enclave in IFP stronghold.
1990	**Natal – Durban**					
18 July	Durban	26	Vigilantes	Commuters	–	Alleged result of sporadic gunfighting between rival ANC and IFP supporting gangs.
1992						
13 March	Umlazi	18	IFP/KZP	Residents	SAP/KZP/ IFP	Attack on Uganda squatter camp.
1994						
11 March	Bhambayi	11	IFP	ANC	–	ANC supporting Congo and Angola settlements invaded.
1990	**Ciskei**					
11 February	Mdantsane	10	Ciskeian soldiers/ SAP	Revellers	–	Attack on revellers celebrating Mandela's release.
1992						
7 September	Bisho	28	Ciskei security forces	ANC supporters	–	Ciskei security forces opened fire on a march of ANC supporters.
1993	**Transkei**					
17 September	Umtata	10	ANC slogan chanters	Stock thieves	–	Well orchestrated atttack on stock thieves.
1996						
5 August	Qumbu	10	Unknown	Residents	–	Revenge for a previous attack on the village of Ntshongweni.
1993	**Western Cape**					
25 July	Peninsula – Cape Town	11	Unknown	Worship-pers	–	Gunmen opened fire and threw 2 hand grenades into St James Church.
1994						
16 October	Khayelitsha	10	Unknown	CATA/ CODESA taxi association members/ protesters	–	Gunmen opened fire in a revival of Western Cape taxi hostilities.
1995	**North West**					
29 January	Orkney	10	Mine-workers	Mine-workers	–	Fighting between 2 rival groups at a hostel at Vaal Reefs Mine.

Statistical summary of major massacres 1990–1996

ANALYSIS BY PERIOD:

January to June 1990	1
July 1990 to June 1991	36
July 1991 to June 1992	15
July 1992 to June 1993	12
July 1993 to April 1994	28
May 1994 to December 1996	11
Total	103

ANALYSIS BY REGION:

PWV/Gauteng	East Rand	33
	Vaal	12
	Soweto	9
	Alexandra	4
	Johannesburg	3
	West Rand	2
	Sub total	63
KwaZulu/Natal:	Midlands	12
	North Coast	9
	South Coast	9
	Durban	3
	Sub total	33
Elsewhere:	Ciskei	2
	Transkei	2
	Western Cape	2
	NorthWest Province	1
	Sub total	7
	Total	103

HRC commissioners/Board members (past and present)

Ms. Brigalia Bam
Mr. Geoff Budlender
Mrs. Mary Burton
Mr. Saad Cachalia
Revd. Dan Chetty
Revd. Frank Chikane
Ms. Josette Cole
Dr. Max Coleman*
Mr. Chris Dlamini
Prof. John Dugard
Mrs. Sheena Duncan
Ms. Maggie Friedman
Mr. Stephen Goldblatt*
Ms. Berenice Jacobs
Ms. Abegail Johannessen
Adv. Pius Langa
Mrs. Joyce Mabudafhasi
Dr. Diliza Mji
Fr. Smangaliso Mkhatshwa
Mr. Titus Mofolo
Dr. Reno Morar
Mr. Silas Nkanunu
Adv. Dullah Omar
Mr. Wesley Pretorius
Dr. Faizel Randera
Dr Thabo Rangaka
Prof. Jeremy Sarkin*
Mrs. Albertina Sisulu
Mr. Howard Varney
Ms. Wendy Watson
Mr. Tom Winslow
Ms. Nomonde Yako

*National chairpersons
**National directors

Researchers (past and present)

Zukisa Bhaku
Jane Connoly
Susie Cowen
Ntokozo Gwamanda
Jenni Irish
Berenice Jacobs
Abegail Johannessen
Sarah Kearney
Patrick Kelly **
Erin Klingele
Wendy Landau
Margaret Levick
Teboho Makhoa
Farida Mangera
Tim Marchant
Phindile Maseko
Nobuntu Mbelle
Joan McGregor
Tony McGregor
Jessica McKay
Linda McLean
Karen Miedzinski
Miemie Moholwana
Eric Pelser
Jonathan Rosenthal
Safoora Sadek**
Elaine Sekhoa
Kubz Sekhonyane
Alison Stent
John Tsalamandris

Interns (past and present)

Maria Saino
Kristian Zitzlaff
Ria Boerema
Patrice Nelson

List of further reading

The HRC since its launch in September 1988 has produced eight different types of publications both regular and occasional. Regular publications include weekly updates, monthly reports, annual reports and special updates. A range of occasional fact papers, special reports and occasional papers have also been produced. Many of these have been incorporated in the present publication. A full list of all documents produced since 1988 is available from the HRC.

The following is a recommended reading list for those interested in acquiring further insight into the repression of the apartheid state.

The War against Children: South Africa's Youngest Victims, 1986, Lawyers Committee for Human Rights, New York

Detention and Torture in South Africa, Foster, Davis and Sandler, 1987, David Philip

The Hidden Hand: Covert Operations in South Africa, Minnaar, Liebenberg, Shutte, 1994, HSRC

Mabangalala: The Rise of Right-Wing Vigilantes in South Africa, Nicholas Haysom, 1986, CALS, Wits University

In the Heart of the Whore: The Story of Apartheid's Death Squads, Jacques Pauw, 1991, Halfway House

Death Squads: Apartheid's Secret Weapon, Patrick Laurence, 1990, Penguin

Apartheid Terrorism: The Destabilisation Report, Johnson, Martin, 1989, Commonwealth Secretariat

Hidden Lives, Hidden Deaths: South Africa's Crippling of a Continent, Victoria Brittain, 1990, Faber and Faber

Apartheid's Contras: An Inquiry into the Roots of War in Angola and Mozambique, William Minter, 1994, Wits University Press

Reconciliation through Truth: A Reckoning of Apartheid's Criminal Governance, Kader Asmal, Louise Asmal, Ronald Suresh Roberts, 1997, David Philip

Subject index

abductions, political 259-261

apartheid in crisis 151-156
– foreign debt crisis 152-154

apartheid laws and structures 148-151

apartheid survival strategies
– structures of apartheid power 200-202
– stakeholders in apartheid power 200-202, 219, 220, 236-242
– strategies 203-206

arrests, political 34, 94, 160, 167

assassinations, political
– list 1974–1989 247-251
– list 1990–1994 252-258

banning and restriction of
– persons 15, 16, 31, 32, 68-73, 74-77
– organisations 18, 19, 33, 85-91
– gatherings 19, 33, 34, 92-95
– publications 19, 20, 34, 35, 95-103
– political activity 20, 35, 36

deaths, political
– emergency 42
– in detention 56-67
– in police custody 67, 245, 246
– by hanging 84
– cross-border 132-134
– during destabilisation 160, 177-179, 209-214, 223-226
– post-elections 231-235
– assassinations 247-258

destabilisation
– statistics 160
– centres of 188-191
– acts of 191-200

detention without trial
– statistics 14, 15, 30, 47-53
– legislation 14, 30, 43-47

– forms of 14, 30, 45, 46
– torture in 14, 47, 53-56
– deaths in 14, 47, 56-67
– hunger strikes 140, 141

disappearances, political 259-261

Emergency, States of
– legislation 14, 38
– declarations 38-40
– regulations and orders 40-42
– deaths during 42

executions, political 17, 81-84

external repression 26, 27, 129-134
– cross-border: raids 132, 133
–   bomb attacks 133, 134
–   abductions 134

foreign mercenaries 184

funerals
– restrictions 19, 95

gatherings
– banning 19, 34, 92-95
– restriction 19, 34, 92-95
– breaking up 19, 34, 93
– legislation 33, 34

hit squads
– definition 22, 118, 168, 169, 185
– activities 22, 23, 119-128, 169-171, 186, 190, 216   (see also assassinations)

imprisonment, political 16
– legislation 35, 36, 77-79
– statistics 80

injury, political
– during destabilisation 160, 179, 214

internal refugees 22

legislation, repressive 14, 28-37, 38-42